The Acceptance and Commitment Therapy Workbook Toolbox

– 3 Books in 1 –

(Includes Over 80 Worksheets for Mental Health!)

*Radical Acceptance and ACT Therapy
Self-Help Guide to Cultivate Mindfulness, Build
Self-Esteem, and Manage Anxiety & Depression*

LIFEZEN PUBLICATIONS

ISBN 9789083397467 (paperback)
ISBN 9789083397474 (hardcover)

A Gift to Our Readers!

FREE DOWNLOAD ALERT!

Download and print our free
**15-Day Mindfulness and Acceptance
(Planner + Journal)!** Just go to
https://life-zen.com to get your gift, or
scan the QR code on this page.

DEDICATION

This bundle is for those ready to embrace themselves as they are, step through fear, and take meaningful action. May you find clarity, strength, acceptance, and peace in every page. Thank you for choosing this journey.

Ava Watters

BOOKS IN THIS BUNDLE
Book 1 – The Radical Acceptance Workbook
Book 2 – The ACT Therapy Workbook for Adults
Book 3 – The ACT Therapy Workbook for Anxiety Relief

ADDITIONAL RESOURCES

BOOK 1:
THE RADICAL ACCEPTANCE WORKBOOK

Transform Your Life & Free Your Mind
with the Healing Power of Self-Love & Compassion

—

Positive Lessons to Treat Anxiety, Self-Doubt,
Shame & Negative Self-Judgment

Book 1 - Table of Contents

Introduction: My Journey from a "Burnout and Breakdown" to Healing and Happiness

"One thing you can't hide - is when you're crippled inside." –
John Lennon

I was returning home from work. I had a business suit on, high heels, a smart-looking handbag on one shoulder, and a laptop case in one hand. I stepped out of my chauffeur-driven car (company-provided) and walked inside the 5-star luxurious hotel where I would stay for the next three months (company-arranged).

I imagine anyone who saw me cross that lobby that day would think I was "successful." If only they knew.

I took the elevator to the 31st floor, fished my room key out of my pocket, and as I slotted it through the door card reader, my tears started falling. Big, fat, ugly tears.

I angrily wiped my tears away, stepped in, and then, just like in previous days, the enormous dark cloud I held at bay all day engulfed me. Even now, I struggle to find the words for what I felt.

I was incredibly lonely, scared, confused, exhausted, unanchored, unbalanced, feeling inadequate... and so many other things. It was like standing still in an eerily silent place while everything inside me was howling in chaos.

At first, I thought I was suffering from extreme loneliness. I was halfway across the world from my husband, family, and friends in a country where I didn't speak the language. But then, I've been away before due to my hectic career, and I never felt this way.

I don't know how I survived the next few weeks, but I did. However, I didn't survive them unscathed. When I returned home, I was different. I was melancholic, struggling to find my footing, and tended to feel the beginnings of a panic attack whenever anything new or different was happening. I felt myself unraveling.

Unsurprisingly, my relationship with my husband was also suffering. Since I didn't understand what was going on with me, I couldn't explain things to him. My roller-coaster of moods created distance between us, and we felt increasingly disconnected.

At the back of all this was the knowledge that my family has a history of Major Depressive Disorder (MDD), and so a part of me thought that maybe I was succumbing to my inevitable fate.

In the end, knowing that depression runs in my family helped me. You see, since I knew about it, I always had an active interest in psychology, particularly anything that involved mental disorders. I would devour psychology books, keep up with the latest developments, and even attend online classes when I had the time. So, when I started to see "signs," I tried to listen to my inner voice. And it said: **I can't breathe. I need space... and time... to just breathe.** So that's what I did. I took some time off to breathe.

I saw a therapist who helped me during those initial dark and troubling weeks. Eventually, I felt it wasn't fully addressing my specific issues, whatever they were. So, I stopped after a few months and started to educate myself about Dialectic Behavior Therapy (DBT) by Dr. Marsha Linehan. (I would enroll and finish her DBT Skills certificate program later.)

DBT initially interested me because of Dr. Linehan herself. She had borderline personality disorder, and I was in absolute awe of her and her achievements in the world of psychotherapy. (I thought, *What a mountain she had to climb!*) As I became more familiar with DBT, I was exposed to the concept of **Radical Acceptance**, which was the principle that truly jumpstarted my mental healing. And as I healed, I found out who I was.

I discovered that I've been a chameleon.

As a child, I was ignored in favor of my younger twin brothers. And I was okay with that, or so I thought. I didn't realize that my coping mechanism for the lack of attention was to be exactly what other people wanted me to be. Mom always wanted a good, obedient, and quiet little girl, so I was that to her. I was "Mommy's good little helper." Dad always wanted an academic achiever, so I was that to him. I was the one who got scholarships throughout my school years. I was "Daddy's genius girl."

I want to say right now that this book is not about blaming my parents, or anyone, for that matter. I was never forced into anything. What moved my decisions was a deep-seated need to be seen, and in my young mind, to be seen meant to be what others wanted me to be.

During my last year of college, my best friend convinced me to take a temp job as a data analyst with her, so I did. I never meant to stay, but apparently, I was good at it. While my friend was let go after a few months, I was offered a permanent job, so I stayed. As the company grew and expanded globally, I grew in position, but I was never passionate about my job. I was just really good at it. Before I knew it, years had passed.

The thing is, you can only betray yourself, your inner spirit, your soul, or whatever you want to call it, for so long.

I wasn't aware that I wasn't living the life I wanted, but something inside me sensed it. After years of being a chronic people-pleaser, being a perfectionist, doing what others expected of me, and seeking approval and validation from others—my mind and body started to shut down. (Later, I would refer to this phase in my life as the time I suffered "a burnout and breakdown.")

So, Radical Acceptance taught me that I've been living my life as "someone," but not fully as myself, not 100% Ava. And since my core personality was to deny who I really was, acceptance in any form was a problem.

Whenever something at work didn't go as planned, I wouldn't accept it and swing between bouts of anger and frustration and feelings of self-doubt and inadequacy.

Whenever my husband and I had a big argument, I wouldn't accept my role in the situation and find ways to blame him.

When a friend betrayed me, I pretended the situation was "beneath me." I didn't want to address it, refusing to accept its impact on my life.

When an immediate family member became toxic and said mean things to me over lunch, I plastered a smile on my face, finished lunch(!), and went home. I was numb and in a daze for days, but I didn't want to talk about it. I told my husband it was nothing and everything would be "fine." And yes, I maintained contact with that family member for a few years.

When a small business I invested in failed, I retreated into myself, recalling and reviewing everything in my mind. I wanted to know what "I" missed and where "I" failed. (This time, I wasn't blaming others. I was self-blaming and self-gaslighting to the extreme.)

Oh, I have so many more examples than I've shared above, but I think the most damaging are the things I told myself in secret. I had this habit where if I tripped, dropped something, or forgot something, I'd silently say, "*Dumb Ava!*" (Later on, I'd realize that despite any displays of outward confidence, I suffered from extremely low self-esteem and was devoid of self-compassion.)

Over time, this constant unacceptance of myself, others, and life events was burying me deeper and deeper into misery. So, when I started to learn more about Radical Acceptance, I embraced it like a lifeline. For once, I let curiosity (not control) lead me because I was desperate to discover why I was so miserable when everything external suggested that I "should" be happy. So, what happened?

Well, it's a very weird feeling to finally get to know and understand yourself. You think you know the person you see in the mirror... but you don't (or at least not fully). People, experiences, and life put layer upon layer upon that person, and it's shocking to be stripped of all of that and see what's lying underneath. But although the journey can be unnerving, it's also very healing.

As I learned to accept myself, Radical Acceptance taught me how to practice acceptance in general. And although that can be frustrating, I realized that acceptance is just another word for "moving forward." (You'll discover why and how in the succeeding pages.)

The "short break" I took became a permanent one. To the shock of everyone around me, I chose not to return to my previous job because I accepted that it wasn't fulfilling me inside. My true passion lies in writing and psychology. I love understanding human behavior, diving into why we do the things we do, why we're in such a stage of so much stress and unhappiness today, and how we can change our lives and be happy and fulfilled. These are the pursuits that move and fulfill me. After decades, I finally met the real "Ava."

In all honesty, when I was learning and applying Radical Acceptance in my life, my only purpose then was to clear the dark clouds enveloping my existence. I never realized how much my life would be transformed!

As I radically accepted myself, others, and life in general, my self-esteem, marriage, and relationships with others improved dramatically. My happiness started radiating outwards, and people who were aware of my troubles asked me what I had done to turn my life around. When I told them about Radical Acceptance, many began to confess their own life struggles and seek my help— and so I did, doing my best to pay forward the gifts that Radical Acceptance gave my life.

Soon enough, more and more people started to get in touch and I found myself writing what I wanted to say so that I could give them a structured approach to Radical Acceptance. My simple "notes" turned to group discussions, which then turned to leading workshops. Before I knew it, I was sitting down and began constructing this book. My goal is that the ripple effect of Radical Acceptance continues to spread, touching the lives of those willing to embrace its transformative power.

So, dear reader, this book is my personal invitation to you to undertake a journey of deep self-discovery through the lens of Radical Acceptance. And in so doing, may your inner healing begin, paving the way for genuine happiness in your life.

Who Should Read This Book

This book is for anyone struggling or who knows someone having a difficult time. It's for anyone dealing with relationship challenges (personal or professional) or emotional challenges (e.g., anxiety, low self-esteem, shame, doubt, feelings of inadequacy, inner turmoil, etc.) and who wants to explore alternative therapies right from the comforts of their own home.

Goal of this Workbook

This book aims to teach you Radical Acceptance and how it can help you get to know, appreciate, and love yourself completely. It also imparts to you how Radical Acceptance can help you cope with negative and heavily unpleasant emotions so you get relief from your emotional suffering. In the end, the main purpose of this book is to help you feel better and live a life of authenticity, true happiness, and purpose—whatever that may look like for you.

How to Use This WORKBOOK

I will say this with as much compassion and honesty as possible: Please get out of your way. Try to put aside your prejudices, preferences, and natural biases. Open your mind, and welcome the ideas in the following pages.

Also, I'm a big believer in the principle that true learning takes place only when knowledge meets action. As such, this book is full of guided worksheets to help you embrace the concepts mentioned in this book.

Your Feelings and Experiences are Valid

During my journey, I would get a bit peeved when people "knew better" than what I was feeling or experiencing; many people gave their opinion (judgment) rather than empathy. So, here's my message to you:

Your truth matters. Your feelings are valid. Your experiences hold significance. Your trauma deserves attention. Please don't let anyone undermine your reality or your voice because you have the absolute right to experience and express your feelings without judgment or dismissal. Embrace your truth and honor your journey no matter how long it takes.

Kindness

Please remember that your Radical Acceptance journey is not a race but a gradual growth and healing process. You might experience ups and downs, progress and setbacks, and struggle with ideas that go against your current beliefs. That's all okay! Be kind and patient during challenging moments because they're part of the journey. Remember to treat yourself with the same kindness and empathy you would offer to a dear friend.

So, dear reader, just at a time when you may want to shut everything and everyone out and deny the chaos and absurdities of this current world, I ask you to open up and embrace acceptance instead. Will you take this step with me?

Ava Watters

Amazon Bestselling Author
Acceptance Therapy Advocate

Part 1: Understanding Radical Acceptance

"Accept yourself, love yourself, and keep moving forward. If you want to fly, you have to give up what weighs you down."
– Roy T. Bennett

In the context of "Radical Acceptance," the term "radical" means complete, thorough, and profound. No *ifs* and *buts*. So Radical Acceptance is an all-embracing and unwavering form of acknowledgment—of yourself, others, situations, etc.

Radical Acceptance encourages accepting reality AS IS without resistance, denial, or judgment, even in the face of challenging situations.

RADICAL ACCEPTANCE

Now, you might be wondering WHY you should radically accept even unpleasant feelings or events, and here's the answer: **to free yourself**.

Imagine painful or challenging situations like having the *flu*. When you're sick, you may think thoughts such as:

I have so many things to do! Why do I have the flu now?
I have travel plans. What if this doesn't clear up by then?
I wonder who gave this to me?!
This is Robin's fault. They had the flu and still attended my party.
I should've known better! Why did I have to go out without a coat?
If you suffer from anxiety, you might even think *OMG, this is COVID.*

Round and round your thoughts go. Amidst all this ruminating, you're essentially *nurturing* your flu (the problem). When we give our problems so much attention, we get stuck in that situation and prolong our suffering.

Radical Acceptance helps you let go of your pain and suffering and focus on taking action to change your situation. So, in the flu scenario above, skip the negative and unhelpful thoughts and ruminations and focus on what you can do to get better instead (e.g., taking medication, drinking plenty of water, getting enough rest, etc.).

So, think of it like this: the longer you deny or refuse to accept something, the longer you'll suffer from it. The sooner you accept, the sooner you can move on to feeling better.

Unacceptance is marinating in a negative situation.
Acceptance is the first step to getting out of one.

Chapter 1. The Foundations of Radical Acceptance

Radical Acceptance isn't "new." It draws from Eastern philosophies like Buddhism and Taoism, which stress accepting the present moment without judgment, cultivating inner peace, and embracing the impermanence of life.

However, as I mentioned at the start of this book, I was introduced to this concept while studying Dialectical Behavior Therapy (DBT), developed by Dr. Marsha M. Linehan in the 1980s.[1] DBT, which incorporates the principles of acceptance and change, emphasizes the importance of Radical Acceptance as a fundamental component of mental healing.

More recently, mindfulness-based approaches, such as Mindfulness-Based Stress Reduction (MBSR) and Acceptance and Commitment Therapy (ACT), have further emphasized the significance of accepting one's thoughts and emotions without judgment.

All of the above practices have highlighted how acceptance without judgment enhances emotional well-being and resilience.

Misconceptions About Radical Acceptance

Even though Radical Acceptance has been around for a while, many people find it difficult to embrace because of all the misconceptions surrounding it. So, let's first clarify what it is and what it's not.

Radical Acceptance IS NOT: Agreement, approval, or consent.
You're not agreeing to anything, saying you're okay with something or someone, or giving consent. You're just acknowledging that a situation exists or has happened.

Radical Acceptance IS NOT: Denial or avoidance.
Radical Acceptance is embracing truth or reality AS IS. You're not trying to deny or avoid difficult situations or negative feelings. You're accepting your awareness of them to find ways to cope effectively.

Radical Acceptance IS NOT: Giving up or giving in.

Accepting a situation doesn't mean you don't want things to improve. When you accept something, it doesn't mean you want it to happen again or that you want the situation to stay that way. It's also not about giving yourself or anyone a "pass." It's acknowledging and embracing the truth of a situation, including all associated emotions.

Radical Acceptance IS NOT: Inaction.

When difficult situations occur, you're not saying you will lie down and be "okay" with it. You acknowledge what happened because it already happened, and you cannot undo the past. Remember, taking action belongs in the future.

Radical Acceptance IS NOT: Suppressing or ignoring emotions.

Radical Acceptance is about allowing ALL feelings to exist. It's about enjoying moments of happiness and acknowledging moments of pain without judgment.

Radical Acceptance IS NOT: Downplaying or trivializing.

This concept doesn't involve underestimating the significance of challenging or distressing experiences. Instead, it supports a deep and nonjudgmental recognition of these experiences, helping you understand how complicated they are and how they make you feel.

Radical Acceptance IS NOT: Dwelling on the past (regrets) or obsessing over the future (fears).

It's about living and feeling the present moment. If you keep reliving the past or are anxious about the future, you're robbing yourself of the present moment. Radical Acceptance is about living in "NOW."

Radical Acceptance IS NOT: Being indifferent or not caring.

Often, being indifferent, detached, or uncaring about something is a sign of deep pain. So much despair that whether you fully realize it or not, you deny the situation by outwardly saying or showing that you don't care. Radical Acceptance is the opposite. It promotes full acceptance of the problem and the pain it's causing, not because you want to be hurt but because you want to be healed.

Radical Acceptance IS NOT: About others.
Your reality is unique to you. As such, you cannot accept for others, only for yourself.

At this stage, I ask you to rethink and redefine the word "acceptance" in your life to:

ACCEPTANCE IS
ACKNOWLEDGING REALITY <u>AS IS</u>

And when it comes to Radical Acceptance:

RADICAL ACCEPTANCE IS
ACKNOWLEDGING REALITY <u>AS IS</u>
WITHOUT RESISTANCE, DENIAL OR JUDGMENT

<u>**The Benefits of Radical Acceptance**</u>

Radical Acceptance is the most liberating concept I've ever come across. At first, I met it with a bit of skepticism (hmmm...), a dash of fear (can I do this?), and loads of uncertainty (not sure about this...). But as I learned and practiced it in my life, I just felt "lighter." Here are some of the key benefits Radical Acceptance offers:

Reduces Stress: Radical Acceptance can help you feel less stressed and anxious. When you accept things AS IS, I can't tell you just how much pressure is taken off your shoulders! No more agonizing about the *this* or *that*, or the *why's* or *why not's* of a situation. Once you accept it, dealing with it gets easier.

Promotes Personal Growth: Radical Acceptance can lead to personal growth and transformation because it fosters a journey of self-discovery and development. It encourages you to face yourself and answer questions such as, *What makes me happy?* Or *What brings me joy?*

When you ask yourself these questions, DON'T be surprised to come up with answers far from your current reality. For example, say that you're a customer service rep, but you used to like baking. In this instance, find ways to bring back baking into your life.

Enhances Self-Compassion: Radical Acceptance encourages deep self-compassion. As you go through the coming pages, you'll go through a journey of self-acceptance and understanding. And in doing so, you'll learn to be kinder and more empathetic with yourself.

Improves Relationships: Practicing Radical Acceptance can enhance relationships by fostering acceptance of others AS IS (instead of what you want or expect them to be). This nurtures genuine understanding and empathy towards others, creating a more harmonious relationship.

Stimulates Emotional Resilience: Radical Acceptance fosters emotional resilience by enabling you to navigate challenging situations with greater ease and inner strength.

Reduces Emotional Suffering: Radical Acceptance can lead to freedom from emotional stress and suffering because often, we unknowingly put these pressures on ourselves by agonizing, or what I call "marinating," in our problems. By unwaveringly accepting reality, even if that reality is uncomfortable or painful, we let go of the need for control and perfection and embrace life's imperfections. From there, we can move forward and work to find solutions to make an unpleasant situation better.

Prevents Self-Gaslighting: Self-gaslighting refers to the act of doubting or questioning your own thoughts, feelings, or experiences, often leading to a distorted perception of reality. It involves internalizing self-doubt to the point where you may dismiss your own feelings or memories, creating a sense of confusion or invalidation within yourself.

If you've ever said any of the following statements to yourself, you might be self-gaslighting. Please go over the list and check the ones that resonate with you.

[ ] Maybe it's all just in my head; everybody says it is.
[ ] I'm overreacting. I'm sure they didn't mean it.
[ ] Oh, you're right. I must be misremembering.
[ ] Why do I make everything worse?!
[ ] It's my fault; I always mess things up.
[ ] No, no, I have no opinions.
[ ] I must be imagining things; it couldn't have happened that way.
[ ] I have no right to complain.
[ ] I'm not good enough for ________________.
[ ] I must have done something to provoke this.
[ ] Why do I always cause problems?!
[ ] I'm just being paranoid; there's nothing to worry about.
[ ] Maybe they're right; I'm not capable of anything.
[ ] I'm too much trouble for others; I should just keep quiet.
[ ] I shouldn't be upset. I make myself a target of jokes all the time.

Self-gaslighting statements undermine your sense of self-worth and reality. Radical Acceptance helps prevent self-gaslighting by teaching you to accept, understand, love, and be proud of yourself. It promotes truth and honesty and, in doing so, helps you see things AS IS without judgment or self-doubt. This practice allows you to establish firm boundaries and trust your perceptions, making it more challenging for others to manipulate your sense of reality.

The Aspects of Radical Acceptance

Radical Acceptance is not a switch you can just turn "On." To make it your second nature, you must cultivate the following qualities:

Mindfulness is nurturing presence in "now." This means not living in the past or the future but living fully in the present moment. (See Chapter 2. Mindfulness: Living in NOW.)

Self-awareness is cultivating a deep understanding of your thoughts, feelings, and behaviors and practicing present-moment awareness. (See Chapter 3. Self-Awareness: I See ME.)

Non-Judgment is approaching situations and experiences with an open and non-critical mindset, allowing understanding, empathy, and facts (not assumptions or opinions) to prevail. (See Chapter 4: Non-Judgment: Breaking Free from the Chains of Criticism.)

Embracing Imperfection is realizing and accepting that perfection is unattainable. Instead, one should focus on the beauty and growth of embracing your flaws and imperfections. See Chapter 5: Embracing Imperfection.)

Letting Go of Control is releasing the need to control external situations or outcomes and instead focusing on developing inner peace and resilience. (See Chapter 6: Letting Go of Control.)

Radical Willingness is cultivating a mindset of openness and willingness to experience life as it unfolds without resistance or attachment to specific outcomes. (See Chapter 7: Radical Willingness.)

Radical Self-Acceptance is learning to embrace your entire being. It's about fostering a genuine connection with your true self and being at peace with who you are and intend to be. (See Chapter 8: Radical Self-Acceptance)

<u>A note about vulnerability:</u>

As you read this book, you might feel vulnerable at certain moments. That's understandable and perfectly okay. Radical Acceptance is not easy; it asks you to embrace your identity, experiences, thoughts, and emotions without any defense mechanisms or shields, which, like me, I'm sure you've been putting up around you for years. So, Radical Acceptance might initially feel uncomfortable or unsettling, but know that this vulnerability is a natural part of self-discovery and emotional healing.

However, please note that being open and vulnerable DOES NOT give anyone license to cause you pain or harm. Ensure that your vulnerabilities are respected and protected by setting and enforcing boundaries.

For example, suppose you feel vulnerable and want to be alone, and a family member drops by unannounced. If this is not helpful, say that you need space and ask the person to drop by some other time. Create a safe space for yourself so you can maintain a sense of emotional security when feeling vulnerable.

Part 2: Bringing Acceptance Into Your Life

"The secret of change is to focus all of your energy, not on fighting the old, but on building the new."— Socrates

"Radical Acceptance" seems simple. But as I learned more about it and practiced it, I realized that even though the concept is easy to grasp, it's difficult to apply because, as adults, we've put up many walls and masks to protect ourselves.

Radical Acceptance asks us to *unlearn* a lifetime of habits. But then again, if these habits, beliefs, and behaviors are not making us happy or are even harming us... why should we keep on doing them? It's like grabbing a hammer and hitting ourselves repeatedly because we haven't learned to put the hammer down. So, let's put the hammer down....

Chapter 2. Mindfulness: Living in NOW

Many people confuse mindfulness with meditation, and that's one of the reasons people don't try it. (*Me, sitting down cross-legged and chanting "Om" for endless minutes?! No way!*) So here's the difference: mindfulness is a quality; meditation is a practice.

Mindfulness is a state of mind; it's something you are.
Meditation is a practice; it's something you do.

So, what IS mindfulness? It's a state of full awareness of the present moment. You're not thinking about anything that has happened (past) or anything you need to do in the next moment (future). You're simply in a state of NOW.

Mindfulness is not easy in today's world because we lead busy lives. We're used to multi-tasking, and thanks to social media and 24/7 news, we're overly stimulated and stressed.

We're also constantly distracted. And although social media and digital technology are partly to blame, research conducted by Harvard psychologists showed that we're so distracted because we engage in constant "mind wandering."[2] Yep, we like to time travel through our minds.

It's waiting in line and thinking about dinner. It's having dinner and thinking about how badly you want to shower and sleep. It's getting in bed and agonizing about all the work you must do tomorrow. And how about that "out of body experience" where someone's right in front of you, talking to you, and the minute they stop and stare at you, you go, "*I'm sorry, what did you say?*" So, if you really think about it, you're hardly ever in the present moment.

Constant mind wandering makes us unhappy, and it can even lead to depression[3] because our focus is on what's NOT happening. To be fair, evolution made us this way.

Our ancestors always had to be on high alert and think about any potential (not present) threat as a way to survive. Unfortunately, even though we're no longer faced with the danger of being eaten alive by predators, there's undoubtedly more stress than ever on the human mind in the form of emotional stress.[4] So, how do you focus more and wander less? Mindfulness holds the key.

When it comes to mindfulness, breath awareness is important. Now, you might be thinking, well, that's easy! Is it?

Most people are *shallow breathers* or *fast breathers*, inhaling through the nose or mouth, trapping air in the chest, and then puffing it out. This means that air doesn't reach your diaphragms.

Daily stress has made humans shallow breathers.[5] It contributes to a host of health problems such as chronic stress, anxiety, inability to think fast, inability to experience quality sleep, fatigue, memory loss, and many others. In contrast, *deep breathing* or *diaphragmatic breathing* promotes less feelings of breathlessness, a more relaxed mind, and better overall well-being.[6]

Deep breathing is an important element of mindfulness because it is an anchor for cultivating present-moment awareness. When you breathe deeply and with intention, you stimulate your body's relaxation response.[7] This process encourages you to shift your focus away from racing thoughts and daily distractions toward only one thing: your breath.

After anchoring yourself to "now," start paying attention to what's happening outside you—one thing at a time.

For example, grab the FIRST object you see. Next, describe it. Don't give any opinion (e.g., *I don't like this shape*); just use descriptive words (e.g., *It's round*). Next, participate mindfully. How are you holding the object? Are you clutching it tightly or holding it loosely? Are you keeping it with one hand or both? Are you holding it at the top, bottom, or middle?

As you can assume, mindfulness doesn't entertain the word "rushed." It's about deliberately taking your time and creating mental space to focus on what's happening inside and outside yourself at any moment. As you go through this book, you'll realize how mindfulness makes you happier, more deliberate, and more empathic.

Worksheet 1: Counting Breath Practice

Just like any new skill, it helps to gradually ease into it. So, for mindfulness beginners, please try this counting breath practice first.

Step 1. Sit or lie down in a comfortable position.

Step 2. Say "One" and inhale slowly through your nose.

Step 3. Say "Two" and exhale slowly through your mouth.

Step 4. Repeat steps 2 and 3 until you reach "Ten."

In all likelihood, somewhere along the way, you'll get lost, distracted, and forget your counting before you reach "Ten." Whenever that happens, start over with "One."

If you find yourself at, say, "18" without realizing how you got there, then you're still not anchored to the present moment. In this case, start over with "One."

This exercise is not about achieving "10," but the mindful journey of getting there. You must be fully aware of EACH of the 10 breaths you take.

Important: Struggling to reach 10 with full awareness? That's okay. Take a break and try again later. Remember, be kind, and have patience with yourself.

Worksheet 2: Mindful Deep Belly Breathing

Deep belly breathing, or diaphragmatic breathing, is a simple yet powerful tool easily incorporated into your daily routine to promote relaxation, reduce stress, and enhance overall well-being. Regular practice can help cultivate a sense of inner peace and emotional balance.

Step 1. Set a timer for 5 minutes. Sit or lie down in a comfortable position.

Step 2. Place one hand on your chest and the other on your abdomen, just below your rib cage.

Step 3. Inhale slowly. Close your eyes and begin to inhale slowly through your nose. As you inhale, focus on expanding your abdomen, feeling it rise as your lungs fill with air. Breathe deeply enough that you feel your abdomen rise more than your chest.

Step 4. Hold your breath briefly at the top of your inhale, holding your breath for a moment without straining.

Step 5. Exhale slowly. Let your breath out slowly and gently through your mouth or nose. As you exhale, focus on allowing your abdomen to fall naturally, feeling it lower as the air leaves your lungs.

Step 6. Repeat steps 3-5. Continue this breathing pattern for several minutes, maintaining a slow and steady rhythm. Pay attention to the sensation of your breath as it travels in and out of your body, keeping your focus solely on the act of breathing.

Step 7. As you practice deep belly breathing, notice any areas of stress or tension in your body. Release any tension you feel with each exhale.

Step 8. When the timer goes off, slowly open your eyes and maintain a sense of calm and relaxation. Notice any changes in your body and mind, such as the release of stress, the relaxation of muscles, a sense that time has slowed down, etc.

Worksheet 3: Mindful Observation Using Your Five Senses

Breathing exercises help you focus. They train you to become FULLY AWARE of ONE act (i.e., the act of breathing).

The mindful observation exercise below takes you a step further. You're not just focused on breathing now. This practice aims to help you cultivate present-moment awareness and deepen your connection with your surroundings. By focusing your attention on the details of your environment—*without judgment or interpretation*—you can become more mindful.

Step 1. Find a quiet and comfortable space to sit or stand without distractions.

Step 2. Pick an object within your surroundings to serve as the target of this observation exercise. It could be a natural object, artwork, or anything that captures your attention.

Step 3. Engage your senses. Start by taking a few deep belly breaths to center yourself and focus your attention on the present moment. Next, use your senses, one at a time, to carefully observe the item you chose.

Step 4. What do you see? Observe the visual details of the object, paying attention to its shape, color, texture, and any intricate patterns or features. Note how the light reflects off the object and how shadows form around it.

Step 5. What textures do you feel? If possible, gently touch the object and notice its surface, temperature, and any unique sensations it suggests. (For example, if it's cool to your touch, it may prompt a slight chill in you.) Focus on the tactile experience and the physical sensations that arise from your interaction with the object.

Step 6. What do you hear? Shift your focus to the sounds near and far in your environment. If the object you chose makes a sound, bring it closer to your ear and focus on what you're hearing. Can you describe the sound? Does the sound remind you of something? If the item doesn't make a sound, extend your focus and notice any surrounding sounds, such as the rustle of leaves, wind against your window pane, a car passing by, etc. Allow these sounds to come and go without attachment or judgment.

Step 7. What do you smell? Pay attention to any scents or aromas present in your environment. Take a few deep breaths and notice any subtle or distinct smells you encounter, whether pleasant, unpleasant, or neutral.

Step 8. What do you taste in your mouth? Perhaps there's the lingering taste of candy or coffee. Try not to engage with the taste; just take note of it.

Step 9. After engaging your five senses, **acknowledge any thoughts, emotions, or physical sensations that arose during this exercise**. For example, how often did you tend to label or interpret your observations? This is normal, especially if this is your first time trying this exercise. Whenever this occurs, gently guide your focus back to the sensory experience.

Step 10. After several minutes of mindful observation, take a moment to reflect on your experience. Think about how the exercise heightened your awareness and deepened your connection with the present moment.

Recommendation: Do this exercise at least once a day until you observe items in an almost "detached" way. Use your senses one at a time and avoid labeling, interpreting, or forming an opinion about what you observe. (Don't observe people yet. Later in this book, there'll be a specific exercise for that.)

Worksheet 4: Notice+Shift+Rewire

Still engaging in a lot of mind-wandering? This Notice-Shift-Rewire (NSR) mindfulness exercise, commonly associated with mindfulness-based cognitive therapy (MBCT) and mindfulness-based stress reduction (MBSR) programs, can help you.[8]

Step 1. Notice

Notice moments when you become "lost in thought." This may be hard to do because, often, you're already in the middle of your mind wandering before you become aware you're doing it. However, you know who you are, so where, when, or with whom do you tend to mind wander?

For example, do you get lost in thoughts under the shower? If so, you might want to try "stepping under the shower" as a cue. It's like telling your mind, *Oh, I tend to mind wander here.* This simple way of putting yourself on notice will help with the next step.

You may also have a "tell" when your mind is wandering. For example, do you tend to look out the window when you mind-travel? If so, make windows your cue.

Step 2. Shift

After noticing your mind wandering, gently redirect your attention to the present moment. This can be focusing on your breath or throwing yourself fully into what you're doing (e.g., showering, holding a cup of coffee, writing an email, etc.) During idle moments like waiting in line, do Mindful Observation Using Your Five Senses to help you re-focus.

Step 3. Rewire

The final step is reinforcing this new present-awareness way of thinking by engaging in it for at least 15 to 30 seconds. Yes, it doesn't take that long to rewire the brain to form a new habit, but you do need to do it often (e.g., at least 3x a day for at least a week). Luckily, you can do this NSR exercise anytime, anywhere!

So, what will happen when you lessen mind wandering and become more mindful?

For one, you'll be shocked at everything you've been missing because of your inattentiveness to the present moment. Second, you'll feel less stressed because you're not constantly worrying about *what was* or *what could be*. You'll feel more alive because you're more connected to what's happening in your life—in real-time.

Meditation Sucks!

So, mindfulness is a character trait, and meditation is one of the ways you can develop it. Ergo, it's in your best interest to engage in meditation. But it sucks, you say.

I have a confession. The first time I tried to meditate, I couldn't do it. I played some relaxing music on YouTube, comfortably sat down, and after a few breaths, I was already thinking of all the work I had to do. So, I stopped and stood up.

The next day, I tried again and gave up again. I don't remember how often I tried and stopped until I had this sobering thought: "Wow, Ava, you can't control your *mind?!*" And it bothered me, that thought.

How am I functioning during the day if I can't control my thoughts and quiet my mind? "Scatter-brained" is a trait I wasn't aspiring to. How can I make "sound decisions" if I can't focus or if I'm not fully aware of what's happening around me? This startling insight changed how I looked at meditation, and I started to think, "*I'm not giving this enough time. I just don't know how to meditate... yet.*"

The more I became open to meditation, the easier it became. Soon enough, I stopped looking at it as a time-waster and started to treat it as a "mind spa." I meditate in the mornings to slowly wake myself up and start my day by filling my mind with positive and intentional thoughts. When I'm feeling stressed, I meditate to release tension. When I'm feeling lost, I meditate to ground myself. Sometimes, I just meditate to give myself a little "mind reboot."

As I talked to family, friends, and people undergoing their own healing journeys, I discovered various other reasons why people think meditation sucks. Following are some of these reasons and why you should perhaps rethink them.

Meditation is boring.

Quick! What do you think meditation looks like? Do you have a picture of sitting down cross-legged and being quiet (or saying "om")? If you want to, you can do that, but plenty of meditation techniques are available. My personal favorite is to do a <u>Walking Meditation</u>. Still, there's also body scan or grounding meditation, guided meditation (following the audio instructions), Transcendental Meditation (TM) (using mantras), movement meditation (e.g., yoga), and others.

By the way, have you done Worksheets 1 and 2? If you have, you have meditated already; those worksheets are examples of breath awareness meditation.

I don't have time.
I get it. We all lead busy lives. However, meditation is highly adaptable and can be tailored to suit your schedule. Moreover, meditation doesn't have to be long at all. Even just a few minutes of mindfulness can yield tangible benefits.[9] Can't you prioritize yourself for even just 10 minutes?

Meditation doesn't do anything.
Countless studies indicate that meditation provides emotional, physical, and mental benefits.[10] However, since we don't see these benefits immediately (no instant gratification here!), we think meditation doesn't do anything. So, please give it time. The benefits of meditation manifest themselves gradually.

Meditation is a religious practice, and I'm not religious.
Although meditation has its roots in Hinduism and Buddhism, it doesn't need to be linked to religion. Instead, think of meditation as a link to YOU, an exercise in stillness, self-observation, and just being.

I'm not comfortable with silence.
Busy lives. Turbulent thoughts. Chaotic emotions. Rush, rush, rush! This is our normal. So much so that meditation, stillness, and silence can be so uncomfortable. However, please note that the goal of meditation is not to eliminate thoughts but to observe them without judgment and that even very

brief moments of mental stillness can profoundly affect your stress and emotional well-being.

I don't need meditation in my life.
Science shows that meditation reduces stress[11], prevents illness[12], helps with weight control[13], improves sleep[14], enhances memory and other mental capacities[15], etc. Don't you want any of these benefits in your life?

Years ago, someone told me that mindfulness and meditation are difficult because, in truth, it's hard to be alone. Ouch! It's hard to give up the screens, the distractions, and the noise because silence is so uncomfortable and deafening.

So, I encourage you to try mindfulness and meditation by leaving you with this thought: BE CURIOUS.

Be curious about how you can be the master of your own mind.
Be curious about the specific benefits you will reap.
Be curious about what you've been missing during the times you haven't been fully present in the moment.
Be curious about the profound sense of relaxation, peace, and clarity that can come from mindfulness.

Worksheet 5: Walking Meditation

Being outdoors in nature does wonders for your stress levels and overall health.[16,17,18] I guess that's why walking meditations are one of my favorites. Here's how you can try it:

Step 1. Find a quiet and safe outdoor location to walk without distractions or interruptions.

Step 2. Stand still for a few moments. Take a couple of deep breaths to ground yourself and be aware of your body and the surrounding environment.

Step 3. Set an intention for your walk. Examples:

I'm going to take a walk to reduce my stress.
I'm going to take a walk to calm my emotions.
I'm going to take a walk to practice mindfulness.

Step 4. Begin your walk. Start walking slowly and comfortably, standing straight, and allowing your arms to hang naturally by your sides.

Step 5. After a minute or two of walking, focus all your attention on yourself, one body part at a time. Start from the top of your head, working your way down to your feet. Examples:

My head feels heavy. Let me de-stress that a bit with a few deep breaths.
My shoulders are tensed. Let me relax them now.
Work your way down to the sensation of your feet touching the ground, noticing the shifting pressure and movements with each step.

Step 6. Practice mindful awareness of your surroundings. Pay attention to the sights, sounds, and smells around you, fully immersing yourself in the present moment and embracing the sensory experiences.

Step 7. Next, practice breath and step synchronization. Coordinate your breathing with your steps, inhaling slowly and deeply as you take a few strides and exhaling gradually as you continue walking. Focus on the rhythm of your breath and steps, allowing them to harmonize and create a sense of flow and continuity.

Note: If you don't have much time, skip steps 5-7 and just do <u>Counting Breath Practice</u> as you walk. Don't rush your steps! Be deliberate and cultivate a focused awareness of each step you take.

Step 8. When you're at the last leg of your walk, reflect on the simple act of walking in peace and the privilege of being able to practice mindfulness. Express gratitude for your body's ability to move and the nature surrounding you.

Step 9. Gradually slow your pace as you approach the end of your walk, allowing yourself to come to a natural stop. (Again, no rushing!) Intentionally delay "next." If you start thinking about what you need to do next, walk even slower and breathe deeply.

Step 10. When you're done, take a moment to stand still and pull that sense of calmness and awareness deeper inside you, intending to continue mindfulness for the rest of your day.

Radical Acceptance requires Mindfulness
because you cannot fully accept something you're not fully aware of.

Mindfulness helps you focus and be 100% present in the moment. Only when you slow down and be mindful can you really understand and see what's inside you and around you. Only then can you fully accept.

Chapter 3. Self-Awareness: I See ME

As you've learned, mindfulness is about complete awareness. This chapter focuses on directing that awareness towards yourself.

Self-awareness means understanding yourself—completely. It's knowing your feelings, thoughts, motives, and why you do what you do (behavior). It's about being attuned to yourself and how you perceive yourself in various situations.

Many of us would like to believe that we know ourselves, but I think we only know bits and pieces, and mostly only the good parts, because it's hard to accept the not-so-flattering ones. Some only see their not-so-good qualities, unable or unwilling to accept the good they have inside them. Self-awareness sees both. It's the ability to completely see and accept who you are—good and bad, strengths and weaknesses, head to toe, left to right, and inside-out.

Here's something I wasn't fully aware about myself.

We were in Canada for a family vacation. My husband and I booked two hotel suites, one for us and one for my mom and younger brothers. My husband was filming as I showed my mom around her suite. In the video, my voice was very high-pitched! NEVER have I envisioned myself having such a voice. A few minutes later, the video showed me talking to my brothers and husband as he was filming, and my voice was audibly softer, more "normal."

After watching the video, I realized something about myself for the first time. I unconsciously, excitedly, raised my voice when speaking to my mom because I wanted her to be pleased with her room. In that startling moment of self-awareness, plenty of previous situations flashed through my mind in which I desperately tried to please her.

As I realized this, I began to ask, *What else? What else am I doing that I'm not fully aware of?* Mind you, not everything will be revealed in one go. You see, self-awareness is an ongoing process of introspection and reflection. It takes time to gain insight into your own patterns of thinking and behaving.

I'd also like to stress that self-awareness is not just reflecting on *previous* situations. Ideally, you're self-aware *in the moment*. You can see and note your feelings, thoughts, motives, and why you do the things you do (behavior)—as you do them.

Now, you might be asking, *Why do I need to understand myself completely?* Well, how can you expect others to do so if you don't? Isn't it a BIG ASK for others to "get" you if you don't "get" yourself?

You might also be wondering, *Why do I need to be aware of my thoughts, emotions, and actions as I do them?* Because wherever you are, you're helping shape your current situation.

Imagine you're in a team meeting at work, and a colleague suggests a new idea. You don't agree, and you're about to say something sarcastic. However, if you're self-aware, you realize *in that moment* that you shouldn't react that way; it's neither compassionate nor professional. This self-awareness allows you to understand how your response might affect the meeting; either you're fostering open discussion and teamwork or creating an atmosphere of resistance.

Here are other reasons why it's important to cultivate self-awareness:

You'll see patterns in your behavior.
Self-awareness enables you to recognize recurring thoughts, emotions, and behaviors patterns. Knowing these patterns will give insight into why you say, think, and behave like you do.

You'll understand your triggers.
By becoming more self-aware, you can figure out what situations or triggers induce strong emotional reactions or resistance in you. And if you know your triggers, you can avoid them, relieving yourself of potential pain and emotional suffering.

You'll be kinder to yourself.
We're usually our own worst critic. We're often ready and willing to see what's "wrong" with us. Self-awareness helps us see the good in us and the good we do. And when we're being impatient, annoying, or downright obnoxious, being self-aware of that is in and of itself a good thing because then we can shift our behavior.

You'll evolve into your authentic self.
Who are you? Do you truly know? As the years go by, many factors greatly influence our lives. We adapt, we change, we transform... but into what? Self-awareness helps cultivate a deeper understanding of who you are right now; not who you were and want to be. Only from a point of pure self-awareness can you decide if you're living life as the real you.

You'll see your relationships improve.
Self-awareness is not just about knowing what's happening inside you. It also entails being fully aware of what you say and think and how you behave towards others.

You'll make better decisions.
Have you ever been so mad that you blurted out something that you immediately regretted? Have you ever been so bored and lonely that you did something you shouldn't have? We've all been there. Emotions drive most of human behavior.[19] But if you're mindfully self-aware, you can give yourself that time and mental space to THINK your emotions through so you can cope with the situation better and make better decisions.

So, self-awareness is about accepting who you are, warts and all. And it's about being aware of what you're thinking, saying, and doing in any situation. It's like being fully awake and seeing yourself as your day unfolds.

Oh, I'm looking at my watch again. I better stop before my boss thinks I don't want to be here.

I'm clenching my hands. I'm upset. It's okay; this situation is beyond my control. Breathe. Breathe. Breathe.

Ready to be more self-aware? Here's a guide to get you started:

Step 1. Engage in mindfulness.
If you remember, mindfulness cultivates present-moment awareness. So, if you're mindful, it's easier to be self-aware. Imagine being extremely angry with someone. Mindfulness gives you that mental space to tell yourself:

Okay, I'm really upset right now. (self-awareness)
Let me calm down before I say something that might worsen this situation.

Step 2. Start journaling.
Maintain a journal to record your daily experiences, emotions, and reactions. This will help you better understand your behavioral patterns and triggers. **Important:** DO NOT judge your feelings or experiences; just describe what happened.

If journaling is not your thing, find a quiet moment at the end of your day, close your eyes, and self-reflect. Explore your thoughts, feelings, and experiences without judgment.

Step 3. Step outside your comfort zone.
Trying something new always brings out the unexpected. Engage in new activities or hobbies that challenge your perspectives and help you discover previously unknown aspects of yourself.

Step 4. Develop strategies for managing your emotions better.
As you become more self-aware, which emotions tend to get the better of you, and how do you normally cope with them?

For example, do you tend to emotionally eat when you're sad? If so, look for healthier ways to deal with sadness, such as investing more time in offline friendships, learning yoga, playing feel-good tunes on Spotify, etc.

Step 5. Ask others for feedback.
Let's face it. When it comes to yourself, you may be biased. So, when you feel strong and courageous enough, ask people you trust to provide constructive feedback and insights into your strengths and areas for growth.

Step 6. Set a personal goal.
As you get to know yourself better, identify clear and achievable personal goals that reflect your *values*.

For example, let's say you realize that you have a deep passion for environmental conservation and sustainability. In this scenario, you might aim to volunteer for local conservation initiatives, use more eco-friendly products in your home, etc. By aligning your goals with your values, you live a life that stays true to your authentic self.

Worksheet 6: Self-Awareness Exploration

Use this worksheet as a guide to explore and enhance your self-awareness. Complete each step mindfully, allowing yourself to delve deeper into your thoughts, emotions, and behaviors.

Step 1. Think of a recent unpleasant situation or undesired outcome.

Example: A misunderstanding with some friends. We discussed having a dinner date, but there was some miscommunication and I didn't arrive on the date. My friends got mad because they thought I blew them off, and I got angry because no one confirmed the dinner plans with me.

What situation did you choose?

____

____

____

____

____

____

Step 2. What did you feel?

Reflect on your emotional state regarding the situation and write down your feelings, acknowledging their presence without judgment or censorship. *Example: I felt annoyed and left out.*

What were your emotions?

____

____

____

____

____

____

Step 3. What thoughts did you have?

Observe your thoughts about the situation without attachment, noticing any recurring thought patterns or themes. Write down any predominant thoughts that come to mind, acknowledging their presence.

Example: I thought it was incredibly unfair to assume I would just know when and where we were supposed to have dinner.

What were your thoughts?

____

____

____

____

____

____

Step 4. What did you do?

Write what you did as a result of the situation.

Example: When they texted me that they were at the restaurant waiting for me, I replied sarcastically. Something like, "Wow, you guys are absolute rock stars at communicating!" After that, I no longer replied to their text messages.

What were your actions?

____

____

____

____

____

____

Step 5. Practice self-awareness.

Reflect on your behaviors and actions, and ask yourself what you would have done differently. If possible, identify any habits or actions you frequently engage in, both positive and negative.

Example: Looking back, I could've sent a quick WhatsApp message asking about the dinner plans. I didn't have to wait for someone to contact me first. Patterns? I guess

I tend to shut down and become uncommunicable when annoyed. I have a pattern of giving the cold shoulder and ghosting people when I'm pissed.

What have you noticed about yourself?

____

____

____

____

____

Step 6. What happened after you acted out your thoughts and emotions?

Reflect on what happened as a direct result of your behavior. *Example: After ghosting my friends, I didn't hear from them for days. They thought I was childish, and I thought they were mean. All in all, it didn't help our friendship.*

What happened?

____

____

____

____

____

Step 7. Did the situation trigger anything in you?

Why do you think the situation evoked such a strong emotional or behavioral response from you? Write down any triggers you noticed.
Example: The situation triggered feelings of being left out and excluded.

What are your triggers?

____

____

____

____

Step 8. Reflect.

Use the space below to write a journal entry, exploring your thoughts, emotions, and behaviors in-depth. Consider how your thoughts and emotions influenced your behaviors and how external factors impact your internal state.

Example: I guess my feelings of being left-out made me send that sarcastic message to my friends.

Step 9. Set personal growth intentions.

Identify specific personal growth and development intentions based on your self-awareness insights from this exercise. Write down actionable steps you can take to promote positive change and foster a deeper sense of self-awareness.

Example: I realize I could've prevented the situation by sending one simple SMS asking about our dinner plans. In the future, I'll be more proactive. Also, when I'm angry, I shouldn't be mean in my responses and ghost people. I should just be honest about what I feel, and if I don't feel like communicating, I should tell them that, too, so they understand me and give me space.

What are your personal growth intentions?

Worksheet 7: Self-Awareness Prompts

Following are a few self-awareness questions to ask yourself to encourage you to reflect and gain insight into your thoughts, emotions, behaviors, and overall self-perception.

Don't answer them all in one sitting. Choose one and dive into it. That is, select one and spend time utterly answering the question, letting your thoughts and answers take you where they want to go. As you go through these prompts, remember to be kind and patient with yourself.

1. How am I feeling right now, and what could be contributing to these emotions?
2. What thoughts have been foremost in my mind today, and how are they influencing my mood?
3. What moments today brought me the most joy, and why did they have such a positive impact on me?
4. What challenges did I encounter today, and how did I respond to them? Were there healthier ways I could have approached these challenges?
5. How did my interactions with others affect how I feel today? How did I contribute or influence the dynamics of each situation?
6. What activities or tasks do I engage in that bring me a sense of fulfillment and purpose, and how can I incorporate more of these activities into my life?
7. In what areas of my life do I feel the most confident, and how can I leverage this confidence in other aspects of my life?
8. What are my main priorities in life? Are my actions aligned with these priorities?
9. What aspects of my life do I find most challenging, and what steps can I take to overcome or adapt to them more positively?
10. How do I typically respond to stress or difficult situations, and are there healthier coping mechanisms I can adopt?
11. What are my long-term goals, and how can I break them down into smaller, achievable steps?
12. How do I prioritize self-care in my daily routine? What else can I do to nurture my well-being?

*Radical Acceptance requires Self-Awareness
because you cannot accept reality AS IS if you don't see yourself AS IS.*

*Life doesn't just happen to us.
We play a role in what happens to us and unless we are fully aware of our
participation in our reality, we cannot radically accept it.*

Chapter 4. Non-Judgment: Breaking Free from the Chains of Criticism

One of the most difficult habits to unlearn is our tendency to judge everything—ourselves, others, song lyrics, TV shows, situations, the world, anything and everything. The irony is that most of us actually hate being judged. And when we're judged, we judge the other person as mean or unreasonable. See the irony there?

To be clear, passing judgment doesn't always mean appraising in the negative. You can judge someone as amazing, music as lovely, a film as groundbreaking, a book as inspiring, etc. So, to be non-judgmental is not about making zero judgments in life. To be non-judgmental is to develop the habit of NOT making negative assumptions. Because unless you know something to be true, accurate, or factual... you're just guessing.

$$Judgment = Opinion$$
$$Judgment = Assumption$$
$$Judgment \neq Fact$$

Also, keep in mind that when we pass judgment, whether positively or negatively, we project aspects of ourselves onto whom or what we're judging. We judge based on that filter called "self." In doing so, we lose objectivity and become blind to the details and nuances of the object we're judging. In short, when we judge, we give others a glimpse of our inner selves.

So, why is it easy for us to judge? There are many reasons for our judgmental nature. Here are some of them:

Cognitive Bias. Cognitive (*mental*) bias (*prejudices*) is judging others based on our preferences, beliefs, or experiences. For example, suppose you're never late, and someone at work's a few minutes late for a meeting. Based on that single event, you may judge (label) your co-worker as "lazy." The issue with cognitive bias is that since we've established ourselves as the "judge" (based solely on OUR preferences), we don't apply the same criteria to our own person. If someone's late, they're lazy (*personality*). If you're late, it's the fault of traffic (*circumstances*).

Social Conditioning. Society and culture play a significant role in shaping beliefs and attitudes. We may adopt judgmental attitudes based on societal norms, stereotypes, or expectations.

Fear of "Different," "New," or the "Unknown." We may judge others because we're exposed to something unusual or different. Fear or discomfort with unfamiliar aspects of life can lead to judgmental attitudes.

Insecurity. Judgmental behavior can sometimes stem from low self-esteem or feelings of insecurity. Criticizing others may serve as a defense mechanism to deflect attention from our perceived shortcomings.

Lack of Empathy. We may be prone to judgmental behavior if we cannot understand others' perspectives or viewpoints. We cannot see their sides, so we'd rather judge them.

Need for Control. Judgment is a way to assert control or establish a sense of superiority. By labeling others as "less" or "wrong," we're, in effect, saying that we're "more" and "right." In this situation, passing judgment provides a temporary sense of power or validation.

Now, just because judgmental behavior is inherent to humans[20,21], it doesn't mean you can't do anything about it. You can develop a non-judgmental behavior. But why should you want to?

For one, research shows that non-judgmental people tend to be happier.[22] That's not really surprising, is it? Imagine a state of being where you're not always calculating, assessing, or judging. That's a lot of stress avoided!

Also, non-judgmental people have better, more stable relationships because they're open to differences, capable of seeing others' points of view, and, as such, are more understanding and empathic. Wouldn't you want to have someone like this in your life? Someone who sees you for who you are and loves you as is?

Further, if you're non-judgmental, you lessen your own emotional suffering. Here's a simple example: imagine waking up and hearing rain outside your window. Your brain immediately judges the day as "dreadful." And that's it; you've set a tone of negativity throughout your day.

But what's the REALITY of the situation?
What's the one true FACT?
It's just raining.

So, **how do you cultivate a non-judgmental attitude?** Would it surprise you that mindfulness and self-awareness have much to do with it?

Mindfulness promotes **present-moment awareness**. And when your mind is preoccupied with NOW, you're less likely to dwell on past judgments or project them onto the future. If you do this one thing, you'll stop starting sentences with, *I "knew" you would...* or *I "knew" you were going to...* because sentences like that mean you're re-living something in the past and judging it to be applicable in the future.

Self-awareness helps you recognize patterns of judgment within yourself. By understanding these patterns, you can work towards breaking the habit of quick, automatic judgments. Using the same sample as above, the minute you start "reliving" something in the past, Notice-Shift-Rewire!

In short, mindfulness and self-awareness promote a pause between stimulus and response. This mental pause allows you to respond to situations with greater thoughtfulness rather than reacting with snap judgments.

Another way to develop a non-judgmental behavior is to **challenge your assumptions**.

When you notice yourself judging, ask yourself, *What else could be true? What can possibly be another reason for this?* Yes, argue with yourself! This is the fastest way to conclude that your judgment is based on an opinion or assumption, not facts.

Also, **develop empathy**. Put yourself in others' shoes and consider, even for a moment, *their* feelings and experiences. Mind you, you don't have to agree. You just have to understand their perspective.

Worksheet 8: What Else?

Judgmental behavior is often about being fixated on a *perceived* specific reason or outcome. However, as mentioned, until you know, you don't know for sure. This reflective exercise will help you develop the habit of giving others the benefit of the doubt.

Step 1. Identify a previous situation where you jumped to a conclusion and easily passed judgment on someone.

Example: I texted a friend to meet for drinks, but they weren't replying. Their "Read Receipt" notification is on, so I saw they read my message. Hours later, still no reply. So yeah, my mind went to several assumptions.

____

____

____

____

____

____

Step 2. What assumptions/judgments did you make?

Examples:
They're deliberately ignoring me.
They don't want to have drinks with me, and they're thinking how to say "no" nicely.
They're already out having drinks with our other friends and don't want me to know about it.

____

____

____

____

____

____

Step 3. WHAT ELSE was true?

Examples: My friend was giving an important presentation at a work meeting and didn't have time to reply to me.

____

____

Whenever you find yourself passing judgment, always ask, "*What else could be true?*" Do this often enough, and you'll cultivate non-judgmental behavior.

Worksheet 9: Empathic People Watching

When we people-watch, we tell ourselves we do so for entertainment, but truly, it's an opportunity to judge others. This exercise is designed to enhance your objective observational skills, foster empathy, and reduce the habit of automatically passing judgment. This activity encourages you to observe people in different situations with a curious and open mindset.

Step 1. Choose a public space like a park, cafe, or shopping mall where people engage in various activities. **Bring a notebook or journal** with you.

Step 2. Find a comfortable spot where you can observe people without feeling or being intrusive. Ensure you have a clear view of different interactions.

Step 3. Begin with a few minutes of **mindful breathing** to center yourself and cultivate present-moment awareness.

Step 4. Now, **watch people** without judgment. Notice their gestures, expressions, and interactions. **Resist forming any immediate opinions**.

Step 5. Be empathic. Put yourself in their shoes. Consider what might be going on in their lives, what emotions they might be feeling, and what their experiences could be like.

Step 6. Write down your observations. Describe only what you see.
Example: I notice a woman walking fast in front of me, a child in tow.

Step 7. Is your mind making any immediate assumptions? If any judgments arise, write them without self-criticism. *Example: I think she's running late, so she's "dragging" her child.*

Step 8. Reflect. Explore where your assumptions came from. *Example: I lived with my father when I was a kid. Apart from work, he always brought me along, and we were always rushing. I was always being dragged somewhere.*

Step 9. Challenge your assumptions. What else could be true?

Example: WHAT ELSE could be true? Maybe the mom I saw wasn't rushing and was just walking fast. Also, now that I think about it, perhaps the child wasn't being dragged at all. The kid had shorter legs, so of course, they'd be walking slower and behind their mother.

Step 10. Move on to observe other people and different situations, repeating steps 4-9. Regular practice can enhance your ability to see the world from different perspectives and cultivate a more open, less judgmental mindset.

Identifying Self-Judgment and Self-Criticism

Although we hate being judged by others, we often judge ourselves and often in a negative light. This is because we've learned that to judge ourselves in the positive (e.g., *I'm looking great today. I'm so kind-hearted. I'm an excellent team leader.*) is being selfish and arrogant.

The problem with self-judgment is, again, we don't just state facts; we're criticizing ourselves. For example, we don't say *I don't know how to play the piano... yet*, we say, *I suck at playing the piano!*

Further, oddly enough, we *prefer* to judge ourselves. This way, we protect ourselves from the harsh judgment of others. Saying *I'm ugly* is less painful than hearing someone else say it. However, even though you think it's less painful, it's not less harmful. When we self-judge and self-criticize, we damage ourselves in so many ways.[23,24,25]

Harms Mental Health. Constant self-judgment contributes to negative thought patterns and can lead to conditions like anxiety and depression.

Lowers Self-Esteem. Excessive self-judgment erodes your self-esteem, making it difficult to appreciate your worth and accomplishments.

Limits Personal Growth. If you keep thinking you're incapable of doing something, chances are, you won't even try for fear of failing. This prevents you from exploring new things and evolving as a person.

Harms Relationships. Judging yourself harshly and constantly can impact your interactions with others, leading to strained relationships and difficulty forming connections. No one likes being around a "downer."

Increases Stress Levels. Constant negative inner chatter is draining! You're harsh on yourself; you blame yourself when things go wrong, even though the situation might be beyond your control, and you constantly second-guess yourself. This can lead to high levels of stress, anxiousness, and an overall decline in your physical health.

Undermines Resilience. You may struggle to bounce back from setbacks if you habitually judge yourself. Instead of thinking *I'll do better next time*, you might think, *Why bother?*

Impairs Decision-Making. A self-judgmental mindset may lead to indecisiveness because you constantly doubt your abilities.

Important: YOU deserve kindness and compassion—always. And there's absolutely nothing wrong with you extending these amazing, healing qualities to yourself. But to achieve this, you need to stop talking yourself down and start talking yourself up.

Silencing your inner critic requires mindfulness, self-awareness, and challenging your negative thoughts. For example, each time you think, " I look old, " take your cue from actress Anne Hathaway and say, "*Aging is just another word for living.*" And instead of looking at your laugh lines, remember all the joyous moments that caused them, and keep smiling!

Here are other tips to put your inner critic into "Silent" mode.

- **Channel positivity** the minute you wake up. Say something like, "Today is a great day to have a great day!"
- **Acknowledge the good in you.** We all have good qualities, so feel free to write down anything and everything that makes you an amazing and unique person. Now, don't overthink this. Examples: I'm good at singing.

I'm organized in the bathroom. I care about my goldfish. (See also the Afformations worksheet below.)

- **Create a positive environment.** Surround yourself with energetic, happy people who see life as "half full," never "half empty." Avoid people and situations that bring you down. Establish and assert your boundaries so you're not "pulled" into anyone's drama.
- **Celebrate your achievements, no matter how small.** For example, "I cooked something I've never cooked before. That's being adventurous, baby. Booyah!"
- **Limit self-comparison.** Avoid constant comparison with others. Your journey is unique, and focusing on your life is more productive. If this entails a digital detox, then so be it!
- **Take care of your body.** A healthy body contributes to a healthy mind.[26,27] Eat and drink well, sleep adequately, and incorporate physical movement daily. This will make you feel and look good, boosting your self-esteem.
- **Practice gratitude.** Regularly reflect on the positive aspects of your life to counterbalance any negative thoughts. (See also The Underrated Power of Gratitude.)
- **Focus less on self-blame and more on solutions.** When things don't go as planned, make a mental jump from *What did I do wrong* to *How can I improve this situation?*

Worksheet 10: Afformations

You probably know positive affirmations already, so what are afformations? Introduced by mental health coach Noah St. John[28], afformations are positive questions you ask yourself.

The goal is to encourage your subconscious mind to find answers and solutions to questions, generating a positive and self-uplifting mindset. In simple terms, you engage your mind in diving deep into what you're good at and why.

Step 1. Ask yourself a positive question.

Examples:
What do I love about myself?
Why am I happy today?
What's the best thing that happened yesterday?
What do I like about my appearance?

What's your question?

____
____
____
____
____
____

Step 2. Engage your mind by writing down at least three positive answers you can think of answering your positive question. For example:

Question: Why is my day filled with joy?
Answers:
a. I appreciate the small moments.
b. I surround myself with positive people.
c. I focus on what I can control.

Answer 1: _______________________________________

Answer 2: _______________________________________

Answer 3: _______________________________________

Answer 4: _______________________________________

Answer 5: _______________________________________

Step 3. Reflect. Take a moment to think about the answers. How do they make you feel? *Example: My answers made me feel grateful.*

____

____

____

____

____

____

Step 4. List down more positive questions related to your initial one.

Examples:
Original question: Why is my day filled with joy?
Related afformations:
- *What else can I do today to bring me joy?*
- *Why do I deserve this happiness I'm feeling?*

Related positive questions:

____

____

____

____

____

____

Step 5. Create a daily afformation practice. Repeat steps 1-4 every day for at least 30 consecutive days. Remember that the questions don't need to be earth-shattering. Simple questions such as "*Why is this cup of coffee/tea making me feel so good?*" are perfectly fine, too. The goal is to keep bringing positivity and good vibes into your life.

*Radical Acceptance requires a Non-Judgmental attitude
because if your mind is preoccupied with labeling yourself, people, things and
situations as good, bad, right or wrong, you cannot accept them for simply
what they are (as is).*

Chapter 5. Embracing Imperfection

In life, we want to do our best. We're on our best behavior for our parents; we put our best efforts at school and at work; we present the best versions of ourselves when dating; we strive to provide what's best for our loved ones; we want to show up day in and day out as the best versions of ourselves.

This quest for "best" often means a pursuit of perfection. The problem is that perfection is a unicorn. It doesn't exist; it's a myth. So, if you live your life to impossibly high standards, you set yourself up for constant disappointment, causing yourself undue stress, burnout, anxiety, and depression.[29,30]

In contrast, embracing imperfection has been linked to greater happiness and better mental health.[31] So, how do you become okay with imperfection if you have a tendency for perfectionism?

Be mindful and live in NOW. Remember, what has happened has already happened. You cannot undo it.

Practice self-awareness. Tell yourself, *"This situation isn't ideal. That's okay. I don't need to react."* Next, **adopt a non-judgmental** attitude. *"This is no one's fault. No one desired this outcome. Now, how can I make this situation better?"*

Go for "flow" instead of perfect. "Flow" is a state of being totally absorbed and focused on something. You're engaging in an activity because of the joy it provides, not because of any desired result you expect. Focusing on "flow" enables you to enjoy the journey rather than being fixated on the destination.

Redefine "perfect." From now on, consider perfection a source of inspiration rather than a goal or established fact. Tell yourself that your goal is to do well, not to be flawless.

Celebrate "unique." Recognize and celebrate what makes you, others, or a situation unique. Keep in mind that if everything's the same, it becomes boring. Quirks and imperfections provide charm and individuality.

Choose freedom and authenticity. You don't need to follow the latest trend. You don't need to be loved by everyone. You don't need to accomplish the perfect project report every single time. You don't have to live up to anyone else's standards of beauty, success, or worth—and vice versa. Once you embrace imperfection, you embrace freedom, the freedom to be yourself.

Learn from undesired outcomes. Embracing imperfection doesn't mean you shouldn't aspire to be better. If things don't go as planned, don't dwell on mistakes or what went wrong. View the situation as a learning opportunity. What lessons can you glean from this? What should you avoid or continue to do in the future? How can this situation contribute to your personal growth?

Worksheet 11: Wabi-Sabi (侘寂)

Wabi-sabi is a Japanese concept that appreciates and finds beauty in impermanence (i.e., everything in life is fleeting) and imperfection. It's a perspective that values simplicity, asymmetry, and the authenticity of materials, so examples of wabi-sabi might be seeing the beauty in broken pottery, appreciating the aged look and ancient folds of an old love letter, etc.

Step 1. Embrace imperfection. Think of a recent situation where something didn't go as planned or was less than perfect. Describe how you initially felt about the imperfection.

Example: Last week, I baked a cake that didn't turn out as perfectly as I hoped. Initially, I was terribly disappointed; all that ingredients, time, and effort!

____

____

____

____

____

Reflect on whether you were able to find beauty or value in the imperfection over time.

Example: I did, actually. I thought I ruined the cake by accidentally adding cardamom instead of cinnamon, but the cake tasted great! As I was annoyed, I wasn't so careful with the icing anymore. Later, I found beauty in the imperfect swirls of the cake icing and considered it a unique creation.

____

____

____

____

____

Step 2. Reflect on the transience or fleetingness of life. Consider a moment or phase in your life that has changed or is changing.

Example: I'm reflecting on a past friendship. Though I'm no longer in touch with this person, I'm not bitter. I appreciate the beauty in the shared memories and the growth I've experienced with that friend.

____

____

____

____

____

____

Step 3. Look for simplicity and authenticity around you. Identify an object or aspect of your life that embodies simplicity and authenticity.
Example: I'm attached to this slightly worn-in book my sister gave me before I left for college. I find beauty in the simplicity of its well-read state, imagining how my sister enjoyed each page as I enjoyed going through them.

____

____

____

____

____

____

List at least three ways you can incorporate more simplicity in your daily life.
Example: de-clutter my bedroom, give away old gadgets, avoid toxic people

Way #1: ____

Way #2: ____

Way #3: ____

Step 4. Appreciate natural materials and flaws. Think about an item you own made from natural materials (wood, stone, etc.). Reflect on the beauty found in that item's natural flaws or imperfections.
Example: I have a small, old, wooden side table with visible knots, grain irregularities, and coffee stains. I love it!

____

____

____
____
____
____

Step 5. Look for asymmetry or irregularities in your environment.
Look around your home and identify an area where asymmetry exists.
Consider how this asymmetry adds character and interest to the space.
Example: My living room has plenty of mismatched sofa pillows. I used to be "bothered" by them. Now, I think they add "character" to my home.

____
____
____
____
____
____

Wabi-sabi encourages us to find beauty in the imperfect, the fleeting, and what is natural (authentic, real). Practice this exercise often to cultivate a deeper sense of appreciation and contentment in your daily life.

*Radical Acceptance requires Embracing Imperfection
because you cannot accept reality AS IS if you expect it to be flawless or if you expect it to be anything at all.*

Life is inherently flawed, and attempting to resist or deny imperfections leads to unnecessary suffering.

Chapter 6. Letting Go of Control

Emotional suffering usually stems from an inability to let go of control. I know a thing or two about this.

In my previous career as a Project Manager, I tended to micro-manage people. I found it extremely hard to delegate. I always followed up on everyone, and I would shift to blaming when something went wrong. I would blame myself, blame others, and I'd even blame fate if I had to. I would blame because I had an extremely difficult time accepting the situation. Emotionally, I was a wreck. I was always on my toes, vigilant of everything. This meant I was almost always stressed and anxious.

As a result, I developed the habit of pulling at my hair (*trichotillomania* or *trich*). It got so bad that I started sporting a very short haircut, telling everyone I preferred it because it meant less time to get ready in the morning. I also pulled, plucked, and tweezed my eyebrows until nothing was left to fix. (I could leave my home without any lipstick, but I couldn't without my eyebrow pencil.)

With Radical Acceptance, I've learned I had issues letting go because of my heightened sense of perfectionism, which was due to fear. I wanted things to be "perfect" because I was afraid of being found out that I wasn't good enough.

Here are some of the other reasons a person may be unwilling or unable to let go of control:

- **Fear of the unknown.** You're hesitant to try "new" because you're uncertain of what might happen. This indicates low self-esteem because you don't trust yourself outside your comfort zone.

- **Need for security.** You live a life of strict routines and planned approaches—designed by you. If the unknown or unexpected happens, your feelings of safety and security are challenged.

- **Perceived signs of weakness**. You may associate "letting go" with giving up or giving in. If you let go, you fear giving others the impression that you're "losing power," are not strong enough to see things through, or are incapable of defending your values and beliefs.

- **Past experiences**. Suppose you've experienced negative consequences as a result of you not having control (e.g., missing an important job interview because your ride was late picking you up). In that case, you might be unwilling to let go of control moving forward.

However, as mentioned above, the inability to let go heaps loads of emotional suffering. So, how do you free yourself from this self-imposed agony?

All the qualities we've discussed—mindfulness, self-awareness, a non-judgmental attitude, and the ability to embrace imperfection—can help you let go of control.

You must also **learn to delegate**, but what does that mean? In my opinion, learning to delegate means learning to trust.

At work, it means trusting that your colleagues have the skills to contribute effectively to a project. In personal relationships, it involves trusting that your partner, friends, or family members are capable and willing to share responsibilities. Ultimately, delegating involves recognizing that you don't have to carry everything on your shoulders. If you don't delegate, you deny others the opportunity to help and involuntarily convey that they are "incapable."

Please note that delegating (trusting) doesn't mean dictatorship. You're not supposed to give instructions but to let others participate in situations with you.

Another way to learn to let go of control is to **stop catastrophizing**, which is the belief that things will go terribly wrong if you're not in charge. So, what do you do? Shift from worst-case scenario thinking and start developing better stories in your head instead. For example, suppose your friends are coming over so you can cook dinner together. Your mind starts to race:

What's the menu? Are we just cooking whatever? Will that work?
What's the timing here? What if the meals are not done at the same time?
My kitchen will get all dirty. I'll have to stay up till 2 AM cleaning!

STOP! What's a better story here?

This is going to be fun. We're going to have a great time!
We need this. This is going to be great for our friendship.
I'm excited to eat something different tonight.

Here's another approach to help yourself let go of control: **develop your self-efficacy**, which is your belief in your ability to accomplish tasks, solve problems, or achieve goals. You see, the more uncertain a situation, the more we try to control it. Imagine all the angst we create for ourselves by trying to time to tame the uncertain or unknown! Instead, release that angst (need for control) and simply enjoy the experience, believing with all your heart and mind that whatever happens, you'll be able to deal with it.

But what about the stress and anxiety you feel inside when you're itching to control a situation? You shift your focus. Shift your mind from thinking about the situation to managing your stress and anxiety (i.e., manage your emotions). How? Firstly, do any of the mindfulness exercises under <u>Chapter 2</u>. Next, try the exercise on the following page.

Worksheet 12: Letting Go for Emotional Release

When you're trying to let go of control, you might experience unpleasant emotions. You might feel resentful, stressed, anxious, angry, etc. The following exercise will help you let go of control by helping you deal with the difficult emotions you might be experiencing as you attempt to release control.

Step 1. Label your emotions. Identify and label the emotions you are currently experiencing. Don't deny or ignore it.
Example: I'm extremely anxious. I'm not used to not being in charge.

____

____

____

____

____

____

Step 2. Accept your emotions. Remember, all your emotions are valid. You have a right to feel what you feel. Accept your emotion, but don't judge it.
Example: I'm anxious. This is what I'm feeling right now, and that's okay.

____

____

____

____

____

____

Step 3. Take a mindful breath. Breathe deeply a few times to relax yourself.

Step 4. Ground yourself. Engage your senses to ground yourself in the present moment. Look around you and identify five things you can see, four things you can touch, three things you can hear, two things you can smell, and one thing you can taste. (See also <u>Mindful Observation Using Your Five Senses</u>.)

Step 5. Body scan to let go of emotions. Did you know that emotions happen in the body?[32] Do a quick body scan (from head to toe) and pay attention to where you're feeling your emotions.

Example: I'm feeling my anxiousness on my shoulders. They're tense and bunched up.

____

____

____

____

____

____

Step 6. LET GO. Focus on the area of your body where you feel the emotion, take a slow and deep breath in, and imagine blowing away your emotion as you slowly exhale. (You can also say the word "Release" or "I release you" as you exhale.) Feel free to stretch, yawn, jump, etc., if you feel like it too.

Do this exercise each time you feel yourself resisting your efforts at letting go of control. It may seem difficult initially, but with constant practice, you'll find yourself going through less emotional distress as you surrender control of situations.

Forgiveness: Letting Go of Control Over Your Emotions

What does forgiveness have to do with surrendering control? In many respects, the difficulty to forgive reflects an inability to let go of control over emotions.

When you struggle to release feelings of anger, hate, jealousy, resentment, bitterness, sadness, etc., you are, in a sense, trying to control those emotions by choosing to hold on to them instead of allowing the natural emotional process to unfold (i.e., acknowledging feelings, accepting them, and then consciously choosing not to let them dictate your well-being).

For example, suppose your partner cheated. You're furious, and you break up. Time has passed, but you're still angry and don't want to forgive them. However, by being unwilling to forgive, you're holding onto your anger and hate. You're choosing to stay in emotional misery and negativity because you cannot let go of control over these emotions.

You might be thinking, *but they don't deserve my forgiveness!* This is where most of us get it wrong. (I know I did.) Forgiveness is, first and foremost, for the benefit of the forgiver (you), not the one being forgiven. By forgiving, you're choosing to let go of unpleasant and unhealthy emotions and energy (negativity) and deciding not to carry it forward with you anymore.

Think of it this way: if you feel bitterness and keep bitterness in your heart, you become a bitter person. But if you feel bitterness and choose to let it go, you can become happy.

Further—and here's something I really had to dig deep for—if you're not willing to forgive, ask yourself what trauma or damage the person or situation triggered in you? Going back to our cheating example, if you cannot forgive them, it's perhaps because you've always had abandonment issues. And rather than accept that you may have low self-esteem or a fear of loneliness, you'd rather stay angry with your ex. After all, "mad" is easier, less painful, and safer than "sad."

So, if you really think about it, to be unforgiving is to be in denial.

I will not forgive you. I will stay angry because this is your fault.
(Translation: I will not forgive you. I will stay angry because I don't want to
deal with feeling abandoned and undesired.)

Important: Forgiving is NOT forgetting, denying, approving, excusing, or condoning. Forgiving is not letting the accountable "off the hook." It's releasing yourself from the hook of emotional negativity and suffering.

While discussing forgiveness with my Radical Acceptance group, someone asked, "*If forgiveness is for me. Can I forgive and not let the other person know?*" I believe you can, especially if you don't want to have any further contact or maintain any form of relationship with them.

We always associate forgiveness with the person who hurt us. I ask you to reframe your idea of forgiveness as a personal, internal, and self-healing process that primarily benefits your emotional well-being. As such, you can forgive privately, focusing on your own peace of mind and emotional release. However, if you believe communicating your forgiveness would bring closure or positively impact your relationship with the other person moving forward, you may choose to do so at your discretion.

If forgiving others is good for you, imagine the healing you accomplish when you forgive yourself.

Unfortunately, for many, forgiving oneself is harder than forgiving others.[33] For one, there are more difficult emotions involved. Research shows that while *anger* is the only significant predictor of unforgiveness, *anxiety, guilt, shame,* and *anger* are associated with self-forgiveness.[34]

Let's flip our example and suppose that you cheated on your partner. Difficulty forgiving yourself may be due to your enormous guilt and shame over what you did. You might be angry at yourself for the situation you caused, and you might feel anxious about your future, not knowing if your relationship will survive the cheating.

Self-forgiveness may also be difficult if you keep thinking about *what could have been* or all the *what-ifs*. This rumination reinforces feelings of guilt and shame and, as such, strengthens any belief you may have that you are "bad."

Judging yourself too harshly or significantly overestimating your responsibility in the situation (i.e., *I take full responsibility. It's all on me.*), as well as believing that you brought this all on yourself (i.e., *I'm weak. I have low morals. I would've cheated sooner or later.*) are also reasons why self-forgiveness may be difficult.

Notice that all the above reasons point to the same thing: You're not letting go of control over your emotions. You're choosing to stay negative instead of allowing the natural emotional process of forgiving yourself to unfold. With self-forgiveness, this natural process means (1) taking responsibility for your actions, (2) exhibiting genuine remorse, (3) sincerely apologizing and making amends, and (4) learning from your mistakes. (See <u>Worksheet 13: The 4 R's of Self-Forgiveness</u>.)

Forgiveness, whether directed to others or yourself, is, for all intents and purposes, acceptance of pain. Something horrible happened, and you're feeling a host of negative emotions. However, staying in that negative state doesn't do anyone any good. To feel better, release yourself from emotional suffering, and heal... you must learn to forgive.

Worksheet 13: Forgiving Others

Step 1. Reflect on the hurt. Take a moment to reflect on the specific actions or behaviors of the person you must forgive. Write down how these actions have affected you emotionally and any residual feelings of resentment or anger.

Example: I asked my best friend of 20 years to help me find a temporary place near them as I had to be there for three months for work. The place was great, but I later learned I was paying 50% more on rent. My "best friend" was pocketing the money. No, I didn't know they took it upon themselves to take a "fee." When I arrived, I even treated them to dinner to say thanks, and they never said anything. I've developed trust issues. I even started to question myself. Like, wow, I don't know how to pick friends?

____

____

____

____

____

____

Step 2. Acknowledge your emotions.
Acknowledge and identify the emotions that have arisen due to the hurt you have experienced. Write down the specific feelings you are experiencing, such as anger, betrayal, or sadness, without judgment.
Examples: I feel angry, dismayed, betrayed, and used.

____

____

____

____

____

Step 3. Practice empathy. Try to understand the perspective of the person who hurt you. Write down any possible reasons or circumstances that may have influenced their actions, fostering a sense of empathy and understanding.

Example: What would drive a person to take money from a friend? I guess if they had debts or health problems for which they need money.

Step 4. Release your resentment. Challenge any lingering feelings of resentment or grudges you may be holding onto. Write down affirming statements that help you release these negative emotions and open yourself up to the possibility of forgiveness and emotional liberation.

Example: I won't stay angry with you anymore. I won't let anger take the better of me. I'm releasing any feelings of betrayal. I won't let this incident completely prevent me from enjoying my other friendships.

Step 5. Write a forgiveness letter. This is optional, but it might help to compose a forgiveness letter addressed to the person who hurt you. Express your feelings honestly and openly, emphasizing your willingness to let go of the pain and move forward with compassion and understanding. Remember, you don't have to send this. This is for you.

Example forgiveness letter to a toxic family member:

I've been reflecting on our relationship, and I find myself carrying a lot of hurt and disappointment. It's not easy to admit, but holding onto these negative emotions is taking a toll on my well-being.

For my own peace of mind, I'm choosing to forgive you for the past. Forgiveness doesn't mean forgetting or condoning hurtful actions, but rather releasing the hold these memories have on my heart.

I'm not sure if I'm going to send you this letter. For now, it's more of a personal reflection; about freeing myself from the weight of resentment.

I hope, in time, we can both find our paths to healing and perhaps even rebuild our relationship. For now, I'm taking steps to focus on my own growth and well-being.

____

____

____

____

____

____

Step 6. Visualize the act of forgiveness. Engage in a visualization exercise where you imagine yourself letting go of the hurt and offering forgiveness to the person who has wronged you. For example, imagine releasing a forgiveness balloon, and as the balloon flies away from you, imagine any unpleasant emotions leaving your body. (If you want, skip visualizing and carry out the act.)

Step 7. Set boundaries for self-protection. Establish healthy boundaries to protect yourself from potential harm in the future. Write down specific actions you can take to set boundaries that prioritize your emotional well-being and prevent similar hurtful experiences from occurring again.

Example: I'll avoid putting myself in a situation involving friends and money. If I ever need help from a friend again that requires money, I'll make sure I verify amounts or pre-discuss with them if there are fees or anything of the kind involved. Honesty and directness will prevent headaches and heartaches later.

____

____

____

____

____

____

Step 8. Embrace your emotional liberation! After forgiving, give yourself some time to get used to it. Afterward, celebrate your journey toward emotional liberation and forgiveness. Write down how forgiving others has contributed to your personal growth, resilience, and capacity for empathy and understanding.

Example: These past weeks, I feel "lighter," as if a burden has been lifted off my shoulders. I also feel that I can enjoy my current friends better; I'm not always on guard or second-guessing their intentions.

____

____

____

____

____

____

Worksheet 14: The 4 R's of Self-Forgiveness

Genuine self-forgiveness is an active process; i.e., there are steps involved. It's not just saying, "*Oh, people make mistakes. I'm human, so I forgive myself.*"

In fact, saying or believing this might indicate a lack of self-awareness over any wrongdoings you may have done. It may also be a sign that you're unwilling to let go of control over your emotions. That is, you're glossing over the issue instead of accepting and addressing it. The following exercise aims to help you attain true self-forgiveness.

Step 1. Responsibility

Take responsibility for your actions. Think of a situation where you made a mistake or did something you regret. Describe the situation briefly.

Example: I made a hasty decision at work without considering the potential consequences. As a result, extra man-hours had to be put in, and the project deadline was not met. The client got mad and left us a bad review online.

____

____

____

____

____

____

Step 2. Remorse

Explore and identify the emotions associated with your actions.

Example: I feel guilty and embarrassed. I was rushing. I should've taken the time to think things through. If I did, the project might not have had issues and finished on time.

____

____

____

____

____

____

Allow yourself to experience and express these emotions fully. Remember, this is not *wanting* to feel further guilt or shame about your mistake. It's allowing your emotions to go through its natural course.

Step 3. Restitution

Consider *practical steps* to make amends or restitution. List actions you can take to repair the harm caused, and then create a plan for implementing these actions.

Example:
    (1) Gather the team for a meeting and apologize sincerely.
    (2) Mention that I'm aware of the negative consequences of my actions.

____

____

____

____

____

Step 4. Renewal

What have you learned from the situation? Identify areas for personal growth and positive change. Set specific goals for self-improvement and commit to them.

Example: I've learned that rushing important decisions is never a good idea. I need to take my time and be more thorough. I also learned that I should always remember that it's not just me involved in a project. My decisions affect other people, so I shouldn't take them lightly.

____

____

____

____

____

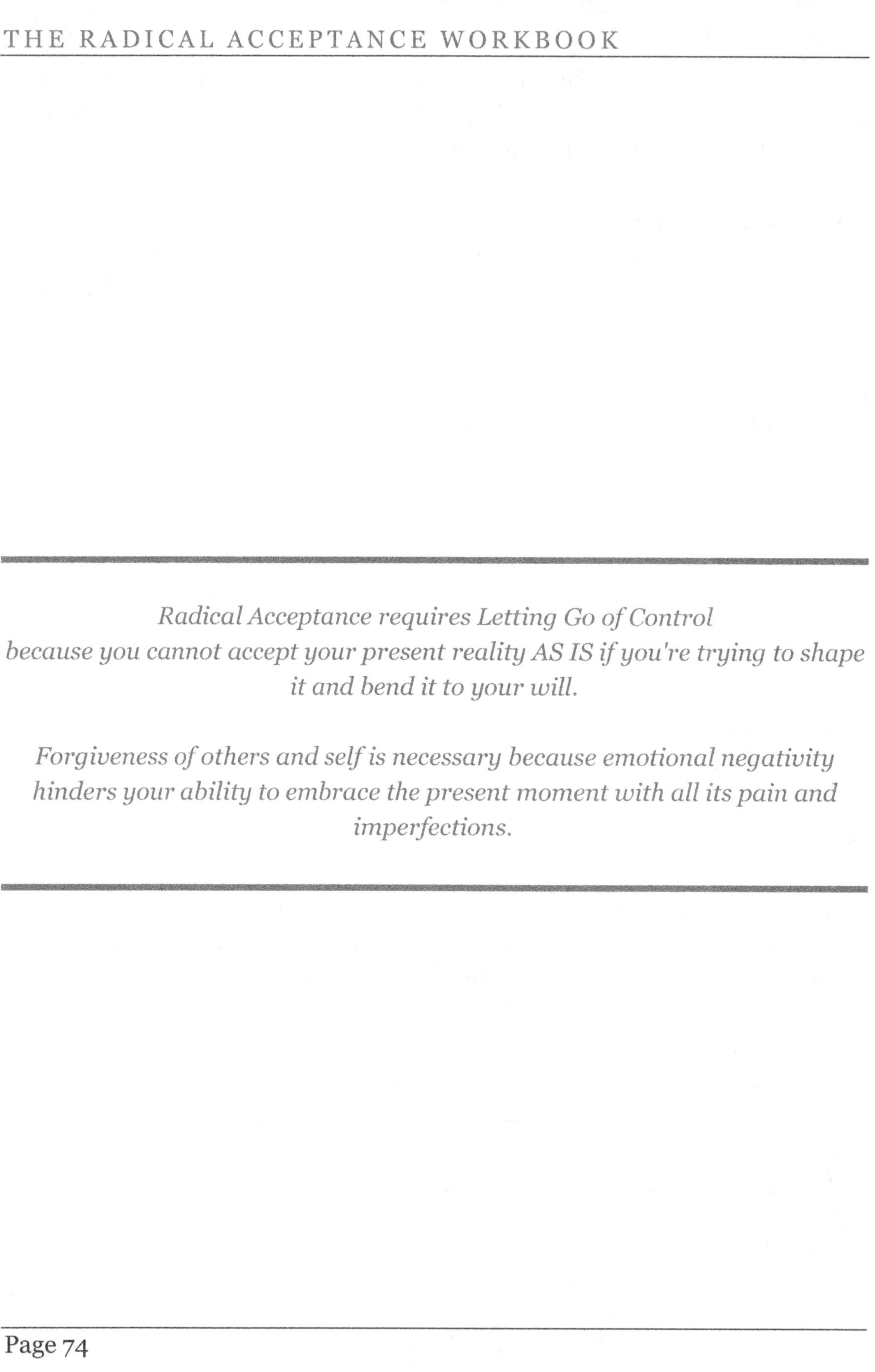
Radical Acceptance requires Letting Go of Control
because you cannot accept your present reality AS IS if you're trying to shape
it and bend it to your will.

Forgiveness of others and self is necessary because emotional negativity
hinders your ability to embrace the present moment with all its pain and
imperfections.

Chapter 7. Radical Willingness

Everything we've discussed so far is meaningless if you're not willing; willing to see reality for what it is, and willing to modify any thoughts, feelings, or habits that are not working for you.

You might think, "*Ava, shouldn't you have mentioned willingness at the start?*" Truthfully, I believe that unwillingness or resistance often comes in the form of *denial*. That is, you may not be seeing or realizing that you're unwilling and, as a result, end your journey before you even start.

However, if you're mindful (*present in the moment*), self-aware (*capable of objectively seeing yourself*), nonjudgmental (*not applying any negative assumptions or opinions*), capable of embracing imperfection (*understanding that healing is not a linear process*), and are okay with letting go of control (*able to trust the process*), then, dear reader, NOW you can be radically willing to accept Radical Acceptance.

Please keep in mind that to experience *unwillingness* is normal. In the context of emotional healing, willingness is the ability to feel emotions without instantly escaping or avoiding them. And dealing with emotions—accepting them, feeling them, and understanding their WHY—can be difficult and painful. So we are unwilling. Unwillingness keeps us "safe."

In the context of life in general, willingness is the ability to openly and actively engage with experiences, challenges, and changes—without resistance.

It means being open to what happens, going with the flow of life, and taking in both the good and bad things with an open heart and mind. Being willing means being ready to learn, change, and grow, knowing that every moment brings new lessons and chances to improve yourself.

As with previous qualities discussed in this book, willingness doesn't mean denying, approving, wanting, or condoning.

For example, suppose you're feeling intense grief due to the loss of a loved one. Willingness is not being "okay" with their death. It's about being willing to feel and experience your grief. Why? To feel better. Willingness to feel grief transforms grief into pain you can endure.

Worksheet 15: Willing Hands

As mentioned, we feel emotions in our bodies. **Willing Hands** is a body-focused exercise often applied in DBT.1 By physically fostering a sense of openness, we can slowly manage our resistance against painful or unpleasant emotions of experiences.

So, don't tense up or ball your hands into tight fists the next time you're in an unpleasant situation and feeling intense emotions (e.g., anger, hatred, shame, guilt, etc.). Instead, deliberately **open your hands, keep your palms up, and relax your fingers**.

If you're still feeling resistance, open your hands slowly–opening or stretching one finger at a time. Next, stretch your hands wide open, fingers apart (almost tensing), and then slowly relax them to a *willing hands* position (relaxed, but open)

Tip: Feel free to combine **Willing Hands** with any mindfulness exercise, such as <u>Counting Breath Practice</u> or <u>Mindful Deep Belly Breathing</u>.

Remember, you're not fighting your emotions or denying them. You're willing to experience them so you can get through them.

Worksheet 16: The Willingness Experience

Often, unwillingness is a sign of fear: fear of the unknown, fear of losing control, fear of being exposed, fear of looking like an idiot, fear of being uncomfortable, etc.

This exercise will help you overcome your fear using a concept called *imaginal exposure*. By imagining how an event will play out, you'll prepare yourself for any eventualities and thus be willing enough to go through the actual experience.

Step 1. What are you resisting? Identify an event (or specific areas in your life) where you have felt resistance or reluctance to engage fully.

Example: A BIG party at work is coming up, and every fiber of my being is unwilling to attend.

____

____

____

____

____

____

Step 2. Why are you unwilling? Reflect on the reasons behind your resistance, acknowledging any fears or uncertainties holding you back.

Example: I'm NOT a conversationalist. I feel very uncomfortable surrounded by people I don't know.

____

____

____

____

____

____

Step 3. Imagine the event. Find a quiet and comfortable space where you will not be disturbed. Sit or lie down. Imagine the event you are dreading as if it were happening right in front of you right now.

Important:

  (1) Don't just imagine your role in the event. Imagine other people, who they are, where they are, and what they say.
  (2) As you imagine the event unfolding in your mind, you might feel resistance or even physical signs of tension and stress. At this stage, label what you're feeling without judgment.
  Example: I'm feeling uncomfortable and anxious.

  ____

  ____

  ____

  (3) Next, mindfully take a deep breath and do <u>Willing Hands</u>.
  (4) Slowly embrace a mindset of curiosity and openness. Do the following:

  Put your left hand over your heart.
  Put your right hand over your left hand.
  Breathe in deeply.
  As you breathe out, say this out loud: "I am willing to feel this feeling of __________, in just this moment. It's okay. This is natural. It's part of the process."

If you feel your resistance is fading, you can proceed to the next step. If not, repeat items (2) to (4).

Step 4. Address the reason for your unwillingness. Reflect on your answer in Step 2 above. Now that you're more open and willing, you can move from the problem to the solution.

Example: I'm not a conversationalist. What can I do:
  (a) Pre-think topics to discuss in advance.
  (b) Bring a +1, so I'm not alone.

(c) *I'll just actively listen! Instead of focusing on what I need to SAY, I'll genuinely listen and ask open-ended questions to keep the conversation going.*

---

*Radical Acceptance requires Radical Willingness
because you cannot accept reality AS IS if you're not fully open and
committed to embracing it.*

*Radical Willingness encourages you to release resistance, let go of the need
for things to be different, and actively engage in the present moment.*

Chapter 8. Radical Self-Acceptance

We all like looking at ourselves in the mirror, but we rarely look beyond what's skin-deep or superficial. Actually, if you think about it, what does the very act of looking in the mirror make us do? We notice everything that needs to be fixed.

Messy hairs need to be combed and put in place, acne needs to be covered up, fine lines need to be erased, and on and on it goes until everything is... *enhanced*. (This is not to say that you shouldn't want to present yourself in a good light. I'm just highlighting how our mind unconsciously shifts to "fix" when we look at ourselves.)

Some of us avoid getting to know ourselves; we fear what we might discover. (*What if the very characteristics we proclaim we don't like (e.g., lying, cheating, close-mindedness, etc.) are the very ones we possess?*) Others, however, already have an idea but refuse to accept it. (*Me? Low self-esteem? Nah, I just don't like putting myself out there, you know?*) Others still are just clueless. (*I don't know why I'm always being passed for promotions!*)

Radical self-acceptance is complete and unwavering unhiding. It means fully and completely accepting yourself just as you are. It's like saying, "*I'm okay, just as I am, with all my strengths and weaknesses.*" Instead of being hard on yourself for not being perfect, you embrace yourself with kindness and understanding. It's a deep and unconditional love for yourself.

However, radical self-acceptance doesn't mean condonement. You shouldn't use it as an excuse for not addressing problematic behavior. (*I'm a chronic liar. That's just who I am. I accept that.*)

It also doesn't mean complacency. It means that you acknowledge that you're a work in progress. You're capable of change; you're capable of learning, healing, growing, and evolving.

For me, at the start of my healing journey, I radically accepted myself as "broken." I was in a state of utter unhappiness. I was experiencing deep internal turmoil, and I didn't know why. Still, I accepted that THAT was my current self. But it didn't mean that I had to stay that way. However, please note that radical self-acceptance doesn't mean you always need to "level up." I suck at anything mathematical, mechanical, or technical, and that's okay. I don't need to learn to be better in those aspects. I'm a capable person even without those particular skills.

So, radical self-acceptance is seeing ALL your strengths and weaknesses. And the only aspects that require change are the ones that hinder your happiness and personal well-being.

Unwavering self-acceptance also means the willingness to see yourself as you are in difficult situations. For example, you and your partner had a big argument. You can't contain your anger and throw a glass against a wall. Your partner is shocked into silence and walks out the door. In the following silence, you replay the argument, and because you're capable of self-awareness, you can see certain points during the fight that contributed to its escalation.

My timing's off. I shouldn't have started this discussion the minute my partner arrived home.
Hmmm, I was the one who raised my voice first.
Throwing the glass against the wall wasn't my best moment.

And now you acknowledge your emotions:
I'm feeling frustrated, angry, and sad. I'm also ashamed for throwing that glass.

Next, you address your emotions:
I feel tightness in my chest over what happened.
What do you do? Address it with mindful breathing.
I'm feeling resistance, a resistance to reconcile and make peace.
What do you do? Address with Willing Hands or practice Walking Meditation. And as you do, visualize the benefits of making peace.

Next, take responsibility for your participation in the situation—without regret, criticism, or judgment.

I participated in that fight. My thoughts, feelings, words, and actions helped escalate it.

Practice radical self-acceptance:

I acknowledge my emotions and reactions during the argument. I'm not going to criticize myself or judge myself because this argument doesn't define me; it's a moment in a much larger journey. I do acknowledge the need to make amends. When my partner arrives home and the timing's right, we'll revisit the topic more positively and healthily.

So, **how do you foster radical self-acceptance**?

Firstly, unwaveringly tune in to yourself. **Mindfulness** and **self-awareness** are keys to getting to know and accepting yourself for who you are. (See also Focusing.) Genuine **self-forgiveness** is also a form of self-acceptance because you're not just saying words (*I forgive myself*) but going through an active process. (See The 4 R's of Self-Forgiveness.)

Self-compassion is another way to radically accept yourself. It's probably the most important thing you should be extending to yourself, but hardly ever do. Why? Because we're our worst critics. If a friend messes up, you'll likely say, "*Hey, you got this! It's all good.*" If you find yourself in the same situation, you'll probably mentally beat yourself up about it—over and over.

However, being harsh or overly critical of your weaknesses or shortcomings doesn't benefit you because you're subconsciously telling yourself you're not "good." (The lack of self-compassion stresses the negative self-impression.) Instead, acknowledge your less-than-amazing qualities and, if it makes you happier or advances your well-being, find ways to change or improve on them.

Self-compassion also entails acknowledging your pain and giving yourself empathy, understanding, and support.

Examples:

I'm doing my best, and that's all I can ask of myself.

I may feel alone, but I'm not alone. I can choose to reach out for help and support.

I don't need to rush my anger/pain/grief/disappointment. I have a right to feel them and go through them.

I regret not always attending my kids' school activities, but it doesn't make me a bad parent.

I mentioned before that I had this habit: if I tripped, dropped something, or forgot something, I'd silently say, *"Dumb Ava!"* I don't do that anymore. Cultivating a nonjudgmental behavior towards myself and self-compassion have completely removed that unhealthy habit.

One of the most amazing aspects of accepting yourself is finding yourself in a scenario where you truly want to learn more! *What more could I do? How can I experience even more happiness and fulfillment? How else can I make a positive impact on the world?*

One way to do this is to **nurture curiosity about yourself** and your inner world. You must be okay with going out of your comfort zone to do this. After all, you cannot discover anything new or different about yourself if you're always doing the same thing. So, ask yourself, *What interesting activities and experiences do I want to try?*

Examples: swimming, baking, taking a weekend vacation with a new friend, sitting alone in a coffee shop to enjoy my own company, hosting a 5-course dinner, etc.

New experience #1: _______________________________________

New experience #2: _______________________________________

New experience #3: _______________________________________

New experience #4: _______________________________________

New experience #5: _______________________________________

Worksheet 17: Focusing

Focusing is an exercise developed by psychologist Eugene Gendlin.[35] It's similar to mindfulness but involves a more narrowed focus on bodily sensations or the "felt sense." The idea is that by unwaveringly focusing on these sensations, you create a non-judgmental space to explore your feelings, encouraging an attitude of curiosity and acceptance.

Step 1. Find a quiet and comfortable space where you won't be disturbed. Take a few deep breaths to center yourself and create a sense of calm.

Step 2. Choose a topic to explore. Identify a specific issue or situation that you want to explore. It could be a challenge, decision, or something that feels unresolved.

Step 3. Initiate awareness. Close your eyes if comfortable and bring your attention inward. Ask yourself, *What am I feeling about this issue right now?* Allow any emotions or sensations to surface without judgment.

Step 4. Locate the felt sense. Pay attention to your body. Where in your body do you feel the intensity or sensation related to this issue? It might be a tightness, warmth, or other feeling. Notice the nuances of this felt sense.

Step 5. Describe the felt sense. Using words, describe the felt sense as precisely as possible. What does it feel like? Is it heavy, light, contracted, expansive? Give it a name or label it if that feels natural.

Step 6. Check for a positive shift. After describing the felt sense, check for any subtle shift or release. Sometimes, simply acknowledging and describing the felt sense can bring positive change.

Step 7. Continue exploring. If the issue still feels unresolved, ask yourself, *"What else is there?"* and repeat the process. Be patient and open to whatever arises.

Step 8. Express gratitude. After focusing, thank yourself for taking the time to explore your inner experience. Acknowledge any insights or shifts, no matter how small.

Step 9. Reflect. Take a moment to reflect on what you've discovered. Consider how this exploration might inform your understanding of the issue or guide your next steps.

Focusing is a gentle and intuitive process, and there's no right or wrong way to experience it. Trust your inner wisdom and allow the process to unfold naturally. And whatever you discover about yourself, remember to be kind and accepting.

Worksheet 18: Self-Compassion Break

Struggling with something? Use this worksheet to guide yourself through a self-compassion break whenever you face challenges or feel overwhelmed.

Step 1. Practice mindful awareness.

What are you going through? Take a moment to acknowledge your current thoughts and feelings. Notice and name the suffering.

Examples:
I'm really struggling in my marriage right now.
I'm drowning at work.
I'm hurting.

____

____

____

____

____

____

Step 2. Establish common humanity.

Recognize that difficulties and challenges are a natural part of the human experience. You're not alone in this world facing struggles. At this very moment, someone is having similar experiences. Check which statement relates to you now, or write your own statement:

[ ] *We all struggle at various points in life.*
[ ] *This experience is just part of being human.*
[ ] *Living includes ups AND downs.*
[ ] *Now that I think about it, what I'm going through will be hard for anyone.*
[ ] *I'm not the only one suffering in this situation. My ______ is likely feeling the same.*
[ ] *I'm not the only one grieving.*
[ ] *We all encounter struggles and moments of self-doubt.*
[ ] _______________________________________

Step 3. Self-kindness.

Offer yourself kindness and understanding. Imagine what you would say to a friend going through a similar situation. Speak to yourself with the same warmth and compassion.

Examples:
I'm struggling, but it doesn't mean I'm giving in. I know I have it in me to make this better.
I give myself kindness. I give myself unconditional love.
I am here for myself.
I made a mistake, but I know in my heart. I'm a good person.

____

____

____

____

____

____

Step 4. Reflect. How do you feel now? Take a moment to reflect on any shifts in your thoughts or feelings after completing your self-compassion break. Notice if there's a greater sense of understanding and acceptance.

Example: I feel better. Just being quiet for a while and giving myself attention has improved my spirits.

____

____

____

____

____

____

Radical Acceptance requires Radical Self-Acceptance because you cannot accept reality AS IS if you're not capable of acknowledging your worth, strengths, and imperfections—without judgment.

Radical Self-Acceptance is the foundation on which Radical Acceptance stands and builds.

Part 3: Navigating Life's Challenges with Radical Acceptance

"Challenges are what make life interesting, and overcoming them is what makes life meaningful." – Joshua J. Marine

Radical Acceptance is *actual reality* acceptance. You see, what you consider as "real" might be your *perceived reality* of what is.

Perceived reality is how you see or believe things to be, while actual reality is how things truly are, independent of personal interpretation. Your thoughts, emotions, and past experiences influence perceived reality. In contrast, actual reality is the objective, factual state of things. It's like wearing glasses; what you see might be influenced by the color of your lenses, but the actual reality remains the same for everyone.

It's hard to shift from perceived to actual reality because of all our conscious and unconscious resistance to what is. Part II: Bringing Acceptance Into Your Life encapsulates all the habits you need to unlearn and all the qualities you need to put in its stead to see and accept actual reality.

Keep in mind that Radical Acceptance is acknowledging reality without putting energy into trying to change it. You might be thinking, *How's that possible? If my current situation (reality) is difficult, painful, or unpleasant, shouldn't I want to change it?* Of course, you should! However, remember that reality is the sum of the past.

For example, suppose you're entering the kitchen with an armful of laundry. You didn't see that your kid's birthday cake has been delivered and is on the kitchen counter. You accidentally knock it over, and now the amazing and expensive birthday cake is on the floor.

What's Radical Acceptance here? The birthday cake is on the floor.

You cannot rewind the previous minutes; ergo, it's pointless and unhelpful not to accept the reality of the situation. It will just bring up negative or unpleasant emotions, which do nothing to remedy the situation.

So, you accept and focus on your next steps to ensure a better outcome. In this example, that might mean cleaning the mess and calling someone to purchase and bring a new cake. In less than an hour, you experience another reality: a great birthday party for your kid.

Chapter 9. Handling Difficult Emotions

Emotions are what make us human. Our capacity to feel a wide spectrum of emotions, from joy and love to sadness and anger, adds depth and richness to our human experience. While some emotions are difficult to experience, they still uniquely shape our understanding of ourselves and how we experience life. Consider the example of grief.

Grieving the loss of a loved one is an emotionally challenging experience. It brings intense sadness, loneliness, emptiness, and sometimes even anger. While these emotions are undoubtedly difficult to go through, they play a crucial role in shaping our understanding of ourselves and the complexity of human connections.

Grieving allows us to confront the depth of our emotions, reflect on the significance of the relationship we had, and ultimately help us navigate the process of healing and finding meaning in life despite the loss. So, even though the emotions associated with grief are challenging, the *grieving process* contributes to a richer and more profound understanding of our own emotional landscape and the intricate fabric of human experience.

Note that the whole grieving process (initial pain/loss -> reflection on the significance/beauty of the relationship -> acceptance or peace with the loss -> healing and moving on with life)[1] is an example of letting the natural process of healing unfold. If you don't radically accept grief, if you hold on to that pain, the pain turns to emotional suffering.

CONTENT WARNING*: The following may be distressing or triggering. Be mindful and take a break when necessary. If you feel overwhelmed, please don't hesitate to ask for assistance or consult a specialist.*

Please choose a difficult emotion you may be feeling now or experience frequently in your life.

---

[1] Please note that this is just an example. The grieving process is different for everyone.

Shame	Inadequacy	Anxiousness / Anxiety
Guilt	Self-Doubt	Grief
Low Self-Esteem	Regret	Unworthiness
Anger	Jealousy	Fear
Other:		

Next, please radically accept the emotion. Place your hands over your heart and say it out loud or just to yourself. For example, *I feel crippled by shame.*

____

____

____

____

____

Take a deep and mindful breath and ask yourself, *Why am I feeling this?* Who or what's triggering this emotion right now? For example, *I've been molested as a child. I mentioned this to a friend, but they didn't believe me. Today, that same "friend" has reached out on FB. It's brought out many buried feelings in me.*

____

____

____

____

____

If you sense negative self-judgments, challenge them with more balanced and compassionate perspectives. For example, *That situation was not my fault. I believe me. I'm more than that experience.*

____

____

____

____

____

Pay attention to your body. Where are you feeling the negative emotion? Breathe deeply into it and release it. If possible, express your feelings in a constructive, releasing way. For example, if you're feeling grief, give yourself a moment to have a big, loud cry. If you're angry, do something physical, such as going out for a vigorous walk or run. If you're feeling shame, write a letter of self-forgiveness.

What do you want to do?

____

____

____

____

____

____

After radically accepting your emotions, visualize yourself feeling lighter as you release yourself from emotional suffering. Note that you may need to do this more than once and use other techniques (e.g., Mindful Observation Using Your Five Senses, Self-Compassion Break, etc.), and that's 100% okay. Radically accepting and dealing with difficult emotions is a process that should not be rushed.

Coping with Change and Uncertainty

Time is always moving forward. Life is constantly changing. And so, recognizing the nature of change and uncertainty is crucial for cultivating Radical Acceptance. Please keep the following in mind:

- **Impermanence.** Change is the only constant in life. Everything, including emotions, relationships, and circumstances, is subject to change. So, open your hands and embrace impermanence instead of trying to grip or hold onto now. Radically accept NOW, but happily welcome NEXT.

- **Unpredictability**. The future is inherently unpredictable. Unforeseen events and circumstances can shape your journey no matter how well you plan. Acknowledging the unpredictability of life fosters resilience and openness to new possibilities.

- **Unknown**. Uncertainty often brings with it the unknown. However, instead of fearing it, Radical Acceptance encourages curiosity and openness. It's thinking that every unknown moment carries the potential for growth and transformation.

- **Adaptability.** Resisting change can only lead to suffering. Why fight the reality that day ends into night, and night gives way to day? Radical Acceptance encourages adapting to change with an open heart. It involves finding the balance between acknowledging the pain of change and recognizing the opportunities it presents.

- **Growth**. Change and uncertainty provide fertile ground for learning and personal growth. Each challenge, setback, or unexpected turn holds valuable lessons. Radical Acceptance involves seeing these experiences as opportunities for development.

Change is an inevitable aspect of life. Radically Accept that reality, and you'll find yourself capable of fully enjoying the richness of the present.

Chapter 10. Building Wonderful Relationships

Your Relationship as a Safe Space

We want this in a healthy, loving, and stable relationship: safety. We don't want to be judged, blamed, scrutinized, or disregarded. To cultivate this safety and security, you and your partner must radically accept each other. If you can't, then the relationship is a disservice to you both because neither of you will ever truly be fulfilled. On the other hand, if you radically accept each other, flaws and all, then you have a relationship you can both consider your sanctuary. For example:

Partner: *I messed up. I was rushing and got a speed ticket.*
Instead of: *Of course you did! (judgment) And how much is that ticket?! (guilt-tripping)*
Say this: *What? Babe, are you okay? You good?*

In this example, nonjudgment and empathy win the day. Imagine the effect this has on your relationship. Imagine how this scenario creates a culture of safety and security where you and your partner can express yourselves authentically and without reservation.

Everyone Is Always Doing their Best

Radical Acceptance in a relationship also means adopting the mindset that **everyone is always doing their best**.

Now, you might be thinking, *No, they're not! If my partner did their best, they wouldn't have gotten a speeding ticket.*

In this example, though, what you're really hopping mad about is the outcome of their intentions. You're angry about the *result* of what happened, not the intent behind their actions. For example, you're pissed about your partner getting a speeding ticket. But what if they drove too fast because they intended to get home to you sooner?

Granted, your partner's best intentions may not always result in the best outcome. (*That speeding ticket is really expensive!*) Still, just like you, they're incapable of predicting the future. So, instead of jumping into an argument about an outcome (*what happened*), try instead to understand their intentions (*what they were trying to do*).

Examples:
Outcome (what happened): Someone dropped and broke an expensive vase.
Possible intention (i.e., what they tried to do): House clean.

Outcome: Someone's late for dinner.
Possible intention: They tried to finish off work to be free with you this weekend.

Accusations = Fears

Often, in the heat of the moment, we might throw out accusations and take it upon ourselves to label our partner's thoughts or emotions.

You just don't love me anymore, do you!
It's ok; admit it. You think our relationship sucks.
I know my weight is bothering you.

However, when you accuse, you're really projecting your own fears.

You just don't love me anymore, do you!
(I'm afraid you don't love me anymore)

It's ok; admit it. You think our relationship sucks.
(I'm afraid I'm losing you.)

I know my weight is bothering you.
 (I'm bothered by my weight, and I'm scared it's affecting us.)

Now, consider what happens when someone is accused. They get *defensive*, right?

You: *You just don't love me anymore, do you?*
Partner: *Huh? Where did THAT come from?!*

So, to prevent this escalation, don't accuse. Radically accept your own emotions and fears and own up to them.

Not: *You just don't love me anymore, do you!*
But: *I feel insecure in our relationship. I'm afraid you don't love me anymore.*

What if your partner is the one who's accusing you? Don't get defensive; see through the statement and reassure their fears.

Hear: *You just don't love me anymore, do you!*
Practice mindfulness...
Say: *Babe, of course, I love you. We're just arguing, and arguments are temporary. This fight has nothing to do with our love for each other. Come here; we're good.*

At this stage, I'd like to repeat that Radical Acceptance is never about approving, denying, ignoring, excusing, or condoning bad or unhealthful behavior—including relationships.

For example, suppose you discovered that your partner secretly withdrew funds from your account to purchase something you never discussed. In this case, practice Radical Acceptance by acknowledging your emotions about the situation and then pausing before reacting.

Also, reflect on your assumptions or expectations about shared finances. Perhaps you and your partner have different beliefs about how money is spent in your relationship to begin with.

Next, apply Radical Acceptance principles toward your partner by adopting a nonjudgmental attitude while discussing the situation. Extend empathy and jointly focus on finding solutions rather than dwelling on the problem. The following is a personal example:

Here's a pet peeve I have with my husband—he forgets. I'm not talking about things like forgetting to take out the trash. We discuss something important, he agrees, and he forgets.

I openly communicated my frustration and told him that when these incidents happen, I struggle with trust. (Notice that I said *"I" struggle with trust*, which is me taking responsibility for my own feelings. If I had said, *Why do YOU always forget?!*, it would be a blaming and judgmental attitude.) How do I know whether he will remember to do something or not? I don't want to second-guess him. So, what do we do? How can we help each other?

My husband suggested noting things on his mobile phone because jotting them down will help him remember them more. And we agreed that if that didn't help, we'd use the BIG whiteboard in his home office. Luckily, we didn't reach that option.

Does this mean he never forgets? He never forgets the really important stuff. I've radically accepted that he will occasionally forget some things or points, and that's okay. I embrace his imperfection because he so readily embraces mine.

The above tips also apply to every relationship in your life, not just intimate ones. For example, say you have a co-worker who consistently takes credit for your ideas during team meetings, undermining your contributions and causing extreme frustration.

In this scenario, radically accept the situation, acknowledge your emotions, and pause before reacting. Next, initiate a private conversation with your co-worker, openly communicating how their actions made you feel. Seek understanding, extend empathy, and then shift the focus of the conversation to finding solutions. For example, state that you would like your co-worker to amend their previous comment and give you credit in the next meeting, attribute the idea to you in a Minutes of the Meeting memo, etc.

Radical Acceptance in relationships also often means establishing and asserting boundaries. Remember, you're part of your reality. You have influence over what happens next, which may mean being clearer and more assertive about your boundaries.

Examples:

No. I don't want to go to your parent's house every Sunday. I'd like us to spend time alone together, or at least I don't want to be forced to come along if I don't want to.

No. I don't appreciate others taking credit for my ideas. Please don't do it again. I WILL speak up immediately the next time that happens.

Hey, bestie, you know I'm here for you, but I can't be your emotional punching bag today. I have problems of my own I need to address right now.

Dealing with Conflict

Despite your and your partner's best efforts, there's conflict between you. That's okay; that's inherent in all relationships. So, how do you accept and address it? Practice **mindful interactions**.

Practice active listening. During discussions with your partner, listen to understand, not to argue. Make it your goal to understand *their* perspective. Think of it this way: you share equal responsibility in your situation. Understanding their 50% enables you to see the whole picture.

Emphatic speaking. When discussing, show empathy by validating your partner's viewpoints. This indicates that you truly heard them, so they'll be more open to hearing you. For example, *I understand you're mad at me for not calling that I won't be home for dinner.*

Speak only from your perspective. When communicating, use "I" statements. Remember, you're sharing *your* perspective.

Examples:
~~You always leave me alone.~~ I feel ignored.
~~You don't spend time with me.~~ I want more time with you.
~~You don't care!~~ I feel sad because I feel like my feelings are being ignored.
~~You don't pick up after yourself.~~ I get stressed when I see clothes scattered on the floor.

I'm Sorry

We've discussed the healing power of <u>forgiveness</u>, but equally, healing is the ability to genuinely apologize and say I'm sorry.[36]

Radical Acceptance has healed me so much that I'm sometimes surprised by all my other changes. I used to have difficulty saying, "I'm sorry." I used to think it was the same as saying "I failed" or admitting I was "less" in any way. But then I learned that being unable to apologize is the perfect example of *avoidant behavior*, which is denying or escaping difficult thoughts, emotions, and situations. Saying sorry made me feel uncomfortable and vulnerable, so instead of owning up to my mistakes, I'd rather just be nasty or find something (or someone) else to blame.

Acceptance is the complete opposite of avoidance, so by fostering Radical Acceptance into my life, I sort of just woke up one day unafraid of saying, "I'm sorry," and those two little words can be oh-so healing for relationships!

For one, saying "I'm sorry" **shows that you're aware of your actions and how they affect your partner.** Unwillingness to apologize is like saying "Hmpf!" to your partner's feelings. In contrast, apologizing shows that you care about your partner's feelings and are ready to try to make things right.

Usually, we don't want to apologize to our partners because we're admitting guilt. If we apologize first, they won't take responsibility for their part in the fight. In truth, our partners just want to hear *"I'm sorry"* for hurting them. So you see, this has nothing to do with guilt or who's at fault. Saying sorry because you're part of an event that caused your partner pain means you care about their feelings. This, in turn, will help your partner feel safe with you and in your relationship.

Saying sorry also **helps rebuild trust and connection**. If your partner feels hurt or betrayed, saying sorry can help validate their feelings and show that you understand and care about them. This can make talking and healing easier, strengthening your connection in the long run.

Further, apologizing **helps avoid future arguments** by admitting you made a mistake and promising to do differently next time.

Relationships are vital to the human experience[37]. Yet, we often find ourselves in conflict with loved ones and get stuck in issues rather than finding ways to improve our connections. Radical Acceptance helps us remove that *"It's complicated"* label we often place on our relationships by fostering understanding, empathy, and open communication. For me, Radical Acceptance is what helped make my relationship a "safe space."

Worksheet 19: Repair and Rebuild Using Radical Acceptance

If your relationship is in a dark place, try this exercise. It will help you acknowledge and embrace the reality of the situation, promoting understanding and providing a foundation for making conscious efforts to move forward.

Step 1. Practice radical self-acceptance.
Begin by practicing Radical Self-Acceptance. Reflect on your feelings, thoughts, and actions related to the relationship. Acceptance of yourself lays the groundwork for accepting others.

Step 2. Acknowledge reality.
Face the current state of your relationship without denial or judgment. Acknowledge the challenges, conflicts, and emotions involved. This step is crucial for understanding what needs to be addressed.

Step 3. Practice mindful awareness.
Take a moment to experience present-moment awareness. Give yourself the freedom to feel your emotions without reservation or judgment. This will help you be mindful and self-aware during conversations and interactions with your partner.

Step 4. Foster open communication.
Initiate open and honest communication. Express your thoughts and feelings calmly, using "I" statements to avoid blame. Encourage the other person to share their perspective without judgment or interruption.

Step 5. Practice active listening.
Practice active listening to truly understand the other person's experiences and emotions. Validate their feelings, even if you don't agree with them. This builds a foundation of empathy.

Step 6. Cultivate empathy and compassion.

Cultivate empathy and compassion for the other person's struggles and challenges. Recognizing that everyone makes mistakes and understanding each other's vulnerabilities is important for healing.

Step 7. Let go of any resentment.

Release resentment and grudges. Radical Acceptance involves letting go of negative emotions tied to past events. Forgiveness, not forgetting, is a powerful tool for moving forward.

Step 8. Set clear and healthy boundaries.

Establish clear and healthy boundaries to prevent recurring issues. Clearly communicate your needs and expectations, and encourage the other person to do the same.

Step 9. Problem-solve together.

Approach challenges as opportunities for collaborative problem-solving. Work together to find solutions that will benefit you both, fostering a sense of teamwork and shared responsibility.

Step 10. Commit to change.

Demonstrate a genuine commitment to positive change. Take concrete actions to address the issues discussed. Consistent effort and a willingness to learn from mistakes are key elements to rebuilding trust.

Step 11. Celebrate progress!

Acknowledge and celebrate progress in the relationship. Recognize positive changes and express gratitude for efforts made by both parties. This reinforces a positive cycle of growth.

Step 12. Seek professional support (if needed).

If your relationship is deeply strained, consider seeking professional support, such as couples therapy or counseling. A neutral third party can provide guidance and facilitate constructive communication.

Repairing relationships with Radical Acceptance is a transformative process that will help you move beyond past hurts and build a stronger, more resilient connection. However, it requires patience, empathy, and a shared commitment to growth. Be kind and forgiving of each other, and don't let setbacks deter you from trying and trying and trying again.

Practicing Radical Acceptance as a Parent

Do you have children? And if so, do you find your parent-child relationship being tested a few too many times? Radical Acceptance can help.

Here's an example situation and how Radical Acceptance can help you as a parent: Your 15-year-old teen came home extremely intoxicated.

Mindfulness.
Accept reality AS IS. Your underage child came home drunk. The situation is not ideal, but it has already happened. You cannot change it. Take a mental pause to let this situation sink in. You have every right to feel your emotions, but you don't have to act on them. Create space between stimulus (situation) and response (your next steps).

Self-awareness.
What are you thinking? What are you feeling? What do you want to say or do? Whatever it is, just be aware of them. See if you're succumbing to any patterns of behavior that are not helpful.

For example, do you want to scold your child? Is this an automatic response (pattern) you have? That is, if your child does something unpleasant -> scold them!

If this is a pattern, is it helpful? Has it ever done any good in the past? What would scolding accomplish *now* when your child is already intoxicated?

Ask yourself if this situation is triggering something in you? Do you have any previous negative experiences or traumas related to alcohol (e.g., a father who came home drunk too often and became abusive)? If so, check that your initial response is not a knee-jerk reaction to your past and, as such, has nothing to do with your child today.

Non-judgment.

Refrain from making unfounded conjectures. Check any biases you may have (e.g., *This is the influence of their new friend at school!*). Also, avoid making sweeping assumptions (e.g., *Oh, now it begins!*). Remember, unless you know for sure, you're just guessing.

Embracing imperfection.

Accept that your child is not perfect (human), has made a mistake, and will continue to make their own mistakes. This is how they'll learn.

Letting go of control.

Let go of the need to control your child's life, even if you believe it's for their own good. This is ONE mistake from which they can learn. There's no need to step in and take over. (Besides, that will just build resentment.)

Radical willingness.

Be willing to accept the effects of this situation on you—and process it.
This is making me afraid that this is not a one-time thing. But, wait, that's not being fair to my child or me.

Be willing to learn from this situation.
I've learned drinking is a trigger.

Be willing to listen and truly hear your child when discussing the matter.

Radical self-acceptance.

This situation doesn't mean you're a bad parent. If you see any shortcomings on your part, practice self-compassion and work on that shortcoming moving forward.

Alright, you've radically accepted the situation and put yourself in the right and helpful frame of mind to discuss what happened with your child.

Remember to actively listen, understand their why, be emphatic, and work together to avoid a repeat of the incident. Here's an example:

Parent: *Hey, can we talk for a moment?*

Teen: *Sure, what's up?*

Parent: *When you came home last night, I could tell you've had a bit to drink. How are you feeling?*

Teen: *I'm okay, just had some fun with friends.*

Parent: *I get it; socializing is a part of growing up. But I'm concerned and want you to know that my concern comes from a place of care, okay? I remember being your age, and I understand the desire to experiment.*

Teen: *Yeah, it was just a party. Everyone drinks nowadays.*

Parent: *I hear you. Parties can be fun, but they can also have consequences. I'm not here to lecture or blame. I want us to have an open conversation. What made you decide to drink last night?*

Teen: *I don't know, everyone was doing it, and I thought it would be cool.*

Parent: *It's natural to want to fit in. I appreciate your honesty. Let's talk about how we can make sure you're making choices that align with your values and keep you safe. What are your thoughts on that?*

Teen: *I guess I should be more careful next time.*

Parent: *That's a good insight. It's good to be aware of the choices we make and their potential impact. If you ever find yourself in a situation where you're uncomfortable, I want you to feel you can reach out to me anytime. I promise: no blaming, no judgment. Okay?*

Teen: *Yeah, okay.*

Parent: *Well, that's it then. Now, go do your homework! Love you, bud.*

In this example, a *consequence* may be necessary (e.g., removing phone privileges for a week, being grounded, etc.). It's your right to impose that as a parent, but ensure your child understands why you're doing it. New boundaries may need to be set, too. Again, discuss and involve your child in the process. This way, they'll be more likely to accept rather than oppose.

Part 4: Living a Life of Radical Acceptance

"Healing is an inside job." - Dr. B.J. Palmer

Chapter 11. Authenticity: You "As Is"

As you embrace Radical Acceptance, you'll find that authenticity follows. As you peel off your mask and strip off layers upon layers of frustrations and expectations, what you're left with is you—as is.

Authenticity can be scary. To be real is to be raw and vulnerable because we share our weaknesses and struggles, too. Authenticity is even uncommon nowadays because social media has rewired our brains to believe and seek the unreal.[38,39]

So, why even seek it? Why be authentic? Because the alternative—to be fake— is exhausting! This is what started my journey. I was so tired and drained from pretending that I suffered a burnout and a breakdown. So, I'll take authenticity and peace anytime.

Everything about Radical Acceptance screams authenticity, so by this page in the book, dear reader, I believe you've already started to slowly meet the real you. Here are some more tips to cultivate authenticity in your life:

Self-reflection. Take time to reflect on your values, beliefs, and aspirations. Understand what truly matters to you and align your choices with your authentic self.

Embrace vulnerability. Be open and honest about your thoughts and feelings, even if it makes you feel vulnerable. Vulnerability fosters genuine connections and allows others to see the real you.

Know your boundaries. Set and communicate clear boundaries that respect your values and well-being. Think of it this way: If you say "Yes," even when you really don't want to, you're not being truthful to yourself and your values.

Express your creativity. Engage in activities that allow you to display your creativity and individuality. Whether it's through art, writing, or other outlets. Find ways to showcase your unique perspective.

Accept your flaws. Embrace your imperfections as integral parts of who you are. Nobody is perfect, and acknowledging your imperfections can lead to greater self-acceptance.

Authentic communication. Be true to your thoughts and feelings in your communication with others. Avoid pretending or conforming to societal expectations if it contradicts your authentic self.

Build authentic relationships. Surround yourself with people who appreciate you for who you are, not how you benefit them. Cultivate relationships where you feel accepted and supported in expressing your true self.

Tip: Focus on building your offline relationships. I find face-to-face interactions and physical presence provide a deeper sense of connectedness. If you have online relationships that do the same for you, great! But don't let it prevent you from exploring offline relationships, too.

Live your values. Identify your core values and strive to live in alignment with them. Your actions and decisions should reflect the principles that matter most to you.

Authenticity is a continual process of self-discovery and self-expression. As life unfolds and you learn and grow, you will change. Embrace who you become, too!

Chapter 12. Cultivating Gratitude and Joy

Cultivating gratitude and joy is important for Radical Acceptance because it shifts your focus from what's lacking or negative to what is positive and present in your life.

Looking back, it amazes me how I lived in fear without realizing it. Afraid I'm not good enough; afraid I have a depression disorder; afraid of being alone; afraid of not being seen; afraid of being too seen; afraid of being idle; afraid of doing too much... on and on it went.

In being afraid of *what could be*, I never enjoyed *what is*. Radical Acceptance changed all that. Today, joy and gratitude define me.

Finding Joy in The Present Moment

People usually interchange joy and happiness, but there's a slight difference. Joy is a state of being (an attitude); happiness is an emotional response to something external.

For example, you wake up, and there's this underlying sense of contentment, fulfillment, and even excitement that exists. That's joy. You go down and see that your partner has been up for a while and has breakfast ready for you. A big smile spreads over your face. That's happiness.

Finding joy in the present moment is about appreciating and fully experiencing NOW. It's like experiencing happiness 24/7 and in HD. It involves letting go of worries about the past or the future and immersing yourself in the current experience.

Mindfulness is key to finding joy in the present moment. Usually, our default setting is "rushed," and we're breathing, thinking, feeling, and acting in "next." But in so doing, we miss everything in "now." Sad, right?

By doing the opposite, by deliberately being fully present in the moment, you can discover joy in simple moments and activities. Whether it's savoring the taste of your favorite food, enjoying a beautiful sunset, or relishing a quiet moment of solitude, finding joy in the present enhances your overall well-being and deepens your connection to life.

I like to think of it this way: finding joy in the present moment is like collecting shells of happiness, resilience, positivity, and all the good stuff. When something unpleasant happens, the situation no longer affects me as much as it used to. Why? What's a pebble of annoyance compared to my jars and jars of collected joy? Here are some tips to cultivate happiness and joy in your life:

1. **Smile often.** If smiling feels unnatural try starting with small, genuine smiles in front of a mirror. Practice until it becomes a more natural and comfortable expression. Remember, even a subtle smile can positively impact your mood and how others perceive you.

2. **Practice mindfulness.** It will help slow you down and focus, and you'll be amazed at all the beautiful things you never truly noticed before.

3. **Get in "flow."** Engage in activities that give you peace and happiness.

4. **Connect with others.** Build your relationships. Here's a tip: What can my friend/partner/colleague\family member do to make me happy right now? And then do that for them.

5. **Take care of your health.** Physical well-being is closely linked to emotional well-being. Ensure you get enough sleep, eat nourishing food, and exercise regularly.

6. **Learn and grow.** When you're in a good place, you think you want to stay there forever, but really, you don't because it becomes boring, stagnant, fixed. What you should be focused on is learning and growing. "New" engages the mind, and it's crucial for happiness.[40,41]

7. **Practice self-care!** Why do we always take care of ourselves last? Self-care is crucial for finding joy because it involves *intentional actions* prioritizing our well-being and overall happiness. (See the bonus section, "51 Self-Care Activities.")

8. **Practice acts of kindness.** Whether big or small, performing acts of kindness for others boosts your happiness![42]

9. **Stay away from "toxic."** Identify and minimize exposure to negative influences, whether in the form of people, places, situations, news, or other media. Surround yourself with positivity!

10. See tip #1.

The Underrated Power of Gratitude

Gratitude is when you feel thankful and appreciative for the good things in your life. It's about recognizing and being glad for the positive experiences, people, or moments that bring you happiness or make a positive impact.

Humans are funny creatures. We want to be happy but focus on what makes us miserable. We often say we want things to be simpler and then complicate our lives.

Cultivating an attitude of gratitude will help you rewire your brain to focus on the good because it enables you to count blessings instead of burdens. It truly has the power to alter your perception of the world.

According to research, gratitude comprises two phases: seeing goodness in one's life (recognition) and giving credit to the external sources of that goodness (acknowledgment).[43]

Phase 1: Recognition. This is when you notice and understand the good things you have in your life. For example, you realize you have a friend who always supports you or remember a time when someone was kind to you.

Phase 2: Acknowledgment. After recognizing the good things, you actively say thank you or appreciate them. For example, you tell your friend how much their support means to you or write a note to express gratitude for someone's kindness.

So, gratitude is not just *Oh, I'm happy for* _______. It's a dynamic process involving intentionally acknowledging and appreciating those benefits. It's like, first, you see the sun shining (recognition), and then you say, "Wow, the sun makes everything brighter, and I'm grateful for that" (acknowledgment and appreciation).

Here are some ways to help you develop an attitude of gratitude in your life. Why don't you put a checkmark on the first three you want to do?

___ **Mindful Moments.**
- Take a few moments each day to appreciate your surroundings.
- Notice the beauty in simple things, like a blooming flower or a clear sky.

___ **Express Gratitude Verbally.**
- Tell the people around you that you appreciate them.
- Say "thank you" sincerely and often.

___ **Random Acts of Kindness.**
- Perform small acts of kindness for others without expecting anything in return. It could be as simple as holding the door open or helping someone with a task.

___ **Gratitude Walks.**
- Take a walk and consciously think about things you're grateful for. Connect your steps with positive thoughts.

___ **Gratitude Jar.**
- Write down moments of gratitude on small notes. Place them in a jar and read them whenever you need a boost.

___ **Reflect on Challenges.**
- Consider the lessons and growth that come from difficult experiences.
- Find something positive even in challenging situations.

___ **Connect with Nature.**
- Spend time outdoors; appreciate nature. Feel gratitude for the Earth's beauty and the life it sustains.

___ **Volunteer Work.**
- Engage in volunteer activities to help those in need. Witnessing the impact of your efforts can be profoundly gratifying.

Gratitude is about consciously focusing on the positive aspects of life, big or small. It's a mindset that can be developed through regular practice and awareness. So, keep at it!

Worksheet 20: Gratitude Journaling

Are you new to gratitude journaling? Here are some prompts to help you get started. Feel free to customize this worksheet to suit your preferences and add additional sections if needed.

Instructions:
1. **Set aside time**. Find a quiet and comfortable place to sit.
2. **Reflect on your day**. Think about the positive aspects of your day.
3. **Express gratitude**. Write down things you're thankful for in the spaces provided.
4. **Be specific**. Include details about each item you list.
5. **Feel the gratitude**. As you write, focus on the emotions associated with each gratitude entry.
6. **Rinse and repeat.** Make gratitude journaling a regular part of your routine.

Date: _______________________

Step 1. Indicate a person or relationship. Write the name or describe a person or a relationship you are grateful for today. Why are you thankful for this person or relationship? Describe specific actions or qualities.
Example: I'm grateful for my husband. He woke up earlier than me, gave me a kiss, and told me he'd wait for me downstairs for breakfast.

____

____

____

____

____

____

Step 2. Identify an experience or achievement. Describe a positive experience or achievement from today. What made this experience special, and how did it contribute to your day?

Example: I got further with my writing project than I thought. I'm grateful for the sense of achievement I feel.

____

____

____

____

____

____

Step 3. Focus on nature or the environment. Reflect on something in nature or your environment that you appreciate. What about this natural element or environment brings you a sense of gratitude?

Example: I appreciate the small wooded area near our home. I'm grateful I can step out and take a refreshing and invigorating walk anytime I want.

____

____

____

____

____

____

Step 4. An act of kindness. Recall an act of kindness that touched you, either given or received. How did this act of kindness impact your day or your perspective?

Example: I always smile and greet people with "Good day" when I'm out for my walks. I think this simple act of kindness has the power to brighten someone's day.

____

____

____

____

____

____

Step 5. Something about yourself. Identify a personal quality or trait within yourself that you are grateful for. How does this quality positively influence your life or the lives of others?

Example: I'm loyal and faithful. I'm grateful for this quality because it's a great foundation for my relationships. This loyalty creates a sense of trust and security for those around me. Although sometimes my loyalty leads me to put others' needs before mine, I appreciate the deep connections it fosters and the strength it adds to the bonds I share with loved ones.

____

____

____

____

____

Step 6. Note a surprise or blessing. Note any surprises or blessings that brought you joy today or recently. What made these surprises or blessings stand out to you?

Example: My best friend baked some cookies and brought me some "just because!" It made me very happy, and knowing they think of me felt great.

____

____

____

____

____

Take a moment to reflect on the overall feelings of gratitude during today's journaling session. Note the positive feelings that come from being grateful, and let them stay with you throughout your day.

Conclusion

"Healing may not be so much about getting better as about letting go of everything that isn't you – all of the expectations, all of the beliefs – and becoming who you are."
– Rachel Naomi Remen

Radical Acceptance can bring so much transformation, healing, and joy into your life—if you accept it. Here's a quick recap.

In <u>Part 1: Understanding Radical Acceptance</u>, we discussed the concept of Radical Acceptance, what it is, and what it's not. There are so many misconceptions about "acceptance." We often link it to agreement, approval, giving in, trivializing, etc. This chapter explains why this is not the case and demonstrates the true meaning of acceptance and its benefits for your life.

In <u>Part 2: Bringing Acceptance Into Your Life</u>, we dive deep into the eight aspects of Radical Acceptance. These are the keys that open the doors of this concept into your life.

- **Mindfulness** is the ability to live in now and simply "be."
- **Self-awareness** is the ability to observe and understand yourself completely and without judgment.
- **Non-judgment** is the skill to resist jumping to negative assumptions. It's the ability to stop guessing and predicting, and developing the skill of always looking for facts.
- **Embracing imperfection** is the art of being perfectly okay with what's NOT perfectly okay.
- **Letting go of control** is the ability to free yourself from any fear of the unknown. It's learning to trust others and yourself.
- **Radical willingness** is the ability to openly and actively engage with experiences, challenges, and changes—without resistance.
- **Radical self-acceptance** is loving yourself—as is.

In Part 3: Navigating Life's Challenges with Radical Acceptance, you learned how Radical Acceptance can be applied to every unpleasant situation or difficulty you find yourself in life. You can use it to handle negative and crippling emotions and apply its principles to improve your relationships.

In Part 4: Living a Life of Radical Acceptance, you discovered how to keep Radical Acceptance a permanent fixture in your life. By shedding your mask, breaking down your walls, being authentic, finding joy in every moment, and cultivating gratitude, you'll find that being a radical accepter is not so hard after all.

As you go through your journey, please always take a moment to track your progress or just to check in with yourself. That, in itself, is important for your self-discovery and growth. (If you need help with this, see Bonus: Radical Acceptance Self-Reflection.)

In my life, Radical Acceptance has been one of the most beautiful and freeing concepts I've ever come across. Each day of learning and applying it meant more weight off my shoulders and less emotional suffering. I hope it's as healing for you as it has been for me.

Bonus: 51 Self-Care Activities

Self-care is essential and personal. Here's a list of 51 simple and rejuvenating options at your fingertips. Each day, try to choose at least one that resonates with you and brings you joy and relaxation.

[ ] **Take a Bubble Bath**: Create a relaxing atmosphere with candles and calming music.

[ ] **Read a Book**: Escape into a good story or explore a topic of interest.

[ ] **Practice Deep Breathing**: Focus on your breath to reduce stress and increase mindfulness.

[ ] **Go for a Walk**: Enjoy nature and get some fresh air.

[ ] **Try Meditation**: Practice mindfulness to calm your mind.

[ ] **Listen to Music**: Create a playlist of your fav feel-good tunes.

[ ] **Journal**: Write down your thoughts and feelings.

[ ] **Unplug**: Take a break from your digital devices.

[ ] **Do Yoga**: Stretch and strengthen your body.

[ ] **Cook a Healthy Meal**: Nourish yourself with good food.

[ ] **Get a Massage**: Relieve tension and relax your muscles.

[ ] **Practice Gratitude**: Reflect on the positive aspects of your life.

[ ] **Have a Picnic**: Enjoy a meal outdoors.

[ ] **Watch a Movie or TV Show**: Have a movie night.

[ ] **Draw or Paint**: Express your creativity on paper or canvas.

[ ] **Take a Nap**: Recharge with a short nap.

[ ] **Visit a Museum**: Explore art and culture.

[ ] **Learn Something New**: Take up a new hobby or skill.

[ ] **Connect with a Friend**: Spend quality time with someone you care about.

[ ] **Visit a Park**: Enjoy green spaces and nature.

[ ] **Plan a Staycation**: Relax at home as if you were on vacation.

[ ] **Dance**: Move your body to your favorite music.

[ ] **Attend a Yoga Class**: Join a class for guided practice.

[ ] **Practice Mindful Eating**: savor each bite.

[ ] **Declutter Your Space**: Create an organized and calming environment.

[ ] **Do a Puzzle**: Challenge your mind with a crossword or jigsaw puzzle.

[ ] **Write Affirmations**: Affirm positive statements about yourself.

[ ] **Go to a Spa**: Treat yourself to a spa day or spa treatments at home.

[ ] **Volunteer**: Give back to your community.

[ ] **Watch the Sunrise or Sunset**: Connect with the beauty of nature.

[ ] **Visit a Farmer's Market**: Explore fresh and local produce.

[ ] **Create a Vision Board**: Visualize your goals and aspirations.

[ ] **Try Aromatherapy**: Use essential oils to create a soothing atmosphere.

[ ] **Go Stargazing**: Enjoy the night sky.

[ ] **Take a Photography Walk**: Capture interesting sights on camera.

[ ] **Attend a Workshop or Class**: Learn something new in a group setting.

[ ] **Do a Digital Detox**: Disconnect from screens for a day.

[ ] **Play a Musical Instrument**: Make music for relaxation.

[ ] **Practice Random Acts of Kindness**: Spread positivity to others.

[ ] **Visit a Botanical Garden**: Surround yourself with beautiful plants.

[ ] **Plan a DIY Spa Day**: Pamper yourself with skincare and relaxation.

[ ] **Practice Tai Chi**: Experience the flowing movements for relaxation.

[ ] **Write a Letter to Yourself**: Reflect on your achievements and goals.

[ ] **Visit a Beach**: Listen to the sound of waves and enjoy the sea breeze.

[ ] **Take a Photography Walk**: Capture interesting sights on camera.

[ ] **Coloring**: Engage in adult coloring books for a creative outlet.

[ ] **Play a Sport**: Engage in physical activity you enjoy.

[ ] **Plan a Digital Detox Day**: Take a break from screens and technology.

[ ] **Do a DIY Project**: Channel your creativity into a craft.

[ ] **Enjoy a Comedy Show**: Laughing is a great stress reliever.

[ ] **Visit a Library**: Explore new books or find a cozy reading spot.

Bonus: Radical Acceptance Self-Reflection

Reflecting on your Radical Acceptance progress is crucial to self-discovery and growth. Take a moment to consider the following aspects:

Mindfulness Practice.
- Reflect on your mindfulness practice.
- Have you integrated mindfulness in your daily life? What do you do? How has it influenced your perspective?

Awareness of Thoughts.
- Reflect on how your thought patterns have evolved since embracing Radical Acceptance.
- Have you become more aware of negative self-talk? Are you better at redirecting those thoughts?

Handling Emotions.
- Evaluate how you manage your emotions now compared to before.
- Are you more capable of acknowledging and accepting your emotions without judgment?

Relationship Dynamics.
- Consider the impact of Radical Acceptance on your relationships.
- Have you noticed changes in how you interact with others? Are your connections healthier?

Self-Compassion.
- Assess your level of self-compassion.
- Are you kinder to yourself in challenging situations? How has this affected your overall well-being?

Response to Challenges.
- Think about how you respond to life's challenges.
- Have you developed a more balanced and resilient approach? How do you navigate setbacks?

Gratitude and Joy.
- Explore the presence of gratitude and joy in your life.
- How often do you consciously acknowledge and appreciate positive moments?

Areas for Further Growth.
- Identify areas where you still encounter difficulties in acceptance.
- What aspects of Radical Acceptance are most challenging, and how do you plan to work on them?

Remember, the journey of Radical Acceptance is ongoing. Celebrate your progress, and use your reflections to guide continued growth and development. Each step forward is a testament to your commitment to a more authentic and fulfilling life.

Audiobook

Enjoyed This Book?
Listen to the Audiobook Version!

If you loved reading this book, why not take the experience to the next level?

With the **Radical Acceptance Workbook** audiobook, you can immerse yourself in the story wherever you are – whether you're driving or relaxing at home.

Narrated by Annete Martin, the audiobook brings radical acceptance to life in a way you've never experienced before!

Why Choose the Audiobook?
- **Convenience**: Listen while multitasking or on the go.
- **Engagement**: Hear the words brought to life through dynamic narration.
- **Flexibility**: Switch seamlessly between reading and listening with most audiobook apps.
- **Great for Auditory Learners!** If you find that you absorb information better by listening rather than reading, this audiobook is perfect for you.

Get Your Copy Today!
The audiobook version is available on Audible here: https://amzn.to/4g2SzDm or scan the QR code on this page.

Thank you for being a reader, and I hope you enjoy the audio journey just as much!

BOOK 2: ACT THERAPY WORKBOOK FOR ADULTS

An Easy-to-Read (No Jargon!) Acceptance & Commitment Therapy Guide for Mindfulness and Mental Wellness

—

Overcome Anxiety, Panic Attacks, Depression & Shame with Practical Exercises

Book 2 - Table of Contents

Introduction

"I. Struggle." – Ava Walters

Every day felt like an endless emotional struggle. I don't remember exactly how it started. I was just always "coping" until I wasn't anymore.

No one knew about it, of course. Every single day, I would put on a brave face and a very "put-together" attitude. At work, people looked up to me for guidance. Friends routinely confided their troubles with me, seeking my opinion or advice. My parents would call me if my younger twin brothers needed more "guidance," my brothers would seek me out whenever they needed a buffer between them and our parents. Ha! If only they all knew how lost I was inside.

> *Later, with therapy, I would realize that my life was this constant cycle of being pulled by different people in different directions. I was always "someone" to someone... but I was never just me. I was never Ava to Ava.*

My husband and I have a great relationship now. But it was a rocky start, a very rocky start. During those early years, I felt I had to "lead." In my head, nothing happens if I don't discuss them, plan them, or address them. Even something as simple as date nights became an issue.

Me: We need to go out and spend some alone time together.
Hubby: Okay. Great.
Me: That's it? Why do I have to think and plan these things? Why do I have to do everything?!

Of course, an argument would follow. Actually, it was often a one-sided argument because I would huff and puff, and my husband would either let me be, try to calm me down, or just give in.

One day, we got into more or less the same argument, and I ended up with the same statements. This time, though, my husband stopped me dead in my tracks.

Me: Why do I have to do everything?!
Hubby: Honey, when will you realize you don't have to?
Me: What the hell do you mean?
Hubby: You think of something and want it addressed NOW and YOUR WAY. You don't give me time to think, give my opinion, or share my plans. You do the same at work until you're all stressed and worn out.

I was rendered speechless. I kept staring at my husband, and he kept looking calmly at me, never breaking eye contract. He wasn't daring me. He was giving me time to process. Looking back, I must have looked like a cartoon character in front of him, a myriad of emotions fleeting over my face. In the end, all I could say was...

Me: Why didn't you tell me your opinion before?
Hubby: Well, during those moments, you already look... frazzled like a busy, stressed bee. I didn't think it was the time to address it. I felt it would make you even more anxious.
Me: You mean it was easier for YOU to handle it that way!
Hubby: Maybe. But...
Me: What?!
Hubby: Well, I didn't want to end up in a bigger fight like the one you're trying to pick right now.

I was rendered speechless—again.

It would be great to say things got all better and rosy afterward. It didn't. People can't just "pivot" from who they are or how they have been living life overnight. So, what changed for me? I hit rock bottom.

You see, stress, anxiety, and deep and difficult emotions don't just flow in and out of you without leaving anything behind. Little by little, situation by situation, year by year... these struggles wear you down. For me, the weight of desperately trying to juggle multiple responsibilities and taking on more and more without ever pausing to catch my breath broke me.

One day, as I sat at my desk at work, surrounded by a mountain of unfinished tasks, I felt a sudden wave of panic wash over me. My heart raced, my palms grew clammy, but I felt oddly cold inside. I stared at one fixed point and tried desperately to bring my breath back to a normal rhythm. When I succeeded, I moved on as if nothing happened. Later that night, I silently asked myself if that was a panic attack... and then I brushed it off. However, as the days turned into weeks and the weeks into months, I found myself experiencing the same thing again and again, with no relief.

At one point, the company I worked for decided to send me overseas for three months. (As a Project Manager by profession, this wasn't unusual; I've done it several times before.) This time, though, things were different.

During the first week I was overseas, I had a mild panic attack, but this time, I felt an enormous dark cloud loom over me. The panic attack decreased, but the dark cloud of gloom stayed with me. Then, one day, as I returned to the hotel where I was staying and entered my room, I just started crying—big, fat, ugly tears. I couldn't stop, and I felt myself unraveling. From that moment on, every single day was a struggle stronger than the day before. Somehow, I survived the three months and returned home, but I wasn't the same.

In addition to the random panic attacks, I felt immensely sad, incredibly alone, often confused, and just bone-deep tired. I attributed the first week to bad jet lag and the second to life, work responsibilities, and pressure. But, when I was still feeling physically and emotionally exhausted by the end of the month, something inside me knew I needed help. I was struggling, and I didn't know what to do.

I met with a therapist, and over our sessions, we concluded that I was suffering from what I now call "a breakdown and a burnout." And this condition stemmed from my relentless people-pleasing and controlling tendencies.

People came to "me" for help when they needed something, which gave me self-worth. It was the only gasoline for my self-esteem. I'm good as long as I was needed and looked like I've got it all together.

Of course, my fears of being found out as "not good enough" and that, in truth, "I don't belong here" developed my need for control. (Yes, that's imposter syndrome.) Over the years, I became consumed with controlling every aspect of my life to ensure I could dictate the outcome. This constant need for control only served to heighten my stress and anxiety. Eventually, I reached a point where I couldn't keep up anymore. My mind and body were exhausted from the constant juggling, coping, and controlling. I ran out of gas.

I'm extremely grateful for undergoing therapy. It helped me understand what I was going through, but sometimes, I felt like it wasn't addressing my specific issues. I felt something missing, as though I was seeing a glimpse of something, but I could not take the next meaningful step forward. So, I concluded my sessions and set out on my own. After some research, I came across Dialectical Behavior Therapy (DBT) by Dr. Marsha Linehan.

As I became more familiar with DBT, I discovered the powerful concept of acceptance (specifically, *Radical Acceptance*), and this proved to be my turning point. Acceptance was the key I've been looking for to unlock me from the cage of my mental and emotional struggles.

Acceptance is so simple, so powerful, yet oh so misunderstood!

You might think, "Acceptance alone won't solve my problems. It doesn't change my circumstances." You know what? You're right. Acceptance isn't the final destination but the necessary starting point for your healing journey. It is what you need to do to *allow* movement from point A to point B.

After discovering the benefits of DBT and taking Dr. Linehan's DBT Skills certificate course, I immersed myself in other types of behavior therapy, including Cognitive Behavioral Therapy (CBT) and Acceptance and Commitment Therapy (ACT). While these three approaches share many similarities, there are also distinct differences. DBT emphasizes mental and emotional skills training and validation, CBT focuses on identifying and challenging negative thought patterns, and **ACT emphasizes acceptance and values-based action**.

This book serves as a compassionate guide specifically focused on navigating the principles and practices of ACT. Why? I believe that truly experiencing the life you want should be based on your values, not the ones dictated by society or others. This was crucial to my mental healing, and I hope it does the same for you.

When I started my journey, I only wanted to "feel better." I never thought I would be radically transformed! It's a bit hard to explain, really. It's like I was going through life, seeing everything in muted colors and carrying this constant weight on my shoulders.

After ACT, my relationship with myself, my husband, other family members, and my outlook in life in general dramatically improved. **I wasn't just feeling better; I was happy.** And you know the thing about happiness, right? It has this tendency to radiate outwards.

Soon, people who knew about my troubles asked me what I had done to turn my life around. I started sharing my journey, and as more and more people reached out, I realized that the best way to live my life was to do my best to pay what I learned forward.

So, dear reader, this book is my personal invitation to you to go on a journey of deep self-discovery and healing with me.

I have been where you are. I know what you're going through. It would be my deepest honor to be of any kind of help to you right now. I offer you the kind of help I desperately needed and received back then.

Who Should Read This Book

This book is for anyone who is struggling right now or wants to support someone who is struggling. Perhaps you're considering therapy but prefer to start with something at home, or you just haven't found the right therapist yet. Maybe you're already in therapy and seek additional support. Regardless, **this book is for you if you want answers and relief**.

How This Book is Different

This book is your modern-day guide to Acceptance and Commitment Therapy (ACT) and how it can help you move from where you are to where you want to be. However, this book takes a rather uncommon perspective in that I've included some elements of Dialectical Behavior Therapy (DBT) and Cognitive Behavioral Therapy (CBT). I've found them to be extremely helpful in my healing journey, and I hope they benefit you, too.

How to Use This Workbook

The chapters in this book build on one another. So please start at the beginning and work your way through.

Also, I firmly believe that learning is knowledge + action. It's not enough to know something; you need to apply it for that knowledge to be useful. That's why each chapter provides guided exercises. As you accomplish each worksheet, you gain a deeper understanding of the concepts discussed and actively integrate them into your life. This integration is where the real transformation happens. It's like learning to swim by jumping into the water rather than just reading about it on dry land.

The Power of YOU

Please don't underestimate yourself. Humans are resilient creatures, so know that you have a remarkable ability to adapt, learn, and evolve in the face of adversity. You CAN break free from mental and emotional suffering and transform.

Also, whatever you're experiencing right now, know that **your truth matters**. Your feelings are valid. Your experiences are relevant, and your struggles deserve attention. Please don't let anyone undercut your reality or your voice. You have the right to feel what you feel and take the time to heal.

Speaking of healing, please always extend kindness and patience with yourself because this will not be a linear process. There will be ups and downs, but I promise you: You'll always be going forward if you stick with the process.

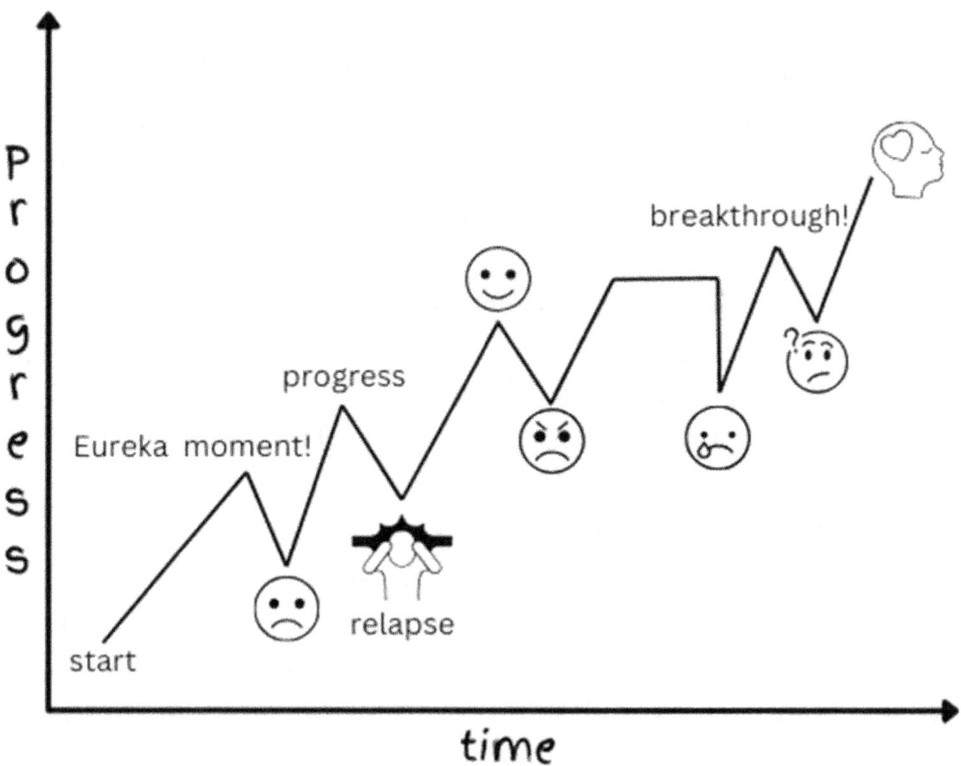

Note: This is just a sample healing journey. You and your circumstances are unique, so yours will most likely look different. Wouldn't it be amazing to discover your own unique path to healing?

Ava Watters

Amazon Bestselling Author
Acceptance Therapy Advocate

Part 1: Acceptance and Commitment Therapy 101

*"Accept yourself, love yourself, and keep moving forward. If
you want to fly, you have to give up what weighs you down."*
– Roy T. Bennett

Chapter 1: What is Acceptance and Commitment Therapy?

Acceptance and Commitment Therapy (ACT) was developed in the late 1980s by psychologist Steven C. Hayes[44] and his colleagues as they were working with people struggling with psychological problems such as anxiety and depression. (Hayes himself is no stranger to anxiety and has, over the years, talked openly about his panic disorder and experience with panic attacks.)

ACT draws from *behaviorism*, which emphasizes the influence of our environment and learning experiences on our behavior. It also incorporates elements of *Cognitive Behavioral Therapy (CBT)* and *Behavioral Therapy*, which focus on modifying maladaptive or unhelpful behavior.

For example, imagine Sarah. As a child, she was bitten by a dog, leading her to fear and thus avoid encountering dogs from that moment on. This avoidant behavior never left her. The thing is, as an adult, Sarah is very much into health and fitness and would love to try running. However, her fear of dogs prevents her from doing this because she fears potentially meeting a dog during a run.

In the above example, behaviorism highlights how Sarah came to fear dogs. By applying CBT and Behavioral Therapy techniques, Sarah might overcome this fear by exploring evidence that not all dogs are dangerous.

Now, you might say this solves Sarah's problems. But that's not entirely true. If you think about it, the above example illustrates a *before-and-after* situation. "Before" is Sarah being afraid of dogs, while "after" is her no longer afraid of them. But what about "during?" How can Sarah address the *exact moments* she's experiencing fear in front of a dog? This is where ACT comes in.

ACT goes beyond traditional behavioral and cognitive therapy approaches by incorporating acceptance- and mindfulness-based strategies to help individuals develop *psychological flexibility.*

Psychological flexibility is similar to the *bamboo principle.* Like the sturdy bamboo tree, you should be capable of bending or adapting to whatever life throws at you (e.g., difficult thoughts, unpleasant emotions, bad experiences, etc.) – without breaking. Or, at the very least, you should be able to bend or adapt to the point that you relieve yourself from mental and emotional suffering.

ACT believes a person lacking psychological flexibility struggles to adapt to life's challenges and may feel stuck or overwhelmed by difficult emotions or situations.

For example, someone with low psychological flexibility will most likely find coping with change or uncertainty challenging. They may become overly anxious or avoidant when faced with new experiences, challenges, or the unexpected, making navigating life's ups and downs difficult. This inflexibility can lead to increased stress, decreased resilience, and overall dissatisfaction and unhappiness with life. How? Well, let's go back to "Sarah."

Imagine that Sarah is happy where she currently lives because she lives in a pet-free apartment building with hardly any dogs in her neighborhood. But what if a great work opportunity comes along that requires her to relocate?

If she has low psychological flexibility, she might not dare to leave her current surroundings and comfort zone. What if she meets a friend or potential partner who loves dogs and lives with one? Sarah might avoid all of these potentially great relationships. One day, she might wake up and feel unfulfilled and unhappy with her life.

Now, you might say the above story is farfetched. But, is it?

Humans are hardwired to avoid the things they don't like, fear, or anything that causes unpleasant or negative emotions.[45] The problem with avoidance is that the trigger is never addressed, so you will almost always think, feel, and behave the same way when encountering it. And the more you do it, over time, what (or who) you're avoiding ends up controlling you.

Psychological flexibility is about being open and accepting of your thoughts and feelings—even the really difficult ones—without letting them rule your life. It means:

1. **You can adapt to "change," "different," or the "unexpected."** Psychological flexibility means you can easily adjust to life's ups and downs. It's about rolling with the punches and coping when things don't go as planned.

2. **You can face challenges that come your way.** Psychological flexibility encourages you to acknowledge difficult thoughts and feelings instead of avoiding or ignoring them. It's like saying, "Okay, I feel really anxious right now, but that's okay. I can handle it."

3. **You are present in the moment.** Psychological flexibility involves mindfulness and awareness of what's happening right now. Instead of worrying about the past or future, it's about staying grounded and focused on the present.

4. **You can choose your actions.** Even when dealing with tough emotions, psychological flexibility helps you focus on what's important. It's about choosing actions that align with your values and life goals, even if it's hard or uncomfortable.

5. **You don't need to be in control.** Sometimes, trying to control everything only makes things worse. Psychological flexibility teaches you to let go of the need for control and accept uncertainty. Instead of being fearful and

uncomfortable, you're okay with the unknown and curious about what may happen.

So, psychological flexibility is like having the mental and emotional agility to navigate life's twists and turns with grace and resilience. Great! But is ACT for you? Studies have shown that ACT has many applications across various aspects of life and can help with the following:

1. **Improves mental health.** ACT is effective in treating various mental health issues, including anxiety[46,47], depression[48], PTSD[49,50], OCD[51,52], and substance abuse[53,54]. It helps individuals develop healthy coping skills to manage their symptoms and improve their well-being.

2. **Reduces stress.**[55,56] ACT teaches mindfulness and acceptance techniques to help individuals cope with stress more effectively. By learning to accept difficult thoughts and feelings and focus on the present moment, people can reduce their stress levels and improve their resilience.

3. **Helps with chronic pain management.**[57,58] ACT is effective in helping individuals cope with chronic pain conditions. By changing their relationship to pain and focusing on value-centric actions, people can improve their quality of life and function better despite pain. (Important: This is not about denying the existence of pain. It's modifying how one relates to pain.)

4. **Boosts work and performance.**[59,60] ACT principles can be applied to enhance performance and productivity in various areas of life, including work, sports, and academics. By clarifying values, setting goals, and taking committed action in line with these values, individuals can achieve their full potential and overcome obstacles that may hinder their success.

5. **Improves relationships.**[61,62] ACT can improve communication and interpersonal skills, leading to healthier and more satisfying relationships. By cultivating acceptance and how to extend empathy and compassion to others, people can strengthen connections and build better relationships with others.

6. **Life transitions.**[63] ACT can be beneficial during major life transitions, such as career changes, relationship changes, or loss. By focusing on values and taking purposeful action, individuals can navigate these transitions with greater clarity and resilience.

7. **Personal growth.**[64,65] Even for those without specific mental health concerns, ACT can be valuable for personal growth and self-discovery. By increasing self-awareness, clarifying values, and fostering mindfulness, individuals can lead more authentic and fulfilling lives.

As you can see, the applications of ACT are diverse. To be honest, I don't see anyone not benefiting from ACT. Our world right now is full of chaos and uncertainty, and stress levels all across the globe are at an all-time high.[66] So, in my opinion, we all need more psychological flexibility, don't you think?

Chapter 2: Successful ACT Therapy at Home

ACT is usually done with a qualified therapist. The number of sessions depends on the nature and severity of the issues being addressed and your goals. However, most individuals see benefits within a relatively short period, often ranging from 6 to 20 sessions.[67,68] (This assumes active engagement between the therapist and the client.) This doesn't mean, though, that self-guided, at-home ACT is not possible.

For self-guided ACT to be successful, approach it with an open mind, a commitment to practice, and a willingness to explore your thoughts, emotions, and behaviors. Don't worry; the following chapters will explain and guide you every step of the way!

Before we begin, let's start with a few exercises to give you a great starting point for your self-guided ACT practice.

Have you ever stepped into a place and immediately felt a sense of peace, calm, or safety wash over you? Perhaps it wasn't the physical space itself but rather a particular item, scent, or memory associated with it that brought you back to a pleasant moment in time.

Our sensory experiences hold incredible power to influence our emotions and state of mind.[69] So, as you embark on this journey of healing and self-discovery, I highly encourage you to begin by creating your own sanctuary—a place where you can retreat during moments of distress or uncertainty.

You can call it your "safe space," your "happy place," or simply your "sanctuary." Whatever resonates with you, the purpose remains the same: to establish a physical or mental refuge where you can find solace, clarity, and peace amidst life's challenges.

Worksheet 1: Physical Safe Space

It's important to carve a space for yourself for your healing journey. This physical safe space can provide a dedicated environment to engage in ACT activities, reflection, and self-care practices. Here's how you can create a physical safe space for self-therapy:

1. **Pick a quiet and private area** in your home where you feel relaxed and safe. This could be a corner of a room, a cozy nook, or a specific chair or cushion where you can sit comfortably.

2. **Remove any clutter or distractions** from the space to create a clean and organized environment. Minimize visual and auditory distractions that could disrupt your focus during therapy sessions.

3. **Create a calming atmosphere** by adjusting the lighting, temperature, and overall "feel" of the space. Use soft lighting, candles, or natural light to create a soothing environment. Consider adding comforting elements such as cushions, blankets, or plants.

4. **Personalize the space** by adding personal touches and meaningful items. Display photographs, artwork, or objects that evoke happy or positive emotions or memories for you. Add elements that reflect your interests, values, and personality to make the space inviting and supportive.

5. **Add therapeutic tools and resources** that support your self-therapy practice. For example, place your journals, notebooks, pens, mindfulness exercises, relaxation techniques, self-help books, or any other resources that resonate with you here.

6. **Set boundaries** to protect your safe space and maintain its integrity. Inform family members about the importance of respecting your privacy during your therapy sessions. Use physical cues such as closing the door and hanging a "do not disturb" sign to signal your engagement in self-therapy activities. (Important: Respect your own boundary by not bringing

your mobile phone inside your safe space. If you must, put it on silent or allow only specific numbers to go through.)

7. Before engaging in any self-therapy session, **take a few moments to ground yourself** in the present moment. If you just "dive in" to therapy, you might find yourself resisting, especially if you're having a long and stressful day. As such, it's best if you can center yourself first. Just breathe deeply for a minute, and with each exhale, imagine yourself moving away from everything and closer to your healing practice.

8. **Establish a routine** to maintain consistency and momentum. Schedule a dedicated time in your calendar for reading this book, carrying out the exercises, self-care and reflection, etc.

9. After each self-guided ACT session, **take time to reflect** on your experiences and insights. Write in a journal about your thoughts, feelings, and observations, and consider any actions or adjustments you want to make moving forward.

10. **Extend patience and kindness to yourself.** Be gentle and compassionate with yourself as you navigate your self-therapy journey. Embrace imperfection and allow yourself to experiment, learn, and grow, knowing that your safe space is always available for calmness, healing, and self-discovery.

Worksheet 2: Mental Safe Space

A dedicated physical safe space you can go to for healing is great, but what if you're experiencing anxiety, distress, or any other unpleasant emotion and you can't access this space? This is where a mental safe space comes in. It's a dedicated room inside your mind to access anytime you need comfort and relief.

1. **Find a quiet and comfortable space** where you won't be disturbed.

2. Take a few deep breaths to **center yourself** and bring your focus to the present moment.

3. Close your eyes and **imagine yourself in a serene and peaceful environment**. This could be a place from your past, a favorite vacation spot, or an imaginary location.

4. **Use your senses to fully immerse yourself in this mental space.** Notice the sights, sounds, smells, and textures around you. Visualize the details of the environment, such as the colors, shapes, and patterns.

   One by one, focus on each of your senses:

   - **Sight**: Visualize the scenery around you. What do you want to see in your safe space? What will bring your calmness and assurance? Are there any specific colors, objects, or landscapes you connect to these positive emotions?
   - **Sound**: Listen to the sounds in your safe space. Are there birds chirping, waves crashing, or gentle breezes rustling?
   - **Smell**: Imagine any pleasant scents in the air. It could be the aroma of flowers, the freshness of the ocean, the earthy smell of the forest, the favorite scent of a loved one, etc.
   - **Touch**: Feel the textures around you. Are you sitting on soft grass, walking on warm sand, or resting against a smooth tree trunk?

- **Taste**: If applicable, imagine the taste of any food or drink that might be present in your mental safe space. It could be a refreshing fruit, a comforting beverage, or any other favorite treat.

5. After establishing your mental safe space, **slowly open your eyes and take a moment to ground yourself in the present moment**. Reflect on how it felt to create and immerse yourself in this safe space. Notice any shifts in your mood, mindset, or overall well-being.

Remember that your mental safe space is ALWAYS available whenever you need it. You can return to it anytime you feel stressed, anxious, or overwhelmed.

Worksheet 3: Kindness Mantras

It would be great if you could get into the habit of entering your physical and mental safe spaces, even during times when you don't need them. For example, when I wake up, I like to take a moment, close my eyes again, and go into my mental safe space for a minute or two. I find that it gives me a little "morning happy boost."

However, you would likely want to enter these safe spaces because you're going through moments of pain, worries, or stress. In these instances, you might encounter resistance. You might say, "I don't have time for this!" or "Why am I doing this?!"

I ask you to take a deep breath and be kind to yourself during these moments. Following is a list of mantras that might help you. Please feel free to write your own, too.

- I will take this time and offer compassion to myself.
- This is me being kind to myself in times of struggle and pain.
- I am resisting. This is okay. This is normal. I'm going to breathe in kindness and exhale resistance now.
- I will take this time to give myself gentleness and understanding.
- I have a heart of kindness and will channel that to myself now.
- I deserve this safe and calming moment.

Worksheet 4: I Want...

This exercise aims to help you establish your intention with your ACT practice. It's important to clearly define what you hope to achieve to have a clearer roadmap for your therapeutic journey. Plus, writing down your intentions can serve as a commitment to yourself.

Important: If you can't list 10 things, that's okay. If you want to write more down, that's fine too. What's important is that you get CLARITY about yourself, your current situation, and what you want for yourself.

Also, please remember that it's normal to see your priorities change (i.e., something you may want right now might turn out to be something unimportant later). As such, you may want to revisit this exercise and do it again later. Now, let's get to the exercise.

Step 1: Write down 10 or more things YOU WANT.

Example: I want to wake up energized and optimistic about my day.

1. ____
2. ____
3. ____
4. ____
5. ____
6. ____
7. ____
8. ____
9. ____
10. ____

Step 2: Write down 10 or more things YOU DON'T WANT.

Example: I don't want to constantly compare myself to my co-worker.

1. ____
2. ____
3. ____
4. ____
5. ____
6. ____

7. ___________________________________

8. ___________________________________

9. ___________________________________

10. ___________________________________

Step 3: Take your DON'T WANT list, and write down what you WANT INSTEAD.

Example:
DON'T WANT: I don't want to constantly compare myself to my co-worker.
WANT INSTEAD: I want to appreciate my unique strengths and abilities without measuring myself against others.

1. ___________________________________

2. ___________________________________

3. ___________________________________

4. ___________________________________

5. ___________________________________

6. ___________________________________

7. ___________________________________

8. ___________________________________

9. ___________________________________

10. ___________________________________

Part 2: The Six Core Principles of ACT

"The secret of change is to focus all of your energy, not on fighting the old, but on building the new."— Socrates

The main objective of ACT is to enhance your *psychological flexibility*, which can be achieved by practicing *Acceptance, Mindfulness, Cognitive Defusion, Self as Context, Values Clarification,* and *Committed Action.*

Acceptance in ACT means acknowledging and embracing your thoughts, emotions, and experiences–without trying to avoid, change, or judge them. It's acknowledging that happiness and sadness both exist in this world. For example, on Monday, you might be bursting with happiness. On Tuesday, you might experience sorrow and pain. Acceptance is acknowledging the Mondays and Tuesdays of life.

Mindfulness involves being fully present and aware of your thoughts, feelings, bodily sensations, and the world around you in the present moment. It's about observing your experiences without judgment or attachment, fostering a sense of clarity and insight.

Cognitive Defusion is about learning techniques to detach yourself from unhelpful thoughts and beliefs by recognizing them as just that–thoughts. They are not facts or rules to live by.

Self as Context in ACT is the "observing self." It's that part of you that notices what you're seeing, doing, saying, and thinking. For example, say you're eating your favorite ice cream flavor. (Mine's pistachio, by the way.) The "engaged self" in this activity is your mouth. The "observing self" is that part of you noticing how much pleasure you get from eating that scoop of ice cream.

Values Clarification represents what matters most to you: your deepest desires, aspirations, and guiding principles. I believe that one of the most common reasons for unhappiness today is that we don't take the time to identify our core values or have drifted so far away from them as the years go by. In ACT, clarifying your values helps you identify the kind of person you want to be and the life you want to live, guiding your choices and actions accordingly.

Committed Action involves taking purposeful steps towards living a life aligned with your values. (No more living based on other people's opinions, wishes, and standards.) It's about setting goals that reflect your values and actively working towards them, even in the face of challenges or discomfort.

These six core principles are interconnected, working together to promote psychological flexibility. In the following chapters, you'll dive deep into these concepts and strengthen your "mental bamboo."

Reminder: The best way to benefit from ACT is to practice its fundamental principles *before* you need them. So, learn them, practice them often, and be proficient in them. If you do, they'll come to your rescue whenever you need them.

Chapter 3: Acceptance

In the context of ACT, acceptance means being open to experiencing all of your thoughts, feelings, sensations, and memories without judgment, avoidance, or criticism.

When we're happy, it's easy to bask in the experience and prolong that feeling of happiness. However, when we encounter something (or someone) that triggers unpleasant or difficult emotions, we want to shut the door at them!

But here's the thing: shutting the door on difficult emotions does not eliminate them. Now, you can choose to stay "inside," but isn't that limiting your world? Isn't that letting life's problems and difficulties control you? Instead, why not try acceptance?

Imagine acceptance as opening the door to life's difficult, negative, and unpleasant experiences–and acknowledging their existence without judgment or resistance.

You accept not because you're "okay" with problems and hardships but because you recognize that they are part of the human experience. No single person in the world is always happy and never has problems. And there's nobody who's always into doom and gloom and never ever smiles. Even people suffering from depression or other mental health conditions have likely experienced moments of happiness.[70]

Why Is It So Hard to Accept?

Acceptance is easier said than done. Sure, the word itself is familiar, but in reality, most people misunderstand the concept, and that's why it's sometimes hard to apply. Here are some of the most common roadblocks to acceptance:

1. **Avoidance.** One of the biggest roadblocks to acceptance is the tendency to avoid or suppress difficult thoughts, emotions, or situations. For example, when you feel anxious about a challenging conversation, you might avoid it

altogether rather than face it head-on. This avoidance may provide temporary relief, but it ultimately prolongs suffering by preventing true acceptance and processing of these experiences.

2. **Fear of Emotions.** You might fear experiencing certain emotions, especially ones you consider negative or uncomfortable. For instance, you might suppress feelings of sadness because you're scared of being overwhelmed by them.

3. **Attachment to Control.** Another roadblock to acceptance is the desire for control over outcomes or circumstances. For example, when faced with unexpected changes in your plans, you might get stressed or anxious and try to micromanage every detail to regain a sense of control. In your mind, "unknown" might result in "bad."

4. **Judgment and Self-Criticism.** You frequently judge yourself harshly and hold yourself to unrealistic standards. For instance, if you make a mistake at work, you might berate yourself for being incompetent instead of accepting that everyone makes errors occasionally. These internal criticisms may fuel self-doubt and even anxiety and depression.[71]

5. **Rumination and Overthinking.** Constantly dwelling on past events or worrying about the future can prevent acceptance of the present moment. Rumination and overthinking keep the mind stuck in loops of repetitive thoughts, making it difficult to let go and fully engage with reality as it is. For example, you might replay a past argument in your mind repeatedly, analyzing every word said and imagining different outcomes.

6. **Social Influences.** External pressures and societal norms can also contribute to roadblocks to acceptance. For example, if you see your friends achieving certain milestones, you might feel inadequate or inferior because you haven't reached the same level of success.

7. **Lack of Awareness.** You may not realize that you're resisting acceptance because you're so accustomed to your habitual patterns of thinking and

behavior. For example, you might not recognize that your tendency to downplay your emotions hinders your ability to accept and address them effectively.

8. **Confusion About the Meaning of Acceptance.** Most people associate acceptance with "I agree" or "I forgive." This is not what acceptance means. Let me clarify this further.

Acceptance doesn't mean you're okay or agreeing with something. In truth, you're not agreeing to anything! You're just acknowledging the existence of a situation, the prevalence of certain emotions, etc. For example, say you and your partner are having an argument. In this scenario, accept that you disagree with each other and that this disagreement is causing you sadness. This practice of acceptance does not equal agreeing with what your partner is saying.

Acceptance is not denying something happened. You're not trying to deny or avoid difficult situations or negative feelings here. You're accepting your awareness of them so you can find healthy ways to cope.

Acceptance is not giving up or giving in. Accepting doesn't mean you don't want things to improve or are okay with it happening again. For example, suppose a friend stood you up for a long-awaited dinner engagement. In this case, accept the fact that your friend stood you up. In the future, set boundaries with this friend for better communication and reliability. Acceptance allows you to acknowledge the reality of the situation without dwelling on negative emotions or becoming consumed by resentment.

Acceptance is not about downplaying or trivializing. Acceptance does not underestimate or undervalue anything. In contrast, it promotes full and unwavering acceptance of challenging or distressing experiences. For example, *I am in pain here. I acknowledge this feeling. I have a right to feel this now.*

Acceptance doesn't mean "I lose." Many people think acceptance means they're wrong (and thus, someone else is right). Acceptance is not about win or lose, or wrong or right. Acceptance is simply acknowledging facts and reality.

At this stage, I'd like to introduce you to a concept I learned while undergoing Dialectical Behavior Therapy (DBT): **Radical Acceptance**.

In my opinion, Radical Acceptance goes just one small step further than ACT's Acceptance concept because it simplifies the principle while simultaneously pushing you to practice complete and unwavering acceptance.

In my experience, Radical Acceptance is one of the most freeing concepts I've ever encountered because it teaches us not to fight reality but simply to accept reality AS IS.

It's unnecessary to think, evaluate, or analyze a situation that has already happened. You cannot go back in time and re-do it, right? So, the best thing you can do is to accept the reality that it happened.

You don't need to overthink or criticize your feelings or reactions to something or someone either. For example, you're anxious about an upcoming event at work. You cannot just click "Close" on emotions, right? The best thing you can do is accept the reality that you're feeling anxious.

Now that we've delved into the complexities of acceptance and cleared up any misconceptions, I hope you're ready to practice acceptance. Here's a quick rundown of how acceptance can benefit your life.

- **Reduces mental and emotional suffering.** Imagine acceptance as this one big "Letting Go" sign. You're letting go of overthinking; you're letting go of control over situations beyond your influence; you're releasing yourself from the grip of uncomfortable and painful emotions. You don't need to suffer from your emotional and mental burdens. You can accept them and, in doing so, reduce their impact on you.

- **Builds resilience.** Acceptance builds emotional resilience by allowing you to move through difficult situations with greater ease and inner power.

- **Enhances emotional regulation.** Acceptance fosters healthier coping mechanisms by encouraging you to respond to emotions with compassion and understanding rather than avoidance or suppression.

- **Reduces stress.** Accepting the present moment AS IS can alleviate stress by reducing the need to control difficult circumstances. For example, suppose a friend's birthday is coming up, and you're stressed about seeing an ex-mutual friend during the birthday party. By radically accepting that your ex-friend will be there, you can move on from "stress" to planning what you should do. Acceptance is a much better coping mechanism for unpleasant situations than stress.

- **Improves your relationship with yourself and, consequently, others.** Acceptance cultivates a kinder and more compassionate relationship with yourself, allowing you to treat yourself with understanding and forgiveness during difficult times. This, in turn, fosters deeper connections and healthier communication patterns, leading to more fulfilling relationships with others.

- **Reduces overthinking and rumination.** Overthinking is generally about the future, and rumination is about the past.

  Overthinking involves excessive dwelling on a particular thought, problem, or situation. It often leads to analysis paralysis, where you become stuck in a cycle of analyzing every detail without reaching a decision. For example, you can't stop thinking about all the possible outcomes of going on a vacation with friends you just met. You're constantly weighing the pros and cons of going or not going without making progress.

Rumination specifically refers to repetitive thinking about distressing thoughts or feelings. You can't help but hit "Replay" on past unpleasant events. For example, you keep replaying a past argument in your mind, obsessing over what was said and how it made you feel, intensifying your negative emotions.

Acceptance reduces overthinking and rumination because it encourages you to unwaveringly recognize your thoughts and emotions–without judgment or resistance–instead of getting caught up in endless cycles of analyzing. Acceptance allows you to make peace with your thoughts and let them pass through your mind without becoming entangled in them.

Acceptance is not only highly beneficial in life, but I consider it the first step in any healing journey. I firmly believe that you must accept your current reality AS IS before you can move to change it.

Acceptance is a skill that takes time and practice to develop. It's not something you can just turn "On," especially if you've been avoiding or judging your thoughts and emotions for a long time. The good news is that with patience and practice, you CAN cultivate acceptance in your life. The following exercises will help you achieve this.

Worksheet 5: Willing Hands

We experience emotions in our bodies. If you're finding it hard to accept a situation, this body-focused practice might help you cultivate a sense of openness within yourself.

Usually, when we're going through an unpleasant or difficult situation, we tend to curl our hands into tight fists. This time, do the opposite. That is, carefully open your hands and palms and relax your fingers.

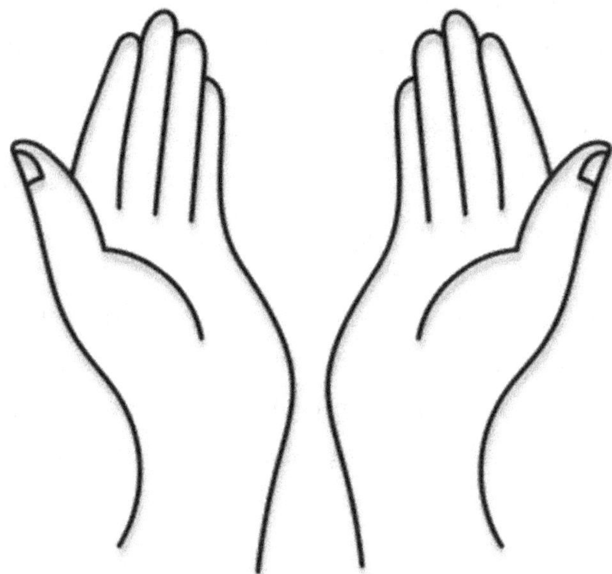

If you continue to sense resistance, slowly open or stretch your hands, one finger at a time, until your hands are open wide and your fingers are wide apart (nearly tensing).

Next, slowly relax to a willing hands position (relaxed but open).

Worksheet 6: Acknowledge, Allow, Accept

This exercise will help you practice acceptance by breaking it down into three simple steps.

Step 1: Acknowledge. Recognize your thoughts, feelings, and experiences without judgment or resistance. This involves acknowledging the reality of your internal and external experiences.

What do you want to acknowledge right now? What's your current reality?

Example: I'm grieving my dog, Charlie. No one understands how deep my pain is now that he's gone.

Step 2. Allow. Once you acknowledge your thoughts and feelings, allow them to be present. Let these thoughts and emotions exist without trying to distract yourself from them. Just sit with the feeling and allow it to pass naturally.

What do you want to allow right now?

Example: I'm allowing my feelings of grief, sadness, and loneliness to exist within me. I have a right to feel these emotions now that my dog is gone.

Step 3: Accept. Accept and make peace with your experiences.

Write down your acceptance statement.
Example: I accept the reality that my best friend is gone. I accept that I'm feeling incredibly sad and lonely right now. I accept that these emotions are part of my grieving process.

Worksheet 7: Non-Judgmental People Watching

It's our nature to judge. We watch something on Netflix and judge it with a thumbs up or down. We hear music and judge it as amazing or "noise." We smell a new scent and judge it as "pleasant" or "unpleasant."

Judging goes against the practice of acceptance because it's a form of control or assessment over something that simply IS. Of course, we're allowed to have an opinion, but acceptance is not about forming an opinion about anything or anyone. It's accepting facts. It's acknowledging reality AS IS.

So, when it comes to unpleasant or difficult thoughts or emotions, try not to label or judge them as "good or "bad" or whether you should feel them or not. Don't analyze, evaluate, or judge. Just allow and accept. The following exercise is one of my favorite exercises to combat judgmental behavior.

1. **Select a public space** like a nearby park, coffee shop, or shopping mall where you can watch people come and go. Bring pen and paper with you. If possible, allow 30 minutes for this exercise.

2. **Sit where you can observe people** come and go. Ensure you have a clear view of different people doing different things, but not close enough that you can hear what they're saying.

3. Look around and notice someone. Pay attention to their gestures and facial expressions. Grab your pen and paper and write down your observations.

    Example: I notice a man walking ahead of a woman who seems to be his wife.

4. Did your mind jump to any assumptions or judgments? If so, write them down. Note: DO NOT criticize yourself for having these thoughts.

    Example: I don't know why, but I got annoyed and judged that the man was not considerate of his wife. I mean, why is he walking away and ahead of her?

5. **Reflect.** Explore where your assumptions might have come from.

Example: I just never saw my dad "walk away" from my mom?

6. **Challenge your assumptions.** WHAT ELSE could be true?

Example: Well, maybe the man and the woman are complete strangers to each other and not a couple at all.

7. Move on to observe other people in different situations. Write down any immediate judgments you form about them, then immediately move on to challenging your assumptions. Continuously do this until your thinking slowly shifts to not forming automatic assumptions about others or until the 30 minutes is up.

8. After this exercise, shift your focus inward and practice self-compassion towards yourself for any judgments you may have made. Acknowledge that it's natural to have thoughts and opinions about others, but also recognize that you can choose NOT to do so.

9. Next, extend compassion to the people you observed. Recognize that everyone is navigating their own challenges and experiences and that you don't know their story or what they're going through that day.

10. Get up and leave the space where you did this exercise. And as you do, release any guilt or negative feelings regarding any judgments you may have made. Recognize that those judgments are simply passing thoughts. Allow them to come and go without getting caught up in them like clouds passing across the sky.

As you go about your day, make a conscious effort to practice nonjudgmental acceptance in your interactions with yourself and others. Notice when judgments arise and gently redirect your attention towards acceptance and compassion.

Chapter 4: Mindfulness (Present Moment Awareness)

Mindfulness is living in the present. It's existing in NOW. It involves paying attention to your thoughts, feelings, sensations, and surroundings—as they are happening—with openness and curiosity.

Instead of getting caught up in worries about the past or the future, mindfulness helps you focus on the here and now. It's like shining a spotlight on your present existence and experience, whether you're eating, walking, or breathing, without letting your mind wander.

The practice of mindfulness is NOT NEW. It emerged as an integral part of Buddhist meditation practices around 2,500 years ago. It was initially developed to cultivate awareness, attention, and present-moment focus to *alleviate suffering* and *achieve enlightenment*.

Most people think mindfulness is just "woo-woo" or nonsense, but I think it makes perfect sense. If you just take a moment to sit and "be," you're giving yourself time; the time you need to mentally and emotionally distance yourself from pain, stress, and whatever negative feelings you're experiencing. (You alleviate your suffering.)

And as you put that distance, you get to see things, situations, and people in a different light. Maybe, just maybe, the situation is not that bad after all. (You achieve enlightenment.)

~~Mindfulness is nonsense.~~
Mindfulness makes perfect sense.

What's the point of mindfulness in ACT? How does it help develop psychological flexibility? Have you ever had a moment where you did or said something, and the second you did it, you were suddenly filled with regret? That's the point of mindfulness: to prevent you from automatically reacting. It gives you the time, space, and opportunity to *think before you act*.

So, imagine mindfulness as a "mental pause button" you can click between "trigger" and "reaction." If you activate it, you give yourself time to focus on yourself, inwardly and outwardly, and to assess what your next step should be.

In real life, trigger+reaction happens fast. For example, if someone hurts you, you hurt back. And then they hurt you back, and then... you get the picture.

But if you're mindful, you can stop, reflect, and assess. At that exact stage of present-moment awareness, you're creating distance between yourself, your strong emotions, and any automatic reactions you want to make. Now, *choice* enters.

As that distance between trigger and knee-jerk reaction grows, alternatives come in. What else can you do? How can you make this situation better? And that, my friend, is *psychological flexibility*, the ability to withstand pain, stress, or the unexpected and shift perspective.

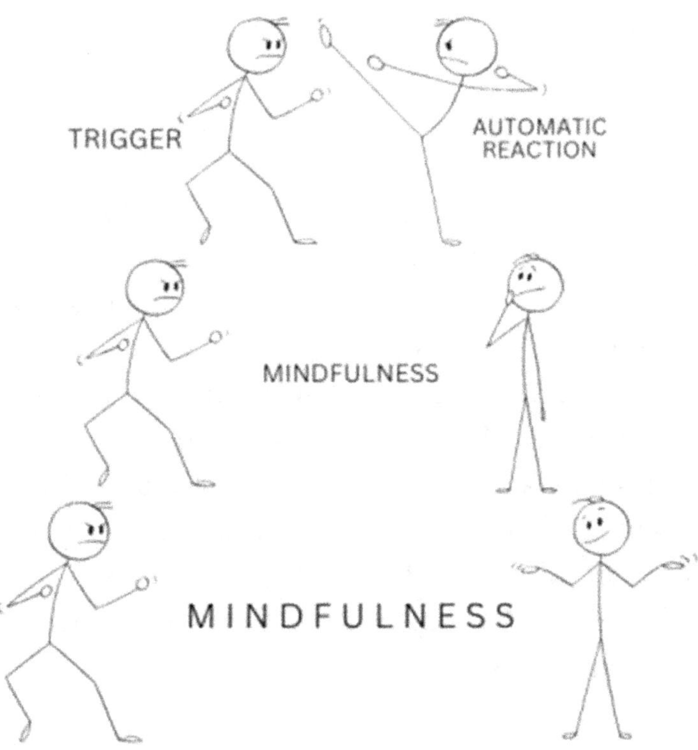

Important: The above image illustrates how mindfulness can help someone not react to a situation in a way that escalates it or makes it worse. This does not mean you're "okay" or "agree" with what happened. Also, your response after mindfulness can be varied. Depending on the situation or trigger, you might do the exact opposite of what you intended (e.g., sit down and calmly engage in a conversation vs. shouting angrily), or you might decide to walk away and return to the situation later. It all depends on the situation and what you want to achieve.

Let's consider another example: Max is stressed at work with deadlines up to his ears when his colleague, Bob, sends him an email on Friday at 4 PM asking him to review a project report due next Monday.

Now, Max is already not a fan of Bob, so his knee-jerk, automatic reaction might be to send a nasty email back saying that he thinks it's crap that Bob is sending the email only now. He might even copy their boss to boot! Max might also pretend he didn't see the email and let everything fall on Bob's shoulders on Monday. Are any of these scenarios helpful in any way? Probably not.

Here's what practicing mindfulness might look like in this situation.

1. **Take a break.** Max gets up, stretches his legs, grabs a cup of coffee or tea, and breathes deeply for a few minutes.
2. **Accept reality as is.** Bob sent a last-minute email asking me to review a report I barely know anything about.
3. **Accept your thoughts and emotions as is.** I'm angry and frustrated right now. That's okay. This is a normal reaction.
4. **Evaluate the next steps.** What's the best way to handle this? What exactly do I want to happen in this situation? The reality is I don't have time for this report, and I want to set a boundary here.
5. **Act accordingly and respond respectfully and tactfully (not angrily and accusatory).**

Dear Bob,

I just read your email. Normally, I would have no issues helping, but it's 4:15 PM, and I have no time to review this report because I also have a couple of mine to go over.

Kind regards and a happy weekend,
Max

As you can see, mindfulness prevented Max from worsening an already stressful situation. He said "No" and set a boundary, and by using simple and direct words that are more factual than emotional, he came across as completely reasonable and professional. Notice the lack of any "blaming" tone in the message as well.

Just like acceptance, mindfulness is a skill that needs to be developed. You may find that getting from "automatic reaction" to "best reaction" takes a long time. However, with constant mindfulness practice, you'll notice that your ability to alleviate your suffering and feel better becomes more efficient over time.

If you find yourself resisting mindfulness, you're not alone. Here are some of the most common roadblocks to mindfulness and what to do about them.

1. **Skepticism or doubt.** This is probably one of the strongest barriers to practicing mindfulness. You may not believe it will work, so you don't want to try it. But imagine this: say someone just met you and decided in that second they don't like you at all. Is that fair? Wouldn't it be better if that person tried to get to know you first? Think of mindfulness as a person you just met.

   What to do: Approach mindfulness with an open mind and a spirit of curiosity. Also, there are many ways to practice mindfulness, so experiment with different techniques to find what works best for you and explore without judgment.

2. **Busy lifestyles.** Everyone is busy. We're always in motion, always doing something, always trying to achieve and move up in life. We've even perfected the art of multi-tasking and dealing with unnecessary interactions. However, none of that erases the fact that we're also stressed and anxious. Wouldn't it be great to be unstressed and unanxious, even for a while?

What to do: Prioritize mindfulness by treating it like a sacred appointment with yourself. Schedule regular times for mindfulness practice, even just a few minutes daily. For example, set an alarm that goes off at the same time each day to remind yourself to take a break or meditate.

Also, look for opportunities to integrate mindfulness into your daily activities. For example, take 5 minutes to mindfully eat breakfast or spend 10 minutes after lunch to engage in mindful walking. Here's some funny advice I received from a mindfulness teacher a few years ago: If you have time to talk, you have time not to talk (and thus, be mindful).

3. **Constant digital distractions.** Focusing on the present moment when you're bombarded with 24/7 non-stop digital distractions is challenging.

What to do: Set digital boundaries by scheduling specific times for digital use and your mindfulness practice. For example, when practicing mindfulness, use features on your phone that limit distractions, such as its built-in Do Not Disturb modes. You can also use tools such as Cold Turkey (for desktops) or AppBlock (for mobile devices) to help you stay focused by blocking phone apps from sending you notifications.

4. **Stress and overwhelm.** Most people tell me they don't have enough time to "waste" on mindfulness because they're too stressed and overwhelmed with life. This is like saying, "I don't want to drink because I'm too thirsty."

What to do: Use mindfulness techniques, such as basic deep breathing or body scan meditation, to manage stress in the moment. You don't need to go "deep" with mindfulness. You don't need to overthink the practice. You can use it as you would take a warm bath or soothing massage to de-stress.

5. **Difficulty with concentration.** When I started my mindfulness practice, I found it hard to be still and concentrate for a few minutes. I found it hard to "not think." But then I had this nagging thought, "Hmmm, I thought I was in control of my mind. Why can't I command it to be still for just a few minutes?!" This thought bothered me because I felt like my mind had too much "noise" that I didn't want. I wanted to reach a stage where I could think clearly without noise or distractions. So, I kept being mindful until I reached this goal. And I know you can, too.

What to do: Be patient with yourself. Let go of any expectations and focus on one thing at a time mindfully rather than trying to juggle multiple thoughts simultaneously. When you practice mindfulness, let go of the word "multi-tasking" and embrace "single-tasking."

For example, if you're listening to music during your practice, just listen to the music and tune out anything else you might hear. If you hear a bird chirping outside, don't let your thoughts follow it. Don't mind-wander. Just say or think "chirp," then return to the music. If you hear a passing car, say or think "car," then return to the music. Do this over and over. In time, you'll find it easier, almost automatic, to ignore external noise.

I like to think of mindfulness as "plugging in" or "recharging." Each time you practice it, imagine giving yourself that energy or juice to refresh your mind and well-being. Just like plugging in your phone to charge its battery, mindfulness allows you to replenish your mental and emotional energy, helping you feel more present, centered, and alive.

So, ready to meet and get to know mindfulness? Following are a few exercises to jumpstart your practice.

Worksheet 8: Box Breathing or Square Breathing

Breathing is basic. We all know this; we all do this. But did you know that you might be breathing the wrong way?

Most people are shallow breathers, inhaling through the nose or mouth and then exhaling it out. We huff and puff, never letting air reach our diaphragms. So, the first thing you need to learn is how to properly breathe deeply. Why? The breath is important in cultivating mindfulness because it serves as an anchor to the present moment.

When you focus on your breath, you bring your attention to the sensations of breathing, which are always in the present moment. (You can't breathe in honor of yesterday or start breathing for tomorrow, right? Breathing is always about NOW.)

So, breathing deeply helps you become more aware of your thoughts, feelings, and physical sensations as they happen—without becoming entangled in them. Plus, the breath is always accessible, making it a convenient tool for practicing mindfulness anytime and anywhere. Let's start!

Step 1: Sit or lie down in a comfortable position. Make sure your spine is straight but not tense. You can place your hands on your lap or sides, whatever feels natural.

Step 2: Inhale slowly and deeply through your nose, counting to four as you breathe in. Feel your lungs expanding as you fill them with air. Try to breathe deeply into your belly rather than shallow breaths into your chest.

Step 3: Hold your breath for four counts. Keep your lungs filled with air, and your body relaxed as you hold your breath.

Step 4: Now, **exhale slowly through your mouth for four counts** as you release the air from your lungs. Feel the tension leaving your body with each exhale.

Step 5: After you've completed your exhale, **pause for another count of four**. This moment of pause allows you to reset and prepare for the next breath.

Step 6: Continue this box breathing pattern for several rounds, maintaining a steady rhythm and focusing on the sensation of your breath. You can do this for a few minutes or as long as you need to feel calm and centered.

Step 7: When you're done, take a moment to reflect. Pay attention to any changes in your body, mind, or emotions. After practicing this exercise, you may feel more relaxed, focused, or grounded.

Make box breathing a daily habit. Studies show that it provides quick stress and anxiety relief, lowers blood pressure, increases focus (not just during practice but throughout the day), and enhances the mind-body connection.[72] The more you practice, the easier it will become to tap into a sense of calm and balance whenever you need it.

Worksheet 9: Mindful Walking in Nature

This exercise offers a multitude of benefits. In addition to training yourself to focus on the present, you interact with nature. Studies show that being outdoors can reduce stress levels, improve mood, and enhance overall well-being.[73] Additionally, walking in nature encourages physical activity. It's a win-win with this exercise.

Step 1: Find a peaceful outdoor location such as a park, forest trail, beach, or botanical garden. Aim for a place with minimal distractions and abundant natural beauty.

Step 2: Before you begin walking, take a moment to **set your intentions** for the practice. For example, write down or say to yourself, "I'm going to take a walk and just be with myself. I want to destress and enjoy my own company for a few minutes."

Step 3: Start by standing still in a comfortable position. Close your eyes if it feels comfortable, and **take a few deep breaths** to center yourself. Feel the sensation of your feet grounding into the earth beneath you.

Step 4: Open your eyes and begin to observe your surroundings. Don't choose what to focus on. Just let your eyes land on something and then try to observe it detachedly. For example, say your eyes land on a nearby bench; describe it. Notice its features (size, length, color, sturdiness, etc.), and try not to form any opinions about it (e.g., that bench looks dirty).

Step 5: Start walking slowly, deliberately paying attention to each step you take. Feel the earth beneath your feet with each stride. Maintain a relaxed and steady pace, allowing your movements to flow naturally.

Step 6: As you walk, **bring your attention to your breath**. Notice the rhythm of your inhales and exhales and how your body moves with each breath. Use your breath as an anchor to keep you grounded in the present moment.

Step 7: Continuously engage your senses as you walk. Notice the intricate details of the natural world around you—the patterns in tree bark, the shapes of clouds, the colors of flowers. Tune in to the sounds of nature, from the songs of birds to the rustling of leaves.

Step 8: You'll inevitably encounter various thoughts, emotions, and sensations during your walk. Practice observing them without judgment. If your mind starts to wander, gently bring your attention back to the present moment and the sensations of walking.

Step 9: At certain moments during your walk, **express gratitude**. You can say thanks for the beauty and abundance of nature surrounding you or simply appreciate your sturdy legs and feet for supporting your every step.

Step 10: When you're ready to conclude your walk, slow your pace and find a quiet spot to reflect. Take a few moments to think about your experience and acknowledge any insights or feelings you had during your walk. Offer yourself gratitude for taking the time to prioritize yourself.

Worksheet 10: Grounding Using Your Five Senses

Mindfulness can also come to the rescue when you're in crisis. When we're in distress, it's easy for our thoughts to spiral out of control. It's like the past, present, and future collide inside you, and you can't stop overthinking or ruminating. One way to press STOP on that rollercoaster of stormy emotions is to bring yourself to the present moment using your five senses.

Step 1: Go to a quiet space where you can sit comfortably without any distractions. It could be indoors or outdoors, as long as you feel relaxed and at ease. There might be situations where you feel you can't just go and leave in the middle of a stressful situation, but you can. Say something like, "This isn't helping me/us. I need to take a break," or "This situation is stressing me. I need to regroup."

Step 2: Sit comfortably on a chair with your feet flat on the floor or cross-legged on the ground. Rest your hands on your lap or knees, whichever feels more comfortable.

Step 3: Take a few deep breaths or practice <u>Box Breathing</u>. Inhale deeply, and imagine any stress or tension moving away from you with each exhale.

Step 4: Now, focus on each of your five senses, one at a time:

- **Sight.** Look around and **notice five things you can see**. They could be objects in the room, colors, or patterns. Take a moment to observe each one without judgment, simply acknowledging its presence.

- **Hearing.** Close your eyes and **identify four things you can hear**. It could be the sound of traffic outside, birds chirping, water splashing, or the hum of appliances in the room. Tune in to each sound and let it wash over you.

- **Touch. Find three things you can touch or feel.** It could be the texture of the fabric beneath you, the coolness of the wall, or the smooth surface of an object nearby. Take a moment to fully experience the sensation of touch.

- **Smell.** Take a deep breath through your nose and **identify two things you can smell**. It could be the scent of flowers, food cooking nearby, or even the freshness of the air. Notice the aroma and how it affects your mood and state of mind.

- **Taste.** Finally, **focus on one thing you can taste**. It could be the lingering flavor of your last meal, the freshness of a mint, or simply the taste of your saliva. Allow yourself to fully experience this sensation, savoring it for a moment.

Step 5: After you've engaged all five senses, take a moment to **return to your breath**. Notice how your body feels now compared to when you started. Allow yourself to bask in the present moment, feeling grounded and centered.

Step 6: Before you end the exercise, take a moment to **reflect on one thing you're grateful for in this moment**. It could be that you're proud of yourself for taking the time to ground yourself to the present moment or something you noticed during the exercise.

Step 7: Take a deep breath and exhale as forcefully as possible. Stand up, stretch, or shake your arms and legs, whatever feels good for you. Next, take one confident step to join the rest of the world again.

Don't rush this exercise. If you need more time to ground yourself, then so be it. You can engage each of your senses again, one at a time.

Mindfulness of Emotions

We're always feeling something. There's not a moment when we're not experiencing an emotion. But when these emotions are the stressful, painful, and difficult kind, we might end up feeling depressed or that there's no hope.

One of the most helpful pieces of advice I received about emotions is this: **No single emotion lasts forever.**

Emotions are transient and tend to fluctuate over time. While some emotions may linger longer than others, eventually, they will fade or shift in intensity. This natural ebb and flow of emotions is a normal part of the human experience.

But WHY do we experience certain emotions? There's an internal process involved as to why we feel the way we do over something or someone.

Step 1: Trigger. This event, situation, or stimulus initiates the emotional response. It could be something external, like a comment from someone, or internal, like a memory.

Example: Sam walks down the street, and someone he knows walks past him without saying hello. This is the trigger.

Step 2: Filtering. Once the trigger occurs, your mind filters it through *your* beliefs, past experiences, and perceptions. This filtering process influences how you interpret and respond to the trigger.

Example: Sam interprets the other person's behavior through the filter of his past experiences. Maybe he's had issues with this person before, so Sam interprets their action as deliberate rudeness rather than a simple oversight.

Step 3: Subjective experience. This step involves your personal interpretation of the filtered information. It's where you assign meaning to the trigger based on your unique perspective, values, and understanding of the world.

Example: Sam feels hurt and slighted by their behavior. Based on his interpretation (filtering), Sam concludes that they don't like him or are intentionally ignoring him.

Step 4: Physiological response. Physiological changes, such as increased heart rate, sweating, or changes in breathing patterns, often accompany emotions. These physical sensations are part of the emotional experience.

Example: Sam's now annoyed by the whole event. His heart rate increases, and he's feeling flushed. This is his body reacting to the emotional distress of being, in his mind, deliberately ignored or snubbed.

Step 5: Behavioral response. Finally, your emotions lead to behavioral responses or actions. These can vary widely depending on the emotion, intensity, and who you are.

Example: Sam might, in the present moment, engage in specific behaviors or reactions (e.g., slamming a door, banging his fist on a table, etc.). In the future, when he sees the other person again, Sam might respond by avoiding eye contact or feeling angry and resentful toward them. This behavior is influenced by the emotions and interpretations he experienced in response to the trigger.

How does knowing this process help you? In the above example, the situation started with "someone not saying hello." Then, it quickly moved on to a personal interpretation of "deliberately being ignored" and feelings of resentment towards the ignorer.

But what does Sam know for sure? What's the FACT here? Someone passed by without saying hello. That's it.

The rest is Sam's *personal interpretation* of the situation. In reality, there could be plenty of reasons why Sam was ignored, none having anything to do with Sam. The other person might have eye problems and was not wearing his glasses that day and missed Sam, or they might be going through something and their mind was preoccupied with their problems.

In short, Sam could have stopped at Step 1: Trigger. He didn't have to go through steps 2-5 and feel bad about the whole thing.

When you are in crisis or distress, it helps to be mindful and aware of how you filter a trigger. It helps to remind yourself that how you see and interpret something may not accurately reflect the situation. When you do this, you prevent emotional and mental suffering.

So what do you do? When triggered, try to label or name the exact emotion you're feeling. This is because what you feel influences your thoughts and behavior. If you can address the emotion first, there's a good chance you can nip any potential negative thoughts and actions you might make.

Worksheet 11: Name that Emotion

Did you know that naming or being able to identify a distressing emotion lessens its intensity, making you better able to handle a difficult situation?[74] The problem is that sometimes, it's hard to pinpoint exactly what we're feeling. For example, what are you feeling RIGHT NOW?

If you're unable to pick one, you might think it's because none of the above six emotions accurately reflect your feelings.

Maybe you're anxious? Confused? Excited? Jealous? Anything else? Whatever it is, understand that it's a totally valid emotion. However, you may not be aware that what you're experiencing is a *secondary emotion*.

Primary emotions (the six above) are our initial reactions to situations. Secondary emotions (or even tertiary ones) are our responses to our primary emotions.

Here's an **Emotion Wheel**. Use it as you go through the following steps in this exercise.

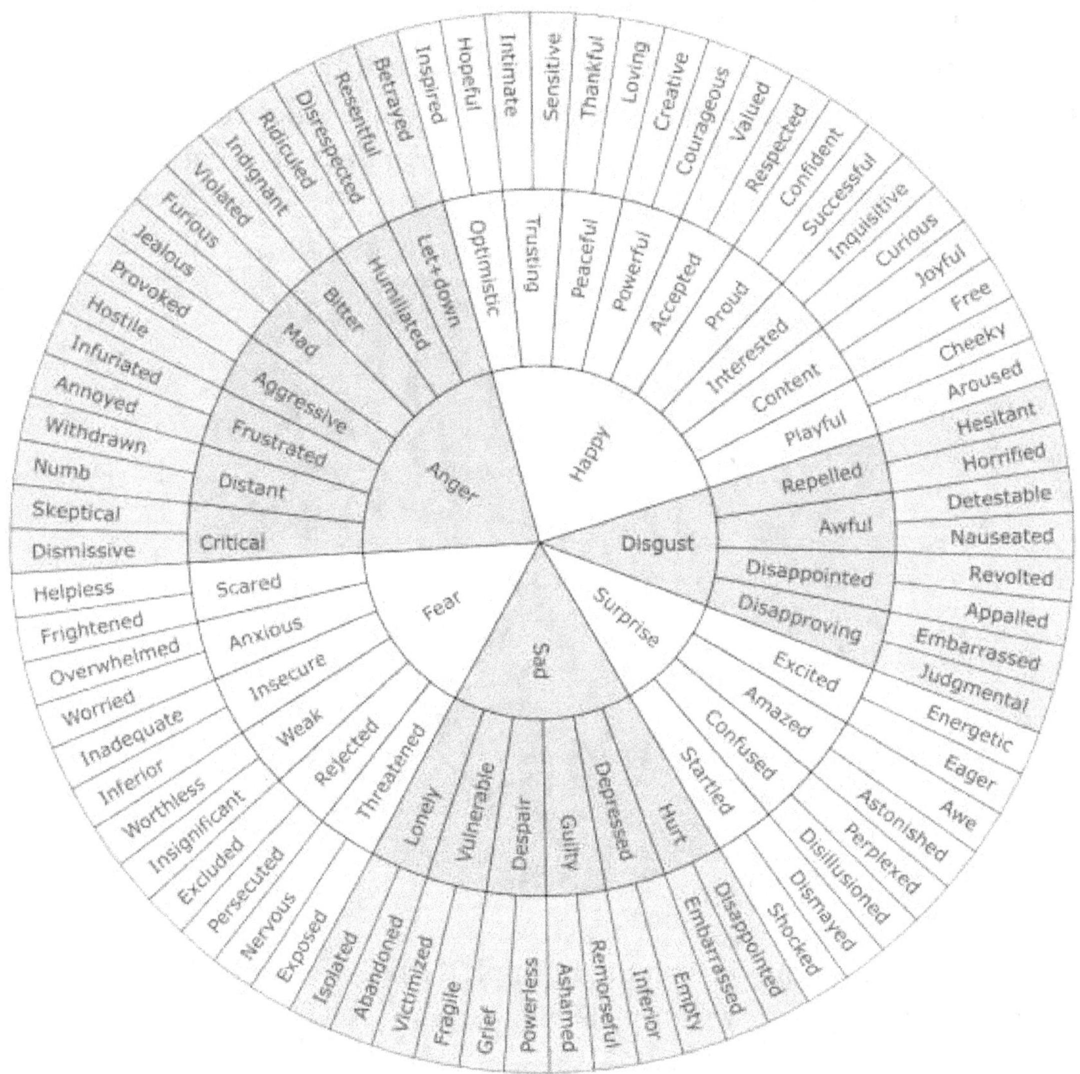

Step 1: Identify a trigger. Think about a recent event or situation that stirred up some strong emotions. It could be something positive, negative, or neutral. Take a moment to recall the details of the event.

Step 2: As you recall the situation, **pay attention to any physical sensations you're experiencing**. Is there any tightness, warmth, or discomfort in certain parts of your body? (Your body often provides clues about the emotions you're feeling.) If you're feeling discomfort, take a deep breath, and as you exhale, say, "Release." Keep on doing this until the negative bodily sensation lessens or evaporates.

Step 3: Look at the outer edges of the Emotion Wheel, and pick the word that describes your emotion RIGHT NOW.

Example: I feel disrespected.
I feel ____.

Move to the inner circle and pick the word that describes your emotion even more.

Example: I feel disrespected -> <u>humiliated</u>.
I feel ____________________ -> ____________________.

In the same section, look at the innermost circle of the wheel and write down the *primary emotion* you see.

Example: I feel disrespected -> humiliated -> anger.
I feel ________________ -> ________________-> ________________.

Step 4: Now that you've narrowed down your primary emotion, **explore what this may mean.** Here's a table to help you.

Happiness	Sadness	Fear
something is important	*something is not right*	*there's potential danger*
Surprise	**Disgust**	**Anger**
a call to focus on new situations	*something is unhealthy for you*	*a need to protect something or fight a problem*

Step 5: Write down what it means to you to be able to name your primary emotion and understand what it means. Does it provide clarity and validation for what you're experiencing?

Reflect on why labeling emotions can help manage and understand your inner world. Write freely, and don't criticize or judge yourself. Let the words flow as you get to the root of your emotions.

Example: When Frank ignored me on the street, I felt disrespected and humiliated. I knew I was angry, but I didn't know that anger meant "wanting to protect something." So, what do I want to protect? My ego, I guess. And if my ego is so easily bruised... do I need to work on my self-esteem?

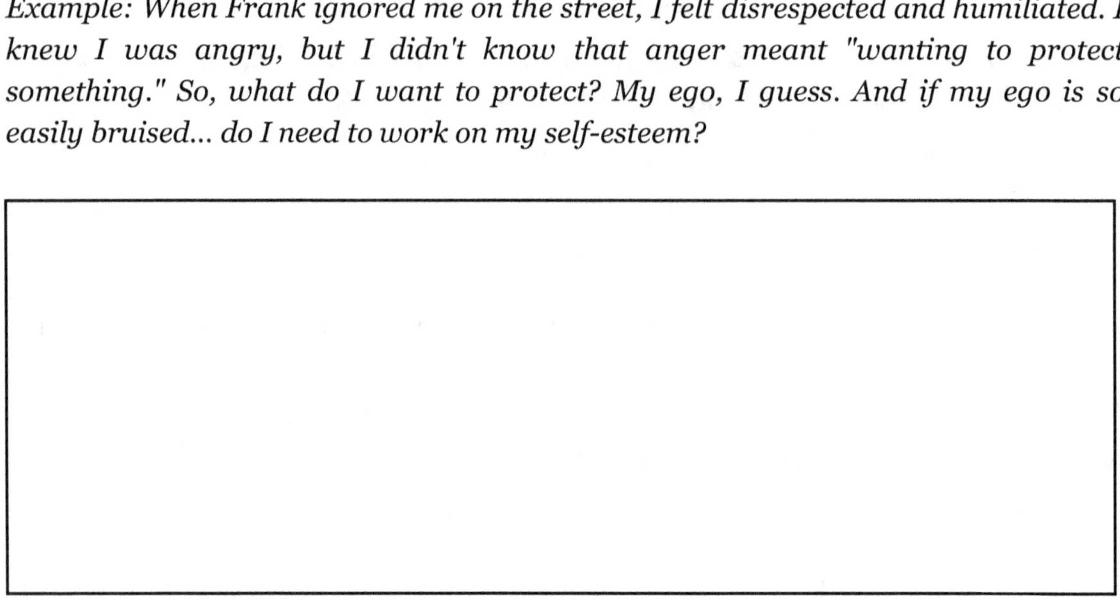

Step 6: After reflecting on your emotion, **consider how you want to express or process it**. This could involve journaling, talking to a friend or therapist, engaging in a creative activity, or simply allowing yourself to feel the emotion without judgment.

The better you can identify and define your emotions, the more effectively you can cope with them. Remember, you have every right to feel your emotions, but you don't necessarily need to act according to them.

Worksheet 12: Mindful Body Scan of Emotions

This exercise aims to cultivate greater awareness and acceptance of the connection between physical sensations and emotional experiences. By systematically scanning your body and exploring sensations with a nonjudgmental attitude, you can learn to recognize and name your emotions more effectively.

Step 1: Choose a comfortable, quiet space to sit or lie down, free of distractions. Ensure you won't be interrupted during the exercise.

Step 2: Sit or lie down comfortably. **Close your eyes and take a few deep breaths** to center yourself.

Step 3: Direct your attention to your physical sensations. Notice the points of contact between your body and the supporting surface. Feel the weight of your body sinking into the chair or bed.

Step 4: Slowly shift your focus to different parts of your body, starting from your toes and gradually moving upward. Notice any sensations, tensions, or areas of discomfort as you scan each body part. Allow yourself to observe these sensations without judgment or the need to change them.

Step 5: As you scan each body part, **pay attention to any emotions or feelings that arise.** You might notice tension in your shoulders, a sense of warmth in your chest, or butterflies in your stomach. Take note of any emotional experiences without trying to analyze or interpret them.

Step 6: If you struggle to identify emotions, practice focusing on specific body parts. For example, if you feel tension in your jaw, gently direct your awareness to that area and notice any associated emotions, such as stress or frustration. You can ask yourself, "Why is my jaw so tense?" and then let the answer come to you.

Step 7: As you become aware of different emotions within your body, **practice accepting** them as valid and natural responses to your internal and external experiences. Allow yourself to feel whatever arises without resistance or judgment.

Step 8: Next, **breathe into your emotions**. With each breath, imagine sending gentle waves of relaxation and acceptance to the areas of your body where you're experiencing emotions. Use your breath to soothe and comfort yourself amid emotional discomfort.

Step 9: After scanning your entire body and exploring the associated emotions, **take a few moments to rest in this state of mindful awareness**. Notice how you feel physically, emotionally, and mentally after completing the exercise.

Step 10: When ready, **gently open your eyes and reflect** on your experience. Notice any insights or observations that arose during the body scan.

Tip: Doing this exercise often may reveal certain things. For example, say that you're often experiencing jaw tenseness. This might reveal that you're often angry. In this case, you might want to think about why you feel this way so often and what you can do to address it.

Chapter 5: Cognitive Defusion (a.k.a. Unhooking)

Here's a story from Elizabeth, or Lizzie, one of my readers.

A painter cousin of mine, James, came to visit one summer when I was about 12 years old. One day, he asked me to "strike a pose," and he'd make a quick sketch of me. I was quite shy, so I just sat there and smiled a little.

After some time, James proclaimed, "Okay. I'm done!" My two older sisters sat beside me eagerly, and James turned his sketch around. It was my "pose," but it was a sketch of Miss Piggy.

My sisters burst into uncontrollable laughter. James was laughing, too. And for some reason, I started "laughing" as well. I guess I didn't want anyone to know just how devastated I was inside. I was embarrassed and angry; all I wanted to do was hide and cry.

One afternoon. One sketch. And I was forever changed.

I started wearing very loose clothes. In my mind, I thought, "No one should ever think my clothes are too tight. What if someone comes over and pinches my "love handles?"

I started to drastically eat less. I threw part of my packed lunch so my mom wouldn't know I wasn't eating all the food she packed for me. But then, most nights, I would binge eat because I was so hungry. Of course, I'd feel very guilty and disappointed with myself after that.

Outwardly, I became even more shy and reserved. (I had only one decent friend in high school.) That feeling of being fat, of being Ms. Piggy, never left me.

As an adult, whenever I would get intimate with someone, the lights MUST be out. I had zero self-confidence in how I looked. During parties, I would demurely say no to food and just "nibble" even though I was dizzy with hunger. What if someone watched me eat and thought, "Wow, what a Miss Piggy."

At work, I was so reserved that I barely voiced my ideas, meaning I often got passed for promotions or recognition. And then three things happened in the span of ONE week that changed everything–again. (But this time, for the better!)

First, my husband saw me in some new clothes and casually remarked, "Babe, that dress is too big for you."

Second, I was at the gym, and as I got out of the shower with nothing but a towel around me, a gym employee said, "Hey, Lizzie, you're... a lot smaller than I thought you were! Why do you always wear baggy clothes out there?"

These instances baffled me. For the first time, I thought, "Am I not as "big" as I think I am?"

Lastly, I ran into a friend I hadn't seen in years. She just got divorced and came back to the neighborhood. We scheduled to meet for coffee a week later, and as we caught up on each other's lives, she shared that she was seeing an ACT therapist to help her through the divorce. "ACT? What's that?" She told me about it, and I was so intrigued that I started researching on my own after that conversation.

I learned many life-changing things with ACT, but particularly enlightening was "cognitive fusion." I realized this is what I've been doing since I was 12.

I was "fused" to the thought that I was Miss Piggy. Actually, to be more accurate, I was fused to the thought that others perceived me as Miss Piggy, and all my actions have followed that thought since then.

I felt a lot of sadness and regret as I learned about this concept. I came to terms with the fact that I heaped a lot of unnecessary shame on myself and did a lot of "hiding." I also regretted my resulting eating habits, which I believe harmed my health. (I'm taking steps to remedy that now.)

I continue to do self-guided ACT at home, practicing cognitive defusion to unglue myself from my "Miss Piggy" belief. I'm not there yet, but I'm hopeful.

ACT proposes that individuals often become fused or entangled with their thoughts. This "fusion" can lead to mental, physical, and emotional distress when individuals believe and behave upon these thoughts without considering their accuracy or helpfulness.

For example, suppose Lizzie hadn't fused to the thought that people saw her as Miss Piggy. In that case, it's highly possible that she would not have drastically changed her eating habits, and her self-esteem would not have plummeted.

Here's another example: suppose you have social anxiety and believe, "If I make a mistake while speaking in public, everyone will think I'm stupid." This thought might become fused with your sense of self, leading you to avoid social situations altogether.

Even if you've had successful presentations in the past, you ignore these facts because your belief is so strong and deeply ingrained. Your assumption that "public speaking mistake = stupidity" constantly influences your emotions and behavior, perpetuating your anxiety about public speaking.

So, how do you unglue or unhook yourself from unhelpful thoughts? You practice cognitive **de**fusion.

Cognitive defusion or mental defusion is about changing the way you relate to your thoughts. Think of your mind as a busy street, with thoughts rushing like cars. Cognitive defusion is like stepping onto the sidewalk and watching cars (i.e., your thoughts) come and go rather than getting caught up in the traffic. By creating distance between yourself and your thoughts, you remove their ability to control or dictate your emotions and actions.

In short, cognitive defusion teaches you that "Thoughts" does not equal "Self." So, to remove or lessen the power or control of "Thoughts," you must learn to put distance between them and the "Self." Why? **Although you are not your thoughts, you can become them**. (What you think, you become.) Cognitive defusion is all about preventing you from becoming your negative thoughts.

"Becoming that person" in ACT is often referred to as the "conceptualized self" or "concretized self."

The **conceptualized self** is how you see yourself based on your thoughts and ideas about who you are. It's like a mental picture of yourself that you create by thinking about your qualities, roles, and how you fit into the world. For example, you might see yourself as a "successful business owner," a "caring parent," or a "good friend" because of how you think about your experiences and what's important to you.

Characteristics: How you think and evaluate yourself shapes your conceptualized self. It includes your personality, accomplishments, and how you see yourself in relationships and society.

Function: Your conceptualized self helps you make sense of your life and guides how you behave and make choices. It's like a mental map that helps you understand who you are and how you fit into the world around you.

The **concretized self** is like being trapped in a rigid idea of who you are. It happens when you get stuck on certain labels or stories about yourself and can't see beyond them. For example, if you've always seen yourself as a "successful professional," you might find it difficult to cope if you face setbacks in your career.

Characteristics: The concretized self feels unchanging and unyielding. You might need to defend this identity, even if it doesn't feel right anymore. It's like being stuck in one version of yourself.

Function: While having a fixed identity can feel secure, it can also hold you back from growing and being true to yourself. It might make you feel stuck or unhappy when life throws you curveballs.

Picture this: Someone feels really sad and lonely. They start to think of themselves as depressed, and their actions follow suit. They withdraw from family and friends and hardly go out anymore. As time goes on, they become deeply fused to this idea that they're not just feeling depressed; they're suffering from depression. The *thought* of being depressed (conceptualized self) becomes a solid part of who they are (concretized self).

So, no, you are not your negative or unhelpful thoughts, but you can become them. And even if you've already started down that path, remember, you can break free and "unhook" yourself from them by practicing cognitive defusion techniques.

Worksheet 13: Thought Labeling

This exercise is designed to help you manage unhelpful thoughts. By learning to label your thoughts, you can create distance and reduce their impact on your mood and behavior.

1. **Find a quiet and comfortable space** where you can sit undisturbed for a few minutes. Take a few deep breaths to **center yourself** and bring your attention to the present moment.

2. Tune into your body and **notice any physical sensations**, such as tension, rapid heartbeat, or shallow breathing. Acknowledge these sensations without judgment or criticism.

3. **Write down your thoughts.** Grab pen and paper and identify the thought or thoughts you want to address. Write down one thought per piece of paper. These might include worries about your future, negative thoughts about yourself, doubts about your performance at work, etc. Important: Write down your thoughts without getting entangled in them. Remember, they are just thoughts, not necessarily facts or truths.

Example: I'm fat and ugly. No one finds me lovable.

Thought, belief, or assumption #1:

Thought, belief, or assumption #2:

Thought, belief, or assumption #3:

4. Next, **label your thoughts**. As you identify your thoughts, practice labeling them **in a neutral and non-judgmental** way. Use simple and descriptive labels to identify the content of your thoughts without getting caught up in their emotional impact. (**Tip**: Remove the word "I" in your labeling.)

Example:
Thought: I'm fat and ugly.
Thought label: negative body image

Thought, belief, or assumption #1:
Thought label #1:

Thought, belief, or assumption #2:
Though label #2:

Thought, belief, or assumption #3:
Though label #3:

5. **Practice acceptance.** After labeling a thought, take a moment to observe it without judgment. For example, say, "This is a thought I'm having today."

6. **Create distance between yourself and each labeled thought.** After practicing acceptance of your thought, stand up and take a physical step back from the thought. Observe the written thought from a distance, like an impartial observer. Remind yourself that The Thought is just a passing mental event, not necessarily a reflection of reality.

7. After labeling and creating distance, **gently let the thought go**. Sit back down, crumple the piece of paper with the thought, and throw it away. As you do so, imagine the thought drifting away like a leaf on a stream or a cloud in the sky.

8. Continue practicing thought labeling for several minutes, allowing yourself to observe and label each thought that arises. If your mind starts to wander or you become distracted, gently bring your focus back to the present moment and resume the exercise.

9. When you're done, take a few moments to ground yourself in the present moment by focusing on your breath or connecting with your senses.

Worksheet 14: Closing Thought Tabs

Here's another exercise designed to help you manage unhelpful thoughts. However, unlike the previous one (Thought Labeling), this exercise asks you to "close" negative thought patterns like closing browser tabs on a computer.

1. **Find a quiet and comfortable space** where you can sit undisturbed for a few minutes. **Close your eyes** and take a few deep breaths to **center yourself** and bring your attention to the present moment.

2. Tune into your body and **notice any physical sensations**, such as tension, rapid heartbeat, or shallow breathing. Acknowledge these sensations without judgment or criticism.

3. **Identify your thoughts.** Imagine your mind as a browser with multiple tabs open. Select a mental tab and identify any thoughts, beliefs, or assumptions that have persisted in your life and may have had a negative or unhelpful impact.

   Example: I always mess things up.

   Keep on doing this step for any other thoughts, beliefs, or assumptions that may have been negatively impacting your life.

4. **Close your mental tabs.** Visualize these thought tabs cluttering your mental space. So, mentally close each negative thought tab in your mind's browser one by one. Visualize clicking on the "X" button and watching the

tab disappear. As you close each tab, say to yourself, "This is just a thought. I am choosing to close the doors on this thought now."

5. **Replace closed thought tabs with positive affirmations.** After closing each negative thought tab, replace it with a positive affirmation or self-affirming statement.

   Example:
   Closed thought tab: I always mess things up.
   Positive affirmation: I also do good, maybe even great, things. And I can learn from any mistakes I make.

6. **Practice self-compassion.** Throughout this exercise, practice self-compassion and kindness toward yourself. Recognize that negative thoughts are a normal part of being human, and it's okay to have them—and to let them go. Offer comfort and reassurance to yourself as you work through the process of closing thought tabs.

7. **Check your mental browser.** Take a moment to check in with your mental browser and notice if any new negative thought tabs have opened. If you notice any new tabs, repeat the process of closing them and replacing them with positive affirmations.

8. When you're done with this exercise, **slowly open your eyes and take a few moments to ground yourself in the present moment** by focusing on your breath or connecting with your senses.

Worksheet 15: Externalizing Thoughts

This exercise is designed to help you manage negative, difficult, or unhelpful thoughts or emotions by externalizing and reframing them. By separating yourself from your thoughts and viewing them from a different perspective, you can reduce their intensity and regain control.

Note: This exercise uses "feelings of loneliness" as an example. Feel free to replace it with whatever thought, assumption, or belief you may be experiencing.

1. **Find a quiet and comfortable space** where you can sit undisturbed for a few minutes. Take a few deep breaths to **center yourself** and bring your attention to the present moment.

2. **Tune into your emotions** and notice any feelings of loneliness that you're experiencing. Acknowledge and validate these feelings without judgment or self-criticism. For example, say to yourself, "I'm feeling alone right now. I feel like there's not a single person in the world who cares for me."

3. **Externalize your thoughts** by imagining them as separate entities outside of yourself. You can name them or visualize them as characters in a story. For example, if you're thinking, "I'll always be alone," you might imagine it as a character named "Lonely Voice."

4. With each externalized thought, **create distance** by mentally placing it outside yourself, like setting it down on a table or putting it in a box. Visualize yourself stepping back from the thought and observing them from a distance, as if you were watching a scene in a movie.

5. **Initiate dialogue** with your externalized thought, addressing it directly as if it were a separate being. For example, ask "Lonely Voice" questions like, "Why are you here?" or "What do you want?" to explore the underlying motivations or beliefs behind your lonely thoughts. For instance, asking

Lonely Voice, "Why are you here?" may reveal that you long to talk to someone right now or you're missing a specific person.

6. Once you've externalized your lonely thoughts, **challenge any associated negative thinking patterns** by reframing the situation more rationally and compassionately.

Example:
Lonely Voice: I feel lonely because no one likes me enough to get to know me.

Reframed Perspective: I feel lonely now, but this feeling doesn't define my worth. It's possible that others may not have had the chance to know me yet, and there are people out there who will appreciate and value me for who I am.

7. **Practice self-compassion.** Throughout this exercise, practice self-compassion and kindness toward yourself. Remind yourself that loneliness is a common human experience. It doesn't define your whole worth or value, and it's a feeling that doesn't have to be permanent.

8. When you finish this exercise, **take a few moments to ground yourself in the present momen**t by focusing on your breath or connecting with your senses. Notice any shifts in your emotional state and any sense of relief or empowerment from externalizing your thoughts.

Worksheet 16: The Defusion Wheel

The Defusion Wheel is a tool to help you gain psychological distance between unhelpful or negative thoughts and yourself. Simply spin the wheel and try out the technique it lands on. Some tasks will be short and easy to do, while others will require effort and time. Now, take a deep breath, keep an open mind, and spin that wheel!

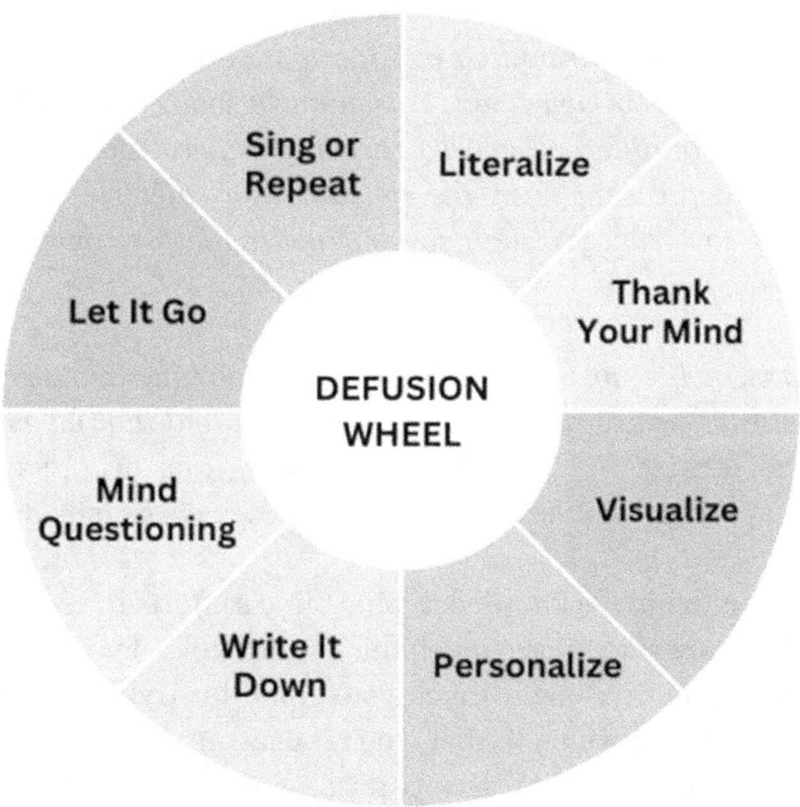

1. **Sing or repeat**. This technique calls on you to sing or repeat the unhelpful thought playfully or exaggeratedly, which can help reduce its emotional impact.

   For example, if you're thinking, "I'm not good enough," you could sing it to the tune of the "Happy Birthday" song, a nursery rhyme, etc. You can also repeat the thought for about 60 seconds in a silly voice. (Think Minions or Chipmunks.)

2. **Literalize.** Treat thoughts literally (i.e., thinking of them as words, symbols, cartoon characters, etc.) rather than allowing them to have their usual emotional impact on you. This helps you see the thought as just words rather than a reflection of reality.

Example:
Unhelpful Thought: "I'm drowning in paperwork!"

Literalizing: Imagine drowning in paperwork, but picture a funny image instead of feeling overwhelmed. You might visualize yourself swimming through a sea of different colored sheets of paper. And then a colleague throws you a life ring from the elevator, the cafeteria, or... it doesn't matter, it's your funny visual, so your colleague (or someone else) can throw it from anywhere!

The point is, by literalizing the thought "I'm drowning in paperwork," you realize that it's just a metaphorical expression and that it's not humanly possible to "drown" in "paperwork." As such, any negative or difficult emotion resulting from the thought should lessen or disappear.

3. **Thank your mind.** Acknowledge your mind's efforts to protect you, even if its methods are sometimes unhelpful. For example, if you're experiencing anxious thoughts, you might thank your mind for trying to keep you safe but gently remind yourself that you're okay in this moment. This is acknowledging the thought without attaching significance to it.

4. **Visualize.** Imagine unhelpful thoughts and beliefs as objects passing by like clouds floating in the sky, cars coming and going on the highway, leaves floating down a river, a favorite slice of cake that, for some reason, you cannot fathom, always disappears way too fast when put in front of you.

5. **Mind questioning.** Instead of dismissing a thought, take a more curious approach towards it. The beauty of this technique is that you can picture your mind as an organ in your body that generates thoughts. This takes you

further away from the Thoughts=Self conviction. Here are some sample questions you can ask your mind.

- *Dear mind, what are you saying? What are you trying to tell me?*
- *Hmmm, is this thought helpful or useful in any way? Why? Why not?*
- *Dear mind, where did this thought come from? Is it based on a past experience? Someone said to me? A fear about the future?*
- *Dear mind, what evidence supports this thought I'm having? What evidence contradicts it?*

6. **Personalize.** Give your unhelpful thought a funny or ridiculous name to reduce its power over you. For example, if you're thinking, "I'll never succeed," you could call it the "Negative Nancy" thought, which helps create distance and lightens the mood.

7. **Write it down.** Take the unhelpful thought and write it down on a piece of paper or in a journal. Seeing it written can help you detach from it and recognize it as just a passing thought rather than an absolute truth.

8. **Let it go.** Practice letting the unhelpful thought pass by without giving it any further attention or importance. For example:

- Imagine the thought as a feather and blow it away.
- Imagine the thought as a speck on your shirt and flick it away.
- Light a match or candle, imagine the flame representing your thought, and blow it out.

Perception vs. Reality

In the realm of cognitive defusion, one of the key concepts to explore is the distinction between perception and reality.

Perception is how we see and understand the world around us. Our past experiences, beliefs, and biases influence it. Now, while our perceptions may feel real to us, they are not always an accurate reflection of reality.

(Unfortunately, our minds can sometimes twist things based on how we see them.)

Cognitive defusion involves challenging the validity and truthfulness of our perceptions. It encourages us to question the stories we tell ourselves and examine whether they align with objective reality or are merely products of our subjective interpretation.

For example, suppose you receive your boss's feedback on a work project. When you open the document, there are several comments, questions, and a hefty dose of corrections. Your initial perception might be that you are a failure and incapable of performing your job well. This perception could trigger feelings of inadequacy, self-doubt, and maybe even anxiety, leading you to avoid similar projects in the future.

Here's a reality check: Receiving constructive criticism is normal for professional growth and development. It doesn't necessarily mean that you're incompetent. For all you know, your boss might have been impressed by your work since the project was a really big and difficult one. By defusing the thought that you are inherently flawed, you can reframe the situation more accurately and constructively.

So, perception and reality are not always synonymous. The following exercises will help you distinguish between the two.

Worksheet 17: I Am...

This exercise aims to help you acknowledge and appreciate the factual aspects of yourself, fostering self-awareness and self-acceptance. By focusing on objective truths rather than subjective judgments, you can cultivate a deeper understanding of your identity and strengths.

1. **Find a comfortable and quiet space** where you can reflect without distractions. Bring pen and paper and create a calming atmosphere by dimming the lights, playing soft music, or lighting a candle.

2. Sit in a relaxed position, allowing your body to unwind and your mind to **focus on the present moment**. Take a few deep breaths to center yourself and release any tension.

3. Start to **reflect on facts about yourself**. Starting each sentence with "I Am," write down factual statements that describe various aspects of yourself, such as your physical appearance, personality traits, skills, talents, accomplishments, and roles.

   Provide Details: Include specific details or examples to support each statement. Instead of generalizing, provide concrete evidence or anecdotes that illustrate the truth of each fact. This adds depth and authenticity to your self-reflection. For example, don't just write down, "I am empathetic," state, "I am empathetic. I often listen carefully to people and try to understand their perspectives."

   Avoid Value Judgments: Refrain from attaching value judgments or interpretations to the facts you list. Focus on describing your true self without assigning labels or evaluating their significance.

   Examples:
   I am fit. My BMI is 20, I run half-marathons, and strength train twice weekly.
   I am punctual. I can't remember the last time I was late for anything.

   I am ____

I am ____

I am ____

I am ____

I am ____

I am ____

I am ____

I am ____

I am ____

I am ____

4. **Practice self-acceptance** by embracing each fact as an integral part of who you are. Recognize that your worth is not determined by external standards or comparisons to others.

5. Take a moment to **review the list** of facts you've written about yourself. Notice any patterns or themes that emerge, highlighting recurring qualities or aspects of your identity. For example, suppose you notice a few facts related to fitness. In that case, it shows that this is a significant area of your life you may be unaware of.

6. **Internalize your truths.** Go over the facts you've identified, allowing them to sink in and integrate into your self-concept. Remind yourself of these truths whenever self-doubt or insecurity arises.

7. **Express gratitude** for the unique qualities and attributes that make you who you are. Appreciate the diversity of experiences and perspectives that shape your identity, fostering a sense of gratitude for your journey.

8. **Be kind and compassionate towards yourself** as you reflect on your list of facts. Offer yourself encouragement and support, acknowledging the value and worth inherent in your identity.

9. **Conclude the exercise with positive affirmations.** Reinforce your self-worth and confidence by saying affirmations such as "I am worthy," "I am enough," or "I am proud of who I am."

Worksheet 18: Socratic Questioning

Sometimes, it's not enough to distance ourselves from negative thoughts about ourselves. We need to challenge it actively!

Socratic questioning is a technique to challenge and reframe negative or irrational thoughts. It involves asking probing questions to help you examine the evidence and validity of your thoughts or perceptions about yourself.

Although traditionally associated with CBT, Socratic questioning also applies in ACT because it promotes mindfulness and cognitive defusion, encouraging you to observe your thoughts with curiosity and openness.

Note: This exercise uses the negative thought "not good enough in a relationship" as an example. Feel free to replace it with whatever thought, assumption, or belief you may be experiencing.

1. **Identify a negative belief** or thought you have about yourself.

    Example: I'm not good enough for my partner.

2. **Explore the evidence.** Examine the evidence that supports this belief. Ask yourself what specific experiences or thoughts have contributed to this belief.

    <u>The Past.</u> Are there any specific situations or events in the past that have led you to believe you're not good enough for your partner? In short, what do you think caused this belief?

Example: I've had many failed relationships before.

The Present. What evidence do you have that supports the belief that you're not good enough for your partner? For example, has your partner ever told you that you're not good enough for them, that you're "less" in any way, etc.

Example: No, not really. I just feel this.

3. **Think about the impact.**

- How is your negative thought affecting your daily life and overall well-being?

Example: I'm so anxious about my partner leaving that I feel unauthentic in this relationship. I feel like I just go along with what they want and don't really know what I want.

- Do you think your negative thoughts affect your partner and how they view your relationship?

  Example: I'm not sure. Maybe they are tired of me assuming the worst all the time in our relationship?

4. **Consider alternative perspectives.** Encourage yourself to consider alternative perspectives that contradict your negative beliefs.

- What evidence do you have that *contradicts* the belief that you're not good enough for your partner? For example, can you think of times when your partner has expressed appreciation or affection towards you?

  Example: Actually, my partner is very affectionate. We go out on date nights, and we cuddle a lot.

- List the positive qualities or strengths that you bring to the relationship.

Example: I'm loyal and loving. I'm empathic and very supportive.

5. **Reframe your negative thoughts** into a more balanced and realistic perspective based on your exploration and analysis.

   - Instead of thinking, "I'm not good enough for my partner," reframe the belief to "I deserve love and respect in my relationship."
   - Focus on affirming your worthiness and value as an individual, independent of external validation from your partner.

6. **Practice self-compassion.** Finish this exercise by extending self-compassion and kindness towards yourself. Remind yourself that it's normal to have insecurities and doubts, but you can challenge and overcome them.

Chapter 6: Self as Context

"Self as context" refers to that part of you that remains constant and unchanged regardless of the thoughts, feelings, sensations, or experiences you may have. It's like the background against which your thoughts and experiences occur.

For example, think of yourself as a vast sky and your thoughts and experiences as passing clouds. No matter how many clouds come and go, the sky remains unchanged, right? Similarly, no matter your thoughts or feelings, the essence of who you are remains constant.

Understanding "self as context" helps you gain perspective on your thoughts and experiences by encouraging you to see yourself as an *observer* of your thoughts rather than being defined by them.

As previously discussed, individuals experiencing mental and emotional distress or who feel like they are living unhappy lives have often reached a stage where they have *fused* a negative thought or belief into their sense of self to the point that they cannot see anything else.

Do you remember Lizzie? Seeing herself sketched as "Miss Piggy" changed her subsequent thoughts, emotions, and behavior. In her mind, Miss Piggy wasn't just a character; Lizzie was Miss Piggy, and Miss Piggy was Lizzie.

This fusion led Lizzie to overlook all the other aspects of her identity and worth. She forgot about her roles as a daughter, friend, colleague, and wife. She lost sight of her great qualities like loyalty, hard work, and reliability. The negative mental associations she carried about herself overshadowed all these positive attributes.

So, in a state of unhappiness, a negative thought, let's call it "X," can dominate your entire identity. However, by applying the "self as context" concept, you can transition into the role of an observer. You are not "X." You are an observer of "X."

By adopting the role of the observer, you become less reactive to challenging thoughts and emotions. Also, remember that as an *observer*, you can be as distant or close to what you're noticing, observing, or witnessing. This means you can shift from a single focus (a single negative thought) to the big picture (your life and everything in it.)

For example, imagine your life like a big stage show you're watching. There are lots of things happening on stage—your thoughts, feelings, and all the stuff you can see, hear, touch, taste, and smell. But here's the cool part: a part of you steps back, sits in the crowd, and watches the show. (You are now the observer or the "Observing Self.")

Sometimes, you might want to focus the stage spotlight on just one thing, like what you do when you focus on your breathing during a mindfulness exercise. Other times, you may want to zoom out and watch multiple things simultaneously. Either way, by being an observer and watching yourself in different situations, you prevent getting too caught up in your own story.

Worksheet 19: Notice-Observe-Watch (NOW)

This mindfulness practice is designed to cultivate present-moment awareness and deepen your understanding of your thoughts, emotions, and sensations—as an observer.

STEP 1: NOTICE.

1. **Find a comfortable and quiet space** to sit or lie down, free of distractions. Close your eyes if it feels comfortable, or maintain a soft gaze.

2. Take a few deep breaths to **center yourself** and bring your attention to the present moment. Notice the sensation of the breath as it enters and leaves your body without trying to control or change it.

3. Slowly **expand your awareness** to include your thoughts, emotions, bodily sensations, and environment. Notice whatever arises in your experience without judgment or attachment.

4. **As you become aware of different thoughts, emotions, and sensations, gently label them in your mind.** For example, "I notice tension in my shoulders," or "I'm aware of sounds in the room."

5. **Approach your experience with curiosity and openness**, as if observing it from a distance. Notice any tendencies to get caught up in particular thoughts or emotions, and gently guide your attention back to the present moment.

STEP 2: OBSERVE.

1. **Shift your focus to observing your thoughts, emotions, and sensations.** Notice their characteristics, intensity, and patterns without trying to change or analyze them.

   For example, you might observe, "This tension on my shoulders. I'm observing that I feel it more on my left shoulder than on my right."

2. **Practice non-attachment.** Allow your thoughts and emotions to come and go like clouds passing through the sky. Avoid getting entangled in the content of your experience or trying to suppress or avoid uncomfortable sensations. For example, say, "I acknowledge this discomfort on my left shoulder."

3. **Notice resistance.** If you encounter resistance or discomfort during this process, acknowledge it with kindness and curiosity. Explore any underlying thoughts or beliefs contributing to your resistance without judgment.

   For example, you might say, "I seem unable to move on from the tension I feel on my left shoulder. I wonder why this is really bothering me. Could I've had this discomfort before and just not realized it?"

4. **Practice accepting** whatever arises in your experience, whether pleasant or unpleasant. Embrace the full spectrum of the human experience with compassion.

STEP 3: WATCH.

1. **Shift to the observer mindset.** Imagine yourself stepping back and assuming the role of the impartial observer of your inner and outer experience. Adopt a detached perspective, as if you were watching a movie of your life unfolding.

2. **Witness your experience.** Watch your thoughts, emotions, and sensations as they arise and pass away in the present moment. Notice the impermanent nature of your experience and the inherent fluidity of your inner world.

3. **Practice detached presence.** Remain anchored in the present moment without getting caught up in the storyline of your thoughts or emotions. If your mind wanders, gently guide your focus back to the present moment.

Imagine yourself as a mountain that remains steadfast amidst shifting weather patterns.

4. **Express gratitude.** Conclude the exercise by expressing gratitude for your ability to observe and witness your experience with mindfulness and presence.

Worksheet 20: The Participant vs. The Observer

This exercise helps you understand the difference between experiencing thoughts and feelings as a participant versus observing them as an impartial observer. Why is this important?

When you're caught up in the role of a participant, it's easy to become overwhelmed by your thoughts and feelings, leading to impulsive reactions and increased distress.

By cultivating the ability to step back and observe your inner experience from a place of detachment, you create space for reflection and insight. This, in turn, influences your behavior. Changing how you perceive your thoughts, feelings, and sensations can change how you act moving forward.

Note: The exercise below uses "chronic pain" as an example. Please feel free to modify it to fit your specific needs.

Important: As with all exercises mentioned in this book, the purpose of this exercise is NOT to deny pain or suffering in life. Acceptance teaches us that these are part of the human experience. This exercise aims to help decrease pain by helping you see it from a different angle.

1. **Find a quiet and comfortable space** to sit or lie down, free of distractions. Take a few deep breaths to center yourself and bring your focus to the present moment.

2. Reflect on the concept of being a participant versus an observer. Being a participant means actively engaging with your thoughts and feelings while being an observer means stepping back and noticing them without judgment.

3. **Identify chronic pain sensations.** Take a moment to tune into your body and notice any sensations of chronic pain that you're experiencing. Pay attention to the pain's location, intensity, and characteristics (e.g.,

sharp, throbbing, etc.). Allow yourself to fully acknowledge these sensations without trying to change them.

Example: I have chronic headaches. I feel heaviness on my head and throbbing pain in the front of my head.

4. **Enter the participant mode.** Visualize yourself fully immersed in the experience of chronic pain. Allow yourself to feel the sensations as if actively participating in them. **Warning**: Doing this may exacerbate the pain. If you feel extreme discomfort, please discontinue.

As you focus on being a participant, notice any thoughts or emotions that arise in response to the pain.

Example: My headache is getting worse. I feel sad and depressed. I'm crying now.

Acknowledge your emotions and experience with kindness and understanding. Say to yourself, "It's okay to feel sad and overwhelmed right now. I'm here for myself. I will get through this challenging moment."

5. **Shift to observer mode.** Change your perspective to that of an impartial observer.

- Take a deep breath, and as you exhale, imagine yourself stepping back from pain sensations and observing them from a distance. Watch your pain as if you're watching something on a screen. Say to yourself, "I am not "pain." I am experiencing pain."
- Observe any accompanying sensations, such as tension, heat, or discomfort, with a sense of openness and curiosity.
- Acknowledge any thoughts or emotions that arise in response to the pain without judgment, allowing them to come and go like passing clouds in the sky.
- Remind yourself that it's okay to feel pain and that you can handle it with mindfulness and compassion.

Tip: Are you experiencing resistance shifting to observer mode? That's natural. Practice Willing Hands to open yourself up to this part of the exercise.

If you prefer a more "active" way of being an observer, great! Research shows that gentle, mindful movement exercises such as yoga, tai chi, or qigong help alleviate pain.[75,76,77,78] For example, when experiencing pain, try yoga, and with each gentle, mindful, and purposeful move, observe how your pain is reacting to your breath and movements.

6. Ask yourself the following **reflective questions**:

- How did your level of involvement influence your pain?
- As a participant, did your pain worsen?
- As an observer, did your pain decrease?

7. Slowly bring your awareness back to the present moment. When ready, return to your day with a renewed sense of mindfulness and self-awareness in managing chronic pain.

8. **Integration.** Consider how you can apply this concept daily with chronic pain. Consider how adopting an observer mindset could help you respond more effectively to pain flare-ups and manage your emotional reactions.

9. **Commit to practicing this exercise regularly**, especially during moments of heightened pain or discomfort. The more you cultivate the ability to observe your chronic pain with curiosity and compassion, the greater your sense of control and resilience will become.

10. If you feel like it, **journal about your experience** with chronic pain and this exercise. Write down insights, observations, challenges, or areas for further exploration.

This exercise is NOT easy. Express gratitude to yourself for being open to exploring your experience with chronic pain in a new way.

Chapter 7: Values Clarification

What are your values? What do you want your life to be about? What kinds of qualities do you want to develop in yourself? What kind of person do you want to be in your relationships?

Your values are the things you consider most important in your life. They're like guiding principles that help you decide what's right or wrong and what you want to focus on or prioritize.

Your values might include honesty, kindness, family, friendship, success, or adventure. They're like a compass that helps you navigate life, making choices and decisions that align with what matters most to you.

Living a values-based life is at the core of ACT. It's one of the main aspects that make this therapy different from all other therapies. ACT emphasizes that if you clarify your values and live according to them, you live authentically. This, in turn, leads to happiness in life.

Unfortunately, not many of us live life according to our values. As a child, we live according to the values of our parents. When we go out into the world, we live life according to the values dictated by society. In relationships, we often prioritize our partners' or peers' expectations and desires over our values. This can lead to feelings of disconnection from our authentic selves and dissatisfaction and unhappiness with our lives.

ACT helps alleviate any mental, physical, or emotional suffering you may be experiencing by teaching you how to align your behaviors with your ideals.

If you're confused about what's truly important to you right now, you're not alone. In reality, few people take the time to pause and reflect on what matters most to them. It's like growing up with values imposed on us like stickers by others, leaving us confused about our own beliefs. Well, it's time to change that. It's time to discover who you are, what you believe in, what you stand for, and what makes you happy.

Worksheet 21: Your 80ᵗʰ Birthday

This short exercise seeks to extract your most significant values by considering what you want others to say about you.

1. Imagine yourself celebrating your 80ᵗʰ birthday surrounded by loved ones, including people who may not be present in your life yet. For example, imagine a partner beside you if you're currently single. You can also imagine future children, grandchildren, or friends you may not have met yet. Picture the venue, the decorations, and the happy atmosphere. Take a moment to soak in the joyous occasion.

2. Imagine each person at your party standing up to say something about you. What do you wish they would say?

Example:
Person: future son or daughter
What I wish they would say: Dad, I love you. I cherish every moment you spent with me playing basketball, even though I knew you hated it! I can only hope to be as amazing a father to my son as you were to me.

Person:
What I wish they would say:

Person:
What I wish they would say:

| Person: |
| What I wish they would say: |

| Person: |
| What I wish they would say: |

3. **Reframe**. Reflect on the toasts you want to hear on your 80th birthday and reframe them into values. For example, suppose you wish your child (or future child) to say, "You were my best friend growing up, Dad. I couldn't

ask for a better role model." This may translate into values such as, "As a parent, I want to listen and always be a part of my child's life."

Birthday wish:
Value translation:

Birthday wish:
Value translation:

Birthday wish:
Value translation:

Birthday wish:
Value translation:

Birthday wish:
Value translation:

4. **Value integration.** After imagining the toasts you want to hear on your 80th birthday and identifying the values they represent, the next step is to integrate those values into your daily life. Consider how you can prioritize these values in your day-to-day actions and decisions.

For example, suppose you want your child to say you were their best friend growing up. This can translate to personal values such as *presence, communication, friendship, trust, quality time,* etc. In that case, think of ways to foster these values now through your actions. For instance, the next time your child mentions a school event, actively listen to foster *communication* and prioritize attending to nurture *presence* and *quality time.*

Worksheet 22: Values Discovery Journey

Even though you might not have taken a moment to deeply reflect and identify your values, it doesn't mean you've never lived according to at least some of them. This exercise aims to "open your eyes" to values you may have already prioritized by reflecting on past events that have brought you happiness.

1. **Reflect on past moments of happiness.** Think about a time when you felt truly happy and fulfilled. What were you doing? What values were you honoring in that moment?

   Example: I remember a time when I volunteered at a local animal shelter and felt a deep sense of joy and fulfillment.

2. **Recall decision points.** Remember a time when you were faced with a decision. What guided you to make the choice you did? What values were at play?

   Example: As a teen, I chose between a part-time job at a café that paid okay and a part-time job walking dogs that paid very little. I picked the second one.

3. **Envision your ideal future or your life in an alternate universe.** What are the most important things to you in that vision? What values do those things represent?

Example: I see myself working as a vet. I associate this with values of compassion, empathy, responsibility, and respect for all living beings. It also probably means I value patience, understanding, and teamwork because I don't see myself working alone in my practice.

4. **Identify common themes.** Reflect on your answers from the previous steps and look for common themes or patterns. For example, if your answers involve "working with others," perhaps *connection,* a *sense of belonging,* and *community* are central to your identity.

5. **Prioritize the values you've identified** based on what feels most authentic and important to you. Consider which values you want to prioritize in your daily life and decision-making. For example, if you want to prioritize *connection* right now, seek daily opportunities to build better friendships and relationships with others. For instance, you might want to improve your active listening skills and develop more empathy in communications.

Important: Prioritizing your values doesn't necessarily mean you need to change jobs and overhaul your life (unless this is what you want to do). Focusing on your values can also mean making daily decisions, even small ones, according to these values. For example, if you value *sustainability*, you might start by avoiding using plastic containers and bags from now on. You can level up later to lead a zero-waste life.

Worksheet 23: Values Cards

In the previous exercise, you were asked to recall specific moments to see which values were important to you. In this exercise, you'll use Values Cards because they present ideals and principles you may not have previously considered. Here's how you can use a values card effectively:

1. Print out the Values table below and cut out each value. Please feel free to add more if you want to.

ADAPTABILITY Being flexible and open to change, easily adjusting to new situations and circumstances.	**ADVENTURE** Embracing new experiences, challenges, and opportunities for growth and exploration.	**ALTRUISM** Acting selflessly and compassionately for the benefit of others without expecting anything in return.
AMBITION Setting high goals and aspirations and striving to achieve one's full potential.	**AUTHENTICITY** Being true to oneself and living in alignment with one's values, beliefs, and identity.	**AWARENESS** Being conscious and attentive to oneself, others, and the environment, fostering mindfulness and insight.
BALANCE Finding equilibrium and harmony between various aspects of life, such as work, relationships, and self-care.	**BEAUTY** Appreciating and creating beauty in one's surroundings, experiences, and expressions.	**CLARITY** Gaining a clear understanding and insight into one's values, goals, and priorities.
COLLABORATION Working cooperatively with others, sharing ideas, resources, and	**COMMITMENT** Dedication and loyalty to one's values, goals, and relationships,	**COMMUNICATION** Cultivating effective and empathetic communication skills to

efforts to achieve common goals.	demonstrating steadfastness and perseverance.	express oneself authentically, listen actively, and foster understanding and connection in relationships.
COMMUNITY Fostering a sense of belonging and connection with others, supporting and being supported by a social network.	**COMPASSION** Showing kindness, empathy, and understanding towards oneself and others.	**CONFIDENCE** Believing in oneself and one's abilities and facing challenges with self-assurance and determination.
CONNECTION Building meaningful relationships and fostering a sense of belonging and community.	**CONTENTMENT** Finding satisfaction and peace with what I have and where I am in life.	**COURAGE** Having the strength and bravery to face challenges, take risks, and pursue one's goals.
CREATIVITY Expressing oneself through imagination, innovation, and originality.	**CURIOSITY** Seeking knowledge, exploration, and new experiences, driven by a desire to learn and understand.	**DETERMINATION** Having strong willpower and perseverance to overcome obstacles and achieve one's goals.
DISCIPLINE Maintaining self-control, focus, and dedication in pursuing one's objectives and commitments.	**EMPOWERMENT** Taking control of one's life and choices and empowering oneself and others to thrive.	**EQUANIMITY** Maintaining emotional balance and composure in the face of challenges and fluctuations.
FAITH Trusting in a higher	**FLEXIBILITY** Adapting to change,	**FREEDOM** Experiencing liberation

power, universal wisdom, or guiding principles, and surrendering to the flow of life.	uncertainty, and challenges with openness, agility, and resilience.	from constraints, limitations, and fears, and living authentically and boldly.
GENEROSITY Giving freely and generously of one's time, resources, and compassion to benefit others.	**GRATITUDE** Appreciating the positive aspects of life and expressing thankfulness for blessings and opportunities.	**GROWTH** Continuously striving for personal and professional development, learning, and self-improvement.
HONESTY Truthfulness and sincerity in communication and interactions.	**HUMILITY** Cultivating modesty, open-mindedness, and a willingness to learn from others and life's experiences.	**HUMOR** Finding and sharing joy, laughter, and light-heartedness, even in difficult or serious situations.
INCLUSIVITY Embracing diversity and welcoming all individuals, regardless of differences or backgrounds.	**INDEPENDENCE** Asserting autonomy, self-reliance, and freedom of thought and action.	**INNOVATION** Embracing creativity and originality, generating new ideas and solutions to old problems.
INSPIRATION Igniting creativity, motivation, and passion through meaningful experiences and connections.	**INTEGRITY** Acting with honesty, ethics, and moral principles, and staying true to one's values.	**JOY** Finding happiness, pleasure, and fulfillment in life's experiences and moments.
JUSTICE Upholding fairness,	**KINDNESS** Showing generosity,	**LOVE** Cultivating deep

equality, and righteousness in one's actions and interactions with others.	compassion, and goodwill towards oneself and others.	connections, affection, and care for oneself and others.
LOYALTY Being faithful, committed, and supportive to one's values, relationships, and responsibilities.	**MEANING** Finding purpose, significance, and fulfillment in one's life and experiences.	**MINDFULNESS** Being present in the moment, aware of one's thoughts, feelings, and surroundings without judgment.
NURTURE Providing care, support, and nourishment to oneself and others for growth and well-being.	**OPENNESS** Embracing new ideas, perspectives, and experiences with curiosity, receptivity, and non-judgment.	**OPTIMISM** Maintaining a positive outlook and hopeful attitude towards the future, even in challenging times.
PATIENCE Practicing tolerance and acceptance of delays, difficulties, and imperfections, fostering endurance and calmness.	**PEACE** Cultivating inner calm, tranquility, and serenity amidst life's stresses and uncertainties.	**PERSISTENCE** Pursuing one's goals and dreams despite obstacles, setbacks, and failures.
PLAYFULNESS Embracing spontaneity, joy, and creativity, engaging in activities for sheer enjoyment and fun.	**PRESENCE** Being fully engaged and attentive in the here and now, and savoring each moment of life.	**PURPOSE** Living with intention, direction, and meaning, and aligning one's actions with one's values and goals.
REFLECTION Engaging in introspection and self-	**RESILIENCE** Bouncing back from adversity, setbacks, and	**SELF-COMPASSION** Treating oneself with kindness, understanding,

examination, learning from past experiences, and gaining insight into oneself.	hardships with strength, adaptability, and determination.	and forgiveness in times of difficulty or suffering.
SELF-DISCIPLINE Exercising control and restraint over one's impulses and behaviors, staying focused on long-term goals.	**SELF-EXPRESSION** Expressing one's thoughts, feelings, and identity authentically and creatively through various forms of communication and expression.	**SERVICE** Contributing to the well-being and happiness of others through acts of service, generosity, and kindness.
SIMPLICITY Embracing a minimalist lifestyle and mindset, focusing on what truly matters, and letting go of excess or unnecessary distractions.	**SOBRIETY** Maintaining abstinence or moderation from substances or behaviors that can impair judgment, health, or well-being.	**SPIRITUALITY** Connecting with something greater than oneself, exploring beliefs and practices that provide meaning and purpose.
STABILITY Cultivating a sense of security, predictability, and steadiness in one's life and environment.	**SUSTAINABILITY** Promoting environmental stewardship and responsible living, ensuring the well-being of future generations.	**TEAMWORK** Collaborating with others towards shared goals, mutual support, and collective success.
TENACITY Demonstrating determination, perseverance, and resilience in pursuing one's objectives and aspirations.	**TRANSPARENCY** Practicing honesty, openness, and authenticity in one's communications and interactions.	**TRUST** Having confidence in oneself, others, and the universe, and believing in the inherent goodness of life.
UNITY	**VITALITY**	**WISDOM**

Fostering harmony, cohesion, and solidarity among individuals and communities despite differences or disagreements.	Nurturing energy, vigor, and vitality in one's physical, mental, and emotional well-being.	Cultivating insight, discernment, and practical knowledge to navigate life's challenges and complexities.
Add another value you want here...	*Add another value you want here...*	*Add another value you want here...*

2. **Select your values.** Spread the Values cards before you, ensuring you can see all the options. Take the time and review each value carefully. Next, select the values that resonate most deeply with you.

3. **Reflect.** Once you've selected your values, think about why you chose those particular values.

- **Explore** how these values align with your goals, dreams, and overall sense of fulfillment. For example, suppose you identified *adventure* as a core value because you love exploring new places and trying new experiences.

   As you explore how this value aligns with your goals and dreams, you might realize that it fuels your desire to travel the world and seek out exciting opportunities for personal growth. You feel most fulfilled when embarking on adventures that push you out of your comfort zone and expand your horizons.

- **Reflect** on past experiences when you lived in alignment with these values and how they affected your well-being. For instance, suppose you have always valued *kindness* because you believe in treating others with compassion and empathy.

As you reflect on past experiences when you lived in alignment with this value, you remember how volunteering at a homeless shelter brought you a sense of fulfillment and purpose. You realize that acts of *kindness* benefit others and contribute to your sense of well-being and fulfillment.

4. **Prioritize your values.** After selecting and reflecting on your values, prioritize them based on their significance and importance. For each value you consider a top priority, ask yourself why?

Example:
Top priority value: trust
Why: I don't want to second guess or doubt my motives or those of others.

Top priority:
Why?

Top priority:
Why?

Top priority:
Why?

5. **Setting goals and taking action.** Use the values you identified as input for goal-setting and action planning. Use the **SMART** technique as defined in ACT (**S**pecific, **M**eaningful, **A**daptive, **R**ealistic, **T**ime-Bound).

Value to prioritize:
Example: honesty

Specific. Clearly define what this value means to you and how you want to incorporate it into your life.

Example: Honesty is extremely important to me, so I will start with myself. I've always struggled to be honest with my parents. I don't always agree with them, but I just give in instead of disagreeing and giving my opinion. From now on, I'll strive to always tell the truth, even when it's difficult.

Meaningful. Why are you doing this? What's the meaning of this goal to you?

Example: I'm tired of giving in and feeling like I never have a voice with my parents. I'm an adult, but I feel like a child with them. Being able to be honest with them means that I'm standing my ground and being authentic.

Adaptive. Do you believe this goal will help you achieve a value-based life? How so?

Example: Yes! If I'm authentic with my parents, I can also strive to be authentic in other areas of my life.

Realistic. Is this goal realistically achievable?

Example: I believe so.

Time-bound: Establish a timeline for achieving your goals. Set deadlines for specific actions or milestones.

Example: Starting next week, I will be honest in all conversations with my parents. I will monitor this in my journal for at least three months.

Important: Regularly review your values and goals to ensure they're aligned with each other. Sometimes, you may realize that you're not prioritizing your most important values or that your goals are not aligned with your values. That's okay. Reflect and adjust, and keep moving forward.

Worksheet 24: Values Bull's Eye

This exercise aims to help you identify and prioritize your core values in the following areas of your life: relationships, work, personal growth, and leisure.

1. **Find a quiet and comfortable space** where you can reflect without distractions. Take a few deep breaths to center yourself and clear your mind.

2. Reflect on the following aspects of your life: *relationships, work, personal growth (health)*, and *leisure*. Consider what is truly important to you in each of these areas. If helpful, reflect on past experiences or moments when you felt most fulfilled and aligned with your values in these areas.

3. Take a piece of paper and brainstorm a list of values that resonate with you. Write down any words or phrases that come to mind without censoring yourself. Consider tangible and intangible values like honesty, creativity, family, health, and adventure. **Tip**: Use the Values cards from the previous exercise.

4. Prioritize your values and identify the **Top 25** that resonate most with you. Rank these values in order of importance, with the most important value at the top and the least important at the bottom.

5. From your Top 25 Values, take your "Value Priority #1" and refer to the Values bull's eye diagram below. Pick a section and ask yourself, "Am I living my life fully by this value in this aspect?" Place an "x" near the circle's center (red area) if you live according to your value. If not, place an "x" away from the center (outer circles).

   Move on to the next section and ask the same question. Keep going till you go through all four areas of your life.

   Here's an example using the value "balance."

In *relationships*, balance means maintaining healthy boundaries, giving and receiving support equally, and prioritizing quality time with loved ones while nurturing independence and individual growth.

In your *work* life, balance involves finding harmony between work and personal life, avoiding burnout, and pursuing opportunities for growth and development while enjoying downtime and leisure activities.

In *personal growth*, balance entails striving for growth and improvement while accepting oneself and practicing self-care. It involves setting goals and challenges while allowing time for reflection, relaxation, and enjoyment.

In leisure activities, balance means engaging in various activities that bring joy and fulfillment while also making time for rest and relaxation. It involves pursuing hobbies and interests that nourish the mind, body, and soul without overcommitting or neglecting other aspects of life.

Here's a sample Values Bull's Eye diagram with the above definitions of what "balance" means in various life aspects.

Value: Balance

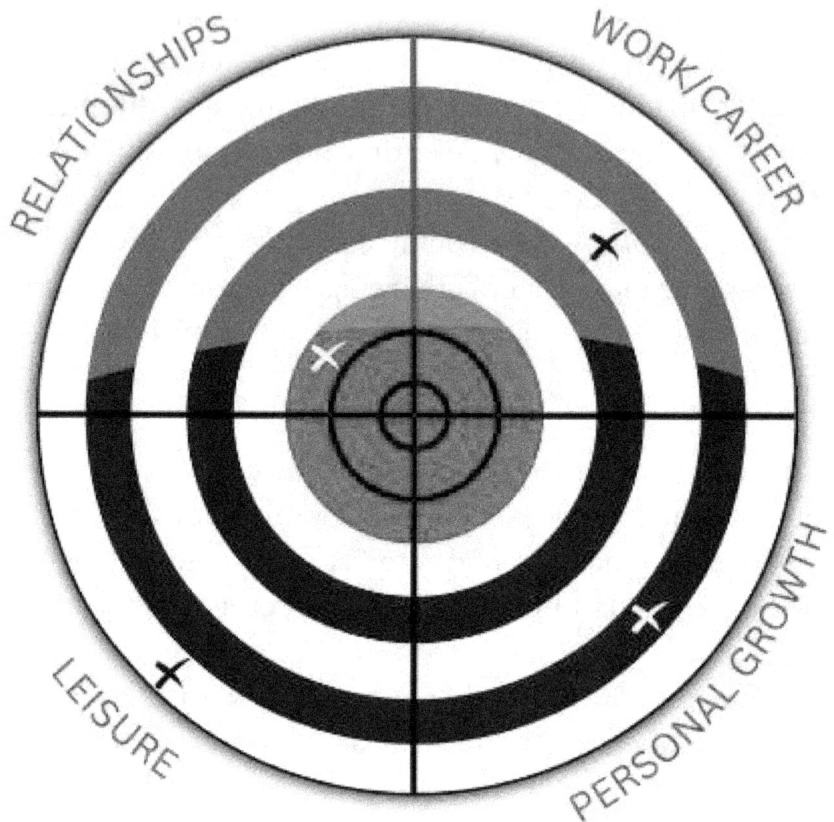

It's your turn to fill out the next diagram.

Value: _______________

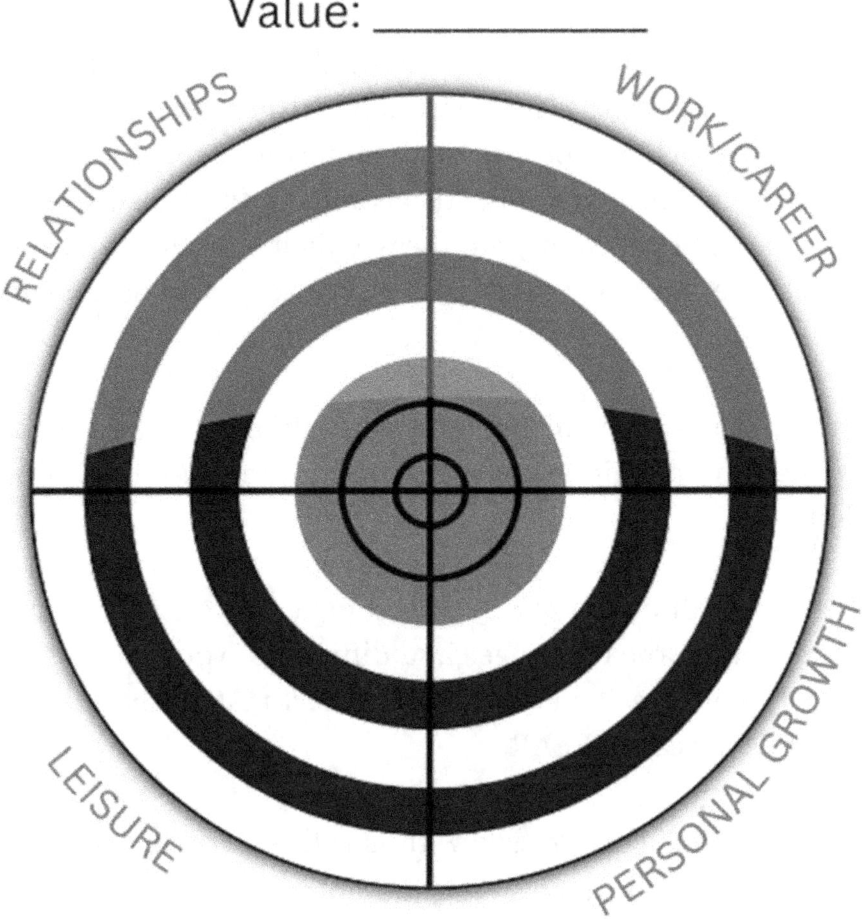

6. **Reflect on alignment.** Look at the diagram you created. Reflect on how well your current lifestyle aligns with a specific value. Are you living by it, or are there areas where you could make adjustments to better align with what matters most to you?

7. **Set value-based goals.** If you notice one life aspect where you're not living fully according to a value, plan and set goals to change that. For example, suppose you're not achieving "balance" in *leisure*. Perhaps you're overcommitting and trying to find time to engage in sports with different groups of friends several times a week and then with your partner on the weekends. In this case, you might want to lessen your weekly commitments so that you (and your body) have time for rest and relaxation.

Chapter 8: Committed Action

In ACT, a life of unhappiness and internal distress is often due to a *misalignment* between your values and actions. For example, if one values *commitment* yet lives a life of procrastination, inconsistency, and indecision, it can lead to inner conflict and dissatisfaction. Similarly, suppose someone values *authenticity* but constantly suppresses their true thoughts and feelings to fit in. In that case, they may experience a sense of disconnection and lack of fulfillment.

So, the key to living a more meaningful and fulfilling life lies in identifying your core values and aligning your actions with them. And yes, that's easier said than done.

Behavioral change is difficult.[79,80] For example, as you read this, you might already think about all the challenges and difficulties you will face. You might even wonder if you have it in you to succeed. In ACT, these psychological barriers to change are called FEAR.

- **F**usion. This is when you struggle with negative thinking, anticipating how your plans could fail or appear unachievable. Before you even begin, you might think this "living according to my values" thing is too tough for you.

- **E**xcessive goal making. Setting goals that exceed your existing resources (e.g., skills, time, money, etc.) might result in swift failure or giving up entirely. Setting realistic goals that correspond to your abilities and available resources is critical.

- **A**voidance of discomfort. Change inevitably brings discomfort, often in the form of anxiety or other challenging emotions. If you're unwilling to tolerate this discomfort, you might stay with what's familiar (comfort zone), even though this doesn't help you achieve your value-based goals.

- **R**emoteness from values. Before you start identifying and working on your goals, ensure they align with YOUR values. Sometimes, our goals are not aligned with our deepest values but rather influenced by external forces (i.e., family, society, what's viral and trending, etc.). If this is the case, it's easier to give up because, well, it's easier to do so when it comes to things we don't truly care about.

Although having doubts and questions (FEAR) is normal, it doesn't mean you cannot succeed. The solution to FEAR is DARE.

- **D**efusion. As mentioned in <u>Chapter 5: Cognitive Defusion (a.k.a. Unhooking)</u>, defusion is about identifying the negative and unhelpful thoughts holding you back in life and unhooking yourself from them.

- **A**cceptance. Do not avoid or deny your painful and unhelpful thoughts and emotions. Accept that they exist so that you can move on from them.

- **R**ealistic aims. If you have a goal for which you do not have the necessary resources, then you have two options. First, you can start with the goal of acquiring the necessary resources you need. For example, if you want to advance at work but need more leadership skills, your first goal should be to acquire these skills. Second, if the necessary resources are unavailable, accept reality's current constraints and modify your goals.

- **E**mbrace your true values. If you find yourself uncommitted or unmotivated about your goals, consider whether the "value" you're attempting to uphold is genuinely important to you. Is this your value or someone else's? If you think the value is important to you, is the action you've chosen to take really connected to it?

Committed action in ACT is acknowledging the existence of FEAR but embracing DARE. It's about taking meaningful steps towards living a life that aligns with your values, even in the face of difficult emotions or challenging circumstances. It is the opposite of *delay* or *avoidance*. It's about making deliberate choices, taking intentional actions, and consistently showing up and engaging in behaviors that align with your values. Further, committed action is not about "thinking" about taking action; it's about taking real action in the real world.

Setting Goals... and Actually Accomplishing Them

According to Russ Harris, author of *The Happiness Trap*[81] and a proponent of ACT, there are four steps to steps to committed action:

Step 1. Choose a life domain that is a high priority for change. Identify an area of your life where you feel dissatisfied or desire improvement. For example, you might choose your *work life* or *career* if you feel unfulfilled or stagnant in your current job.

Step 2. Choose what values you wish to pursue in this domain. Determine the core values that are important to you in your chosen domain. These values represent what truly matters to you in that area of your life. For example, if you choose your career, your values might include *creativity, growth, making a positive impact,* etc.

Step 3. Develop goals that are guided by those values. Set <u>SMART</u> (**S**pecific, **M**eaningful, **A**daptive, **R**ealistic, **T**ime-Bound) goals that align with your chosen values. These goals should reflect the kind of life you want to live in that domain. Using the career example, if your value is *creativity,* your goal might be to *pursue a job that allows you to express your creativity regularly.*

Step 4. Take action mindfully. Actively engage in activities that move you closer to your goals while staying present and aware of your thoughts, feelings, and sensations. In short, as you engage in an activity, be 100% present in that moment. Don't think of the past or the future; just be in NOW. For example, suppose your goal is to be more creative at work. In this case, you might take mindful action by brainstorming new ideas during team meetings and being fully present and attentive to the creative process.

Worksheet 25: Committed Action

In this exercise, you will apply the four steps of "committed action."

Step 1. Identify the life domain that is a high priority for change. Note that you might need to break down this particular aspect of your life further and assess which one(s) have priority.

Example:
Life domain: relationships
Particular aspects: romantic relationships, friendships, family connections, professional relationships
Priority for change: family connections

Life domain:
Priority for change:
Priority for change:

Step 2. Choose what values you wish to pursue in this domain.

Example:
Life domain: relationships
Priority for change: family connections
Values: honesty, trust, communication, respect, empathy, support

Step 3. Develop goals that are guided by those values. Based on your prioritized values, brainstorm specific goals you want to achieve in this domain. Remember, your goals should be in alignment with your values. Use the SMART (**S**pecific, **M**eaningful, **A**daptive, **R**ealistic, **T**ime-Bound) technique.

Life domain: _______________________________

Example: relationships

Priority for change: _______________________________

Example: family connections

Value to prioritize: _______________________________

Example: communication, harmony

Specific. What are your specific goals regarding this value? Be as detailed as possible.

Example:

- *I will improve communication with my siblings by regularly asking them for lunch. Preferably, at least one lunch date every other week.*
- *I will start my invites next week, for Saturday, 12 noon, at Café ACT.*
- *If one can't make it, I will NOT cancel and still hold the lunch date with those who can.*
- *I will not be discouraged if an intended lunch date doesn't push through. We all have busy lives, after all. Instead, I will ask them out again the following week.*
- *I accept that I have no control over the conversation during these lunches. There will be times when it's all fun and when we disagree with each other. I will do my best to practice patience and open-mindedness and encourage them to do the same.*

Meaningful. Why are you doing this? What's the meaning of this goal to you?

Example: I want to communicate better with my siblings because we're always getting into misunderstandings over the most trivial things! And yet, even though they're trivial, I feel enormous sadness and anxiety over them.

Adaptive. Do you believe this goal will help you achieve a value-based life in this domain? How so?

Example: Yes. By fostering more and better communication with my siblings, I believe there will be fewer misunderstandings between us, which is better for my mental well-being.

Realistic. Is this goal realistically achievable?

Example: I believe so. We all live in the same city, so meeting for lunch every other week or once a month is possible. We also all have jobs, so paying for lunch shouldn't be a problem.

Time-bound. Establish a timeline for achieving your goals. Set deadlines for specific actions or milestones.

Example:

- *I will start my invites next week, for Saturday, 12 noon, at Café ACT.*
- *I will initiate these lunch dates for at least three months.*
- *After three months, I'll assess if our communication and harmony have improved.*

Step 4. Take action mindfully. Practice present-moment awareness while engaging in the activities that enable you to achieve your value-based goal.

Example: I will treat these lunch dates with my siblings as "sacred time." No answering calls, no checking of emails, etc. I will actively listen when someone speaks and politely ask them to do the same when I have something to share.

Worksheet 26: Values-Based Exposure

In the previous exercise, you identified your life values and listed the steps you want to take to live according to them. Good for you!

Now, there might be times when certain goals require you to confront uncomfortable or even feared situations. For example, you might need to assert yourself in a challenging conversation at work to uphold your value of *honesty*, or you might need to push through your fear of public speaking to pursue your value of *making a difference in your community*. This is where Values-Based Exposure (VBE) comes in handy. It will help you face your fears while staying true to your values.

1. **Identify your value-based goal.** Start by identifying the goal you want to achieve.

   Example: I want to be better at initiating conversations.

2. **Identify the values associated with your goal.**

   Examples: connection, communication, authenticity, courage, growth

3. **Choose a target situation.** Choose a specific situation or scenario where you struggle to initiate conversations due to anxiety, fear, low self-esteem, etc. This could be initiating conversations with strangers, colleagues, acquaintances, or potential friends. Start with a situation that feels challenging but manageable.

Example: Initiate a conversation with a co-worker I like.

Target situation:

4. **Set clear action steps.** How do you intend to meet your goal? Be clear and specific with what you intend to do. For example, your goal might be to initiate a conversation with at least three new people in a social setting within the next week. Make sure your goals are realistic and achievable within your current comfort level.

Action steps:

5. **Prepare mindfully.** Prepare yourself mentally and emotionally for the exposure exercise. Practice mindfulness techniques to stay present and grounded in the moment.

6. **Visualize success.** Take some time to visualize yourself successfully doing your action steps. For example, if one of your action steps is to talk to three strangers today, imagine yourself feeling confident, relaxed, and engaged as you approach others and start conversations. Visualizing success can help build confidence and reduce anxiety.

7. **Begin with small, low-pressure exposure tasks.** Take small steps to gradually build confidence and momentum. For example, suppose your objective is to be better at initiating conversations. In that case, you might want to start with initiating very brief conversations with people you encounter in everyday situations, such as asking a cashier how their day is going or complimenting a coworker on their work.

8. **Challenge avoidant behaviors.** Identify any avoidance behaviors you engage in to avoid doing what you set out to do. For example, if you're uncomfortable initiating conversations, you might often avoid eye contact, stay glued to your phone, or leave social situations early. If so, challenge yourself to gradually reduce these avoidance behaviors during the exposure exercise by planning ahead.

AVOIDANT BEHAVIOR	PLAN
Example: I usually avoid eye contact.	*Example: Practice making brief, intentional eye contact with people in low-stress situations, such as with friends or family.*

AVOIDANT BEHAVIOR	PLAN

9. **Accept discomfort.** Accept that discomfort and anxiety are normal parts of the exposure process. Instead of trying to avoid or suppress these feelings, practice willingness to experience them fully while still acting in line with your values. (**Tip**: Try Willing Hands.) Remind yourself that feeling discomfort is normal, but it is temporary.

10. **Remember your values.** Reflect on how the activity aligns with your values throughout the exposure exercise. Notice how participating in the activity brings a sense of fulfillment, even if they feel challenging or uncomfortable in the moment.

11. **Celebrate successes.** Celebrate each success and milestone you achieve during the exposure exercise, no matter how small. Acknowledge your courage and progress in facing your fears and taking steps toward your goals. Reward yourself with self-care activities or positive affirmations to reinforce your efforts!

12. **Reflect and adjust.** After completing the exposure exercise, reflect on your experience and what you've learned. Identify any insights or lessons gained from the process and areas for improvement or adjustment. Use this feedback to refine your approach and set new goals for future exposure exercises.

Worksheet 27: Living in the Future

As you engage in "committed action," it's normal to experience setbacks. However, the key to success is to "keep your eye on the ball." That is, you must not lose sight of what you're trying to achieve, and one of the best ways to do that is to visualize yourself in the future, living your value-based life.

1. **Find a quiet and comfortable space** where you won't be disturbed. Close your eyes and take a few slow, deep breaths to **center yourself**.

2. **Bring to mind a valued intention or goal** that you've been working towards. It could be anything from improving relationships to advancing your career or personal well-being. Visualize this goal clearly in your mind.

3. **Envision yourself successfully living out this value or intention.** Picture yourself taking action in alignment with this value, with no obstacles standing in your way. Imagine feeling confident, capable, and fulfilled as you pursue your goals.

4. **Pay attention to how it feels to succeed in this area of your life.** Notice any feelings of satisfaction, pride, or contentment within you. Allow yourself to fully **immerse in the positive emotions associated with living according to your values**.

5. Take a moment to acknowledge any thoughts, emotions, or physical sensations that arise during this visualization. **Notice how your body and mind respond to the experience of success and fulfillment.**

6. **Shift your focus to the external environment in your visualization.** Notice any changes in the world around you resulting from achieving your goal. For example, suppose your goal was to improve communication and connection with your partner. In this case, imagine your relationship now that you've achieved this goal.

7. Take as much time as you need to **fully immerse yourself in this visualization** and experience the rewards of living in alignment with your values. When you're ready to conclude the exercise, slowly open your eyes.

8. Grab a pen, a piece of paper, or a journal, and jot down all the positive outcomes and insights you discovered during this exercise. Reflect on how you can carry these lessons forward and continue to pursue your values with clarity and purpose.

Part 3: Moving Forward with ACT

"Challenges are what make life interesting, and overcoming them is what makes life meaningful." – Joshua J. Marine

Chapter 9: ACT Maintenance and Growth

As you continue your journey with ACT, focusing on maintenance and growth is essential to sustain your progress and further enhance your psychological flexibility. Remember that, as with any life skill, you need to consistently apply what you've learned until it becomes a habit.

The following exercises explore strategies for deepening your understanding of yourself and your values and how you can further integrate ACT principles into your daily life.

Worksheet 28: Your Life Compass

This exercise helps you continually live a life of value-based intention and purpose. It allows you to look at your life and all its aspects— *family, intimate relationships, work or career, health, leisure, social life, education, and spirituality*—the core values you want to apply to them and reflect on your desired life direction.

1. Each box below represents an aspect of your life. In each box, write down:

- The values most important to you.
- The people who matter most.
- Who you want to be.
- Your current strengths and qualities.
- Other strengths, qualities, or skills you want to develop or acquire.
- Your goals.

Note: If a box feels irrelevant right now, leave it blank and return to it whenever you feel it's appropriate. It's fine if the same words appear in multiple boxes; this can help you pinpoint essential values.

2. **Priority.** After completing all the boxes, rate each box according to their priority in your life.

3. **Values adherence.** After completing all the boxes, return to the first box and reflect on the values you wrote down. Next, rate your current level of adherence to these values on a scale of 0 to 10, with 0=not adhering at all and 10 for extremely adhering.

4. After rating your value adherence for all the boxes, reflect on what you wrote.

- What is this Life Compass exercise telling you?
- Based on your rating, what are the most essential aspects of your life?
- Are you living according to your life priorities?

- Say you prioritize "Family" above all. What's your value adherence rating for that life aspect? Are you content or happy with this self-rating? If so, do you have any other goals you wish to add? If not, review or revise your goals.

Here's an example:

FAMILY	**_Priority: 2_**
Values: _love, respect, communication, support, unity, compassion, forgiveness, responsibility, acknowledgment, gratitude_	**_Adherence: 6_**
People who matter most: _mom, dad, siblings, and grandma Ellie_	
Who I want to be: _I want to be part of my family again. I left home early, and it seemed like I left and never looked back. I want to change that._	
Current strengths and qualities: _I'm a committed person. I'm also loving even though I don't always show it. I can also be very giving._	
Strengths, qualities, and skills I want to develop: _Better communication, more time for family, gratitude._	
Immediate goals. _Something modest, basic, and achievable within the next 24 hours._ • _Call mom!_ • _Ask if I can visit next weekend._	
Short-term goals. _Targets that can be accomplished within the next few days or weeks._ • _Visit family and STAY the whole weekend._	
Medium-term goals. _Targets that can be completed during the following few weeks or months._ • _Stay in touch. Call my parents every weekend._ • _Invite my sisters to visit me this summer._	

> ***Long-term goals.***
>
> *Targets that will be achieved in the following months or years.*
>
> - *Improve my relationship with my parents.*
> - *Build my non-existent relationship with my older and younger sisters.*

Now, it's your turn.

FAMILY	Priority:
Values:	**Adherence:**
People who matter most:	
Who I want to be:	
Current strengths and qualities:	
Strengths, qualities, skills I want to develop:	
Immediate goals. *Something modest, basic, and achievable within the next 24 hours.*	

<table>
<tr><td colspan="2">

</td></tr>
<tr><td colspan="2">

Short-term goals.

Targets that can be accomplished within the next few days or weeks.

</td></tr>
<tr><td colspan="2">

Medium-term goals.

Targets that can be completed during the following few weeks or months.

</td></tr>
<tr><td colspan="2">

Long-term goals.

Targets that will be achieved in the following months or years.

</td></tr>
</table>

INTIMATE RELATIONSHIPS	Priority:
Values:	Adherence:

People who matter most:
Who I want to be:
Current strengths and qualities:
Strengths, qualities, skills I want to develop:
Immediate goals. *Something modest, basic, and achievable within the next 24 hours.*
Short-term goals. *Targets that can be accomplished within the next few days or weeks.*

Medium-term goals.

Targets that can be completed during the following few weeks or months.

Long-term goals.

Targets that will be achieved in the following months or years.

WORK | JOB | CAREER	Priority:
Values:	Adherence:
People who matter most:	
Who I want to be:	

<table>
<tr><td></td></tr>
<tr><td>Current strengths and qualities:</td></tr>
<tr><td>Strengths, qualities, skills I want to develop:</td></tr>
<tr><td>Immediate goals.
Something modest, basic, and achievable within the next 24 hours.</td></tr>
<tr><td>Short-term goals.
Targets that can be accomplished within the next few days or weeks.</td></tr>
<tr><td>Medium-term goals.
Targets that can be completed during the following few weeks or months.</td></tr>
</table>

Long-term goals.

Targets that will be achieved in the following months or years.

HEALTH (Mental, Physical, and Emotional)	Priority:
Values:	**Adherence:**
People who matter most:	
Who I want to be:	
Current strengths and qualities:	
Strengths, qualities, skills I want to develop:	

Immediate goals.

Something modest, basic, and achievable within the next 24 hours.

Short-term goals.

Targets that can be accomplished within the next few days or weeks.

Medium-term goals.

Targets that can be completed during the following few weeks or months.

Long-term goals.

Targets that will be achieved in the following months or years.

RECREATION | LEISURE	**Priority:**
Values:	**Adherence:**
People who matter most:	
Who I want to be:	
Current strengths and qualities:	
Strengths, qualities, skills I want to develop:	
Immediate goals. *Something modest, basic, and achievable within the next 24 hours.*	
Short-term goals.	

Targets that can be accomplished within the next few days or weeks.

Medium-term goals.
Targets that can be completed during the following few weeks or months.

Long-term goals.
Targets that will be achieved in the following months or years.

SOCIAL LIFE	Priority:
Values:	Adherence:

People who matter most:

Who I want to be:

Current strengths and qualities:

Strengths, qualities, skills I want to develop:

Immediate goals.

Something modest, basic, and achievable within the next 24 hours.

Short-term goals.

Targets that can be accomplished within the next few days or weeks.

Medium-term goals.

Targets that can be completed during the following few weeks or months.

<table>
<tr><td colspan="2"></td></tr>
<tr><td colspan="2">Long-term goals.
Targets that will be achieved in the following months or years.</td></tr>
</table>

SCHOOL | EDUCATION	Priority:
Values:	**Adherence:**
People who matter most:	
Who I want to be:	
Current strengths and qualities:	

Strengths, qualities, skills I want to develop:

Immediate goals.

Something modest, basic, and achievable within the next 24 hours.

Short-term goals.

Targets that can be accomplished within the next few days or weeks.

Medium-term goals.

Targets that can be completed during the following few weeks or months.

Long-term goals.

Targets that will be achieved in the following months or years.

FAITH | SPIRITUALITY	**Priority:**
Values:	**Adherence:**
People who matter most:	
Who I want to be:	
Current strengths and qualities:	
Strengths, qualities, skills I want to develop:	
Immediate goals. *Something modest, basic, and achievable within the next 24 hours.*	

Short-term goals.

Targets that can be accomplished within the next few days or weeks.

Medium-term goals.

Targets that can be completed during the following few weeks or months.

Long-term goals.

Targets that will be achieved in the following months or years.

After doing this activity, print it out and keep it. During tough or challenging moments, take it out to remind yourself of your values and your life goals. It will help you "stay true" during challenging times.

Also, life is ever-changing. Your priorities, the values you associate with them, and your goals might change, so it's good to reflect and re-evaluate every now and then.

Chapter 10: Self-Guided ACT

You have learned A LOT, delving deep into the principles of ACT and gaining invaluable insights into yourself. Feeling overwhelmed and perhaps even inclined to take a break and let everything sink in is normal.

When you're ready to dive back in, you might be unsure where to begin. That's why I've crafted a special 30-day ACT Plan to guide you on your continued journey of growth and self-discovery.

Worksheet 29: Your 30-Day ACT Plan

This 30-day ACT plan is a guide. Its goal is progress, not perfection. So, keep to the plan as much as possible, but if setbacks happen, that's okay. Just get back up and keep on going!

Week 1: Building Awareness and Acceptance

Days 1-3:

Day 1: Spend at least 10 minutes practicing mindfulness, focusing on your breath or body sensations. (**Tip:** Select any of the mindfulness exercises mentioned in Chapter 4: Mindfulness (Present Moment Awareness)

Day 2: Engage in mindfulness and notice any negative thoughts or emotions that arise during the day without judgment. Accept these thoughts AS IS. (**Tip:** If you find yourself resisting acceptance, re-read Chapter 3: Acceptance.)

Day 3: Write down three things you struggle to accept about yourself or your life and reflect on how these things might be holding you back or keeping you in a cage of unhappiness. Reflect on how acceptance can free you from mental and emotional suffering.

Days 4-7: Start practicing cognitive defusion.

Day 4: Reflect on any negative thoughts you might be having about yourself and then label them as "Thoughts." Remind yourself that you are not your thoughts. They are not facts. Your thoughts are mental events coming and going like clouds in the sky. (**Tip:** Experiment with techniques from Chapter 5: Cognitive Defusion (a.k.a. Unhooking) and find what works best for you.)

Day 5: Engage in a pleasant activity mindfully, paying attention to the sensations and emotions it brings. Notice how doing the things you love or are passionate about brings you joy. If you observe unhelpful thoughts, practice cognitive defusion and let these thoughts pass without judgment.

Day 6: If any negative or unhelpful thoughts arise, distract yourself by making it a game and using the Defusion Wheel exercise. Notice how distancing yourself from difficult emotions or situations makes you feel better, allowing you to move forward.

Day 7: Journal and list down your unique skills and positive qualities. If any negative thoughts arise, don't try to deny it or push it away. Instead, say aloud, "Ah, I'm having this thought that I'm ______." Then, mentally place the thought outside yourself, like putting it in a box and visualizing placing that box in another room.

Week 2: Clarifying Values

Day 8-10:

Day 8: Randomly pick one of the "life boxes" you filled out in the <u>Life Compass</u> exercise in the previous chapter. Are you living in alignment with the values you wrote in this box? If not, think of ways to align your daily decisions and actions with the values you indicated in the "life box" you chose.

Day 9: Randomly choose one value to focus on today and set one small, meaningful act or goal related to it. For example, suppose you picked the value *discipline*" In this case, a small goal might be to ensure you drink 8 glasses of water today.

Day 10: Randomly choose one value to focus on today and set one small, meaningful act or goal related to it. However, this time, involve others. They don't need to know what you're doing. The objective is to extend the value to others. For example, suppose you picked the value of *kindness*. In this case, a small goal might be to genuinely smile at three people today or do a small favor for someone.

Days 11-14:

Day 11: Practice kindness and self-compassion to yourself today. Acknowledge and soothe any pain or difficulties you may be going through.

Day 12: Notice any behaviors driven by fear or avoidance, and consider how they conflict with your values. For example, suppose you're avoiding talking to a friend with whom you recently had a misunderstanding. In that case, you might be going against values such as *communication, connection,* and *forgiveness.*

Day 13: Pick an important personal value. Take one small action aligned with your chosen value, even if it feels uncomfortable.

Day 14: Pick an important personal value. (You can use the same one as yesterday's.) Take one small action aligned with your chosen value, even if it feels uncomfortable. Reflect on how it felt to act per your values. Did it bring a sense of fulfillment or purpose?

Week 3: Committed Action

Days 15-17:

Day 15: Set aside time to create a **<u>SMART</u>** (**<u>S</u>**pecific, **<u>M</u>**eaningful, **<u>A</u>**daptive, **<u>R</u>**ealistic, **<u>T</u>**ime-Bound) goal related to a value you've identified.

Day 16: Break down your value-based SMART goal into smaller action steps and schedule them throughout the week.

Day 17: Practice self-compassion and acceptance if you encounter obstacles or setbacks in pursuing your goal.

Day 18-21:

Day 18: Engage in a mindfulness exercise to connect with yourself today.

Day 19: Take action on one of the steps you identified on Day 15, even if it's challenging.

Day 20: Notice any internal barriers (e.g., self-doubt, fear) that arise and practice acceptance of these feelings.

Day 21: Reflect on any progress on your SMART goal and celebrate your achievements, no matter how small.

Week 4: Integration and Maintenance

Days 22-24:

Day 22: Review your values and goals and consider if any adjustments are needed based on your experiences. (**Tip:** Reflect on Chapter 7: Values Clarification and Chapter 8: Committed Action.)

Day 23: Engage in a values-based activity that brings you joy or fulfillment.

Day 24: Practice gratitude by reflecting on three things you're grateful for.

Days 25-28:

Day 25: Revisit your mindfulness practice and spend 15 minutes in mindful awareness.

Day 26: Reflect on how your relationship with difficult thoughts and emotions has shifted since starting this journey.

Day 27: Write a letter to yourself, acknowledging your efforts and commitment to growth.

Day 28: Plan for ongoing practice beyond the 30 days, setting intentions for continuing to integrate ACT principles into your life.

Day 29-30: Reflection and Celebration

Day 29: Spend time reflecting on your 30-day journey with ACT. What have you learned about yourself? What changes have you noticed?

Day 30: Celebrate your accomplishments and commit to ongoing growth and self-compassion. Consider sharing your experience with a supportive friend or journaling about your insights.

Conclusion

"Healing may not be so much about getting better as about letting go of everything that isn't you – all of the expectations, all of the beliefs – and becoming who you are."
– Rachel Naomi Remen

Life can be overwhelming at times. It's full of ups and downs. Now, the "ups" are great, but when the "downs" occur, that's when you need to have *psychological flexibility*. When you can sway with the wind, roll with the punches, and stand up and adapt, that's when you thrive.

Our thoughts are very powerful. What we think we become. And I think this is where we often trip ourselves in life. We don't realize that the "Thought" stage is not yet the "Fact" stage, yet we behave as though it were. As such, our thoughts become a self-fulling prophecy.

Now, if the thoughts are positive and helpful, great! (That's why positive affirmations work.[82]) However, when our thoughts are unhelpful, painful, negative, or harmful, we set ourselves up for an unhappy life.

When people ask about ACT, I tell them I learned it in therapy. However, I also told them that I think ACT skills benefit anyone and everyone at any time in their lives. Why? We cannot erase stress, problems, and challenges. They are inherent to the human experience. However, these events don't have to overwhelm us or knock us to the ground. We can just... sway, stand right back up tall, and keep moving forward.

Here's a quick recap of ACT:

In Part 1: Acceptance and Commitment Therapy 101, you learned about the history of ACT, what it's all about, and how it can help you find relief from your current life situation. You also learned how to prepare yourself for your ACT self-guided practice.

In <u>Part 2: the Six Core Principles of ACT</u>, you discovered the skills you need to develop to foster psychological flexibility.

- **Acceptance** is learning to acknowledge your current situation AS IS without trying to control, evaluate, or judge it. You learned that Acceptance is the door that opens your life to change.

- **Mindfulness** is present-moment awareness. It's living in NOW and not feeling, thinking, and behaving based on the past or the future.

- **Cognitive Defusion** involves letting go of negative self-talk and beliefs. It's about unhooking, ungluing, and distancing yourself from unhelpful thoughts or stories you associate with yourself.

- **Self as Context** teaches you to be an "observer" of your thoughts instead of being controlled by them.

- **Values Clarification** is taking a step back and evaluating what YOU truly consider important in this life. It's time for self-discovery and life realignment.

- **Committed Action** is about taking concrete, intentional steps to live a value-based life. It's taking real action in the real world to live life according to your values.

In <u>Part 3: Moving Forward with ACT</u>, you were given the tools to help you maintain and sustain the progress you've made with ACT.

Psychological flexibility. I often think about what that phrase means to me.

When I started my journey, I just wanted all the negative stuff (e.g., pain, depression, loneliness, feelings of inadequacy, confusion, etc.) to STOP overwhelming me. But when I got to *cognitive defusion* and *values* clarification, my life opened up. All of a sudden, I had clarity.

I learned that I was unnecessarily attached to unhelpful (and, in many instances, even *false*) ideas about myself, and I needed to distance and release these beliefs from my being. I also shockingly discovered I was not living up to my values or what I considered important. I was living based on what others wanted and expected. I was living *their* values. No wonder I was so confused and unhappy!

Ultimately, I can only be grateful for what I've learned. Why? Because now, I'm happily living the life I truly want to live. I sincerely hope that you achieve the same.

BOOK 3:
ACT THERAPY
WORKBOOK
for
ANXIETY RELIEF

A Simple Acceptance & Commitment Therapy Toolbox to Help Reduce Stress, Panic Attacks, Worry and Depression

Includes 30+ Mindfulness and Coping Strategies

Book 3 - Table of Contents

Introduction

"Panic attacks feel like you're stuck in a nightmare, and the only escape is to wake up, but you can't." — **Unknown**

I was 12 years old when I had my first panic attack (at least, that's the one I remember). It was a normal, boring afternoon; I was helping my mom put dishes in the dishwasher when I started feeling really dizzy out of the blue. I stood perfectly still, trying not to throw up, but I could feel my heart racing, and I couldn't catch my breath.

My mom was not the nervous and dramatic type, so instead of fussing over me, she simply asked, "What's wrong?" I said the first thing that came to my head:

Me: I'm scared.
Mom: Of what?
Me: I don't know.

My mom then proceeded to ignore me as if nothing happened. I managed to get a glass of water and sit. My younger brothers were screaming their heads off in the living room, so my mom left the kitchen, and that was that. I can't describe it, but I couldn't forget what I felt. I felt *fear* as if I were shivering inside.

About a year later, I was sitting in the car with my dad when I had another panic attack. He was dropping me off a swimming date with some girlfriends.

Me: Dad...
Dad: Yeah?
Me: I'm... nervous. (I was dizzy, my heart was racing, I was finding it hard to breathe, and I had that feeling again. I was scared and felt cold just beneath my skin.)
Dad: Huh?
Me: I can't... get... out of the car.

Dad: Ava, you're a great swimmer. There's nothing to be scared about, honey.
Me: I...
Dad: Your friends are waiting inside.
Me: Dad...
Dad: Ava!!!

I was startled. I whipped my head around to look at my dad, and oddly enough, although I could see his impatience, focusing on him made me calm down. I managed to get out of the car, and everything was on autopilot.

Go meet friends, walk to the changing rooms, and change clothes. People surrounded me, but I could barely hear them. I jumped into the pool and swam and swam and swam. By the time I got out of the pool, I was exhausted but was back to myself again.

Over the years, I have experienced moments like this. And with each episode, a "secret fear" was building slowly but surely inside me. You see, I knew my family had a history of mental health issues on my mother's side.

Growing up, there were always whispers about my cousin Ellen, who "stayed home all the time." Later, I would learn she had Major Depressive Disorder (MDD). When I was about eight, we visited my grandparents and met Uncle Frank, my mother's oldest brother, for the first time. I remember thinking it was odd to meet an uncle I never heard of before. Later, I would learn that Uncle Frank had schizophrenia. These events scared and scarred me because although my mom never exhibited any signs of mental health problems, I was just always scared I would get them. That's why I never forgot my first panic attack.

For the record, Uncle Frank leads a productive life. He has a job and lives on his own. However, he continues to experience schizophrenic episodes at various stages in his life, usually brought on by severe stress and anxiety.

Looking back, I'd say that my unaddressed fear of developing mental health problems contributed to... well, my mental health problems. (Yep, the irony!)

This unaddressed fear (no one talked about mental health in my family) made me constantly stressed and anxious inside. I had two younger twin brothers who were the center of the family's attention, which led me to develop an intense desire to be "seen." As a result, I became whatever people wanted me to be. I became a master at people-pleasing. However, since I was only ever trying to please others and be seen, I was always afraid that people would find out I was a fraud. This led to my controlling and perfectionist tendencies. And I've been doing all of these—for years.

Of course, one can only keep the façade for so long. I realize now that as each year passed, **I kept piling mental and emotional weight on my shoulders... until I couldn't anymore.**

I found out the hard way that when you live with unaddressed stress and fear and seek nothing but external validation, you lose yourself bit by bit until there's hardly anything left to lose.

It all came to a head when I was in my mid-30s and suffered what I now call "a burnout and a breakdown."

My career was my "cover." As an International Project Manager, I zigged and zagged across the globe, giving the impression that I was successful and that I'm someone who's got it all together. Ha! Inside, I was a wreck.

I felt like I was constantly swinging wildly between arrogance and self-doubt or between brief moments of calm and intense bouts of anxiety. At the slightest problem in my career or personal life, my mind would become an immediate battlefield where the fear of failure and the pressure to maintain my "successful" image waged a relentless war.

One day, while abroad and alone, I suffered another panic attack. (By this time, I was already used to having them now and then.) This time, however, I felt an enormous dark cloud loom over me. My anxiety subsided, but I couldn't shake my melancholy. Right around the third week, I returned to the hotel where I was staying, and as I entered my quiet suite, I started crying—and I couldn't stop. This scared me. Somehow, I knew it was different this time. Inside, I felt like I was drowning.

I don't know how, but **I survived** the three months I was away and returned home. **But I wasn't the same.**

My panic attacks became more frequent, I had this deep, unshakeable sadness, and I felt just bone-deep tired. So I did the best thing I could've ever done—I reached out for help.

I met with a therapist, and over our sessions, we learned that I was going through burnout, which was already at the cusp of a breakdown. And that underlining this condition was **years of unaddressed anxiety**.

I learned that I fit the description of high-functioning anxiety to a T! My people-pleasing, controlling, perfectionistic, and other tendencies all pushed me to overextend myself in every aspect of my life, leaving me incapable of ever taking a freaking break! However, persistent worries about "dropping the ball" (at home and work), always wearing a mask for the outside world, and constant self-doubt had been silently eroding my mental health for years.

To be honest, recognizing this connection was both eye-opening and validating! It explained why I felt so overwhelmed and why my attempts to simply "push through" weren't working.

I'm incredibly grateful for going through therapy. It was what I needed to see and understand what I was going through. However, I sensed that it wasn't enough. I felt something was missing. It was as if I was seeing a glimpse of something, but I couldn't take the next crucial step towards it. Something was blocking me, but I didn't know what. So, I wrapped up my sessions and set out on my own. After some research, I came upon Dr. Marsha Linehan's Dialectical Behavior Therapy (DBT).[83]

DBT taught me a concept called Radical Acceptance[84], which was my healing turning point. Acceptance was the critical step I was missing!

After learning about the benefits of DBT, I was so captivated that I enrolled in Dr. Linehan's DBT Skills certificate course. From that moment on, I've immersed myself in other forms of therapy, such as Mindfulness-Based Stress Reduction Therapy (MSBR), Cognitive Behavioral Therapy (CBT), and Acceptance and Commitment Therapy (ACT).

I learned that while these therapies have similarities, they also significantly differ.

- MSBR focuses on mindfulness to alleviate stress,
- DBT emphasizes mental and emotional skills training to instigate change,
- CBT focuses on identifying and challenging negative thought patterns to modify behavior, and
- ACT emphasizes acceptance and values-based behavior to improve mental and emotional resilience.

This book is a non-technical (no jargon!), easy-to-understand, and compassionate guide to help you explore and apply ACT for anxiety relief. I'll share with you how ACT helped me accept my anxious thoughts (rather than deny, ignore, or bury them as I have been doing for years). I'll also share with you how ACT helped me develop *psychological flexibility*, which enables me to bounce back better and faster from anxiety episodes.

You'll also discover how ACT helped me live a happier life. I learned that **unhappiness is usually due to a mismatch between what we're doing and what's truly important to us.** This is exactly what I've been doing for years(!), and in this book, I'll guide you on how to finally live the life YOU want (not the life based on what family or society dictates). This was crucial to my healing, and I hope it does the same for you.

When I started my journey, I just wanted to feel better and get some relief from my anxiety. I never thought I was going on this wonderful journey of self-discovery, healing, and transformation. **Today, I don't just feel better, I'm happy.**

Happiness has this way of radiating from you, and the people around me certainly saw the difference. It all started at a BBQ party one summer evening...

One of my best friends had round, wide eyes when she saw me enter their backyard with my husband. Later that evening, she asked:

Friend: Ava, what have you been doing? You look amazing!
Me: Thanks! I feel amazing. And you know I haven't been for a long time.
Friend: I know, but I'm glad to see you this way. What happened? What did you do?

I shared the story of my healing journey for the first time that night. As more saw me, asked me, and reached out, I felt that the best way to live my life was to try to pass on what I'd learned.

So, dear reader, this book is my personal invitation to you to go on a healing journey with me and find relief from anxiety. Together, we'll explore the steps and practices that helped me, hoping they will bring you the same sense of peace and well-being.

How is This Workbook Different?

This book is your simple, modern-day, and "usable in real life" guide to Acceptance and Commitment Therapy (ACT). However, I have a confession: this book is NOT limited to ACT. I've included certain aspects of MSBR, DBT, and CBT that I believe are important in dealing with anxiety. These elements have been important to my healing, and I hope they benefit you, too.

How to Use This Workbook

The chapters in this book build upon one another. Please start from the beginning and work your way through.

Also, I believe that learning is information + action. Simply knowing something isn't enough; you must put what you learn into practice for it to truly make a difference. That's why each chapter in this book includes practical, self-guided exercises. These activities are key to turning the knowledge you get in this book into real-world skills. This hands-on approach is where true transformation takes place.

Content Warning

We'll be tackling anxiety in detail, and some of the real-life stories, topics, and exercises here may trigger you. Stress, distress, loss, conflict, trauma (past and recent), health problems, etc., are examples of such content. Please be aware of these and other topics that may concern you. Also, never hesitate to ask for help or consult a specialist if you feel overwhelmed.

Safety While Reading

Working through anxiety can sometimes get intense, so it's important to take steps to ensure you feel safe and comfortable while engaging with the content. Here are some tips to help:

- **Create a Safe Space.** Find a place where you feel at ease, like a cozy chair or a quiet spot in your home. Choose a place that feels safe, peaceful, and secure.

- **Set Reading Boundaries.** As you read and do the exercises, take breaks when needed and stop if you start feeling overwhelmed. Your well-being comes first.

- **Practice Self-Care.** Take care of your physical and emotional needs. Get enough sleep, eat well, stay hydrated, and do activities that make you happy and relaxed.

- **Create a Safety Plan.** Know what to do if you feel unsafe or overwhelmed. Some ideas:
  - Stop and take a break.
  - Call or message a friend or family member.
  - Go to a safe, calm place.
  - Listen to soothing music or watch something comforting or funny.

Lastly, as you go through this journey, please **always extend patience and kindness to yourself** because this will not be a linear process. Just like me, you'll face ups and downs, but I promise you: If you stick with the process, you'll always move forward.

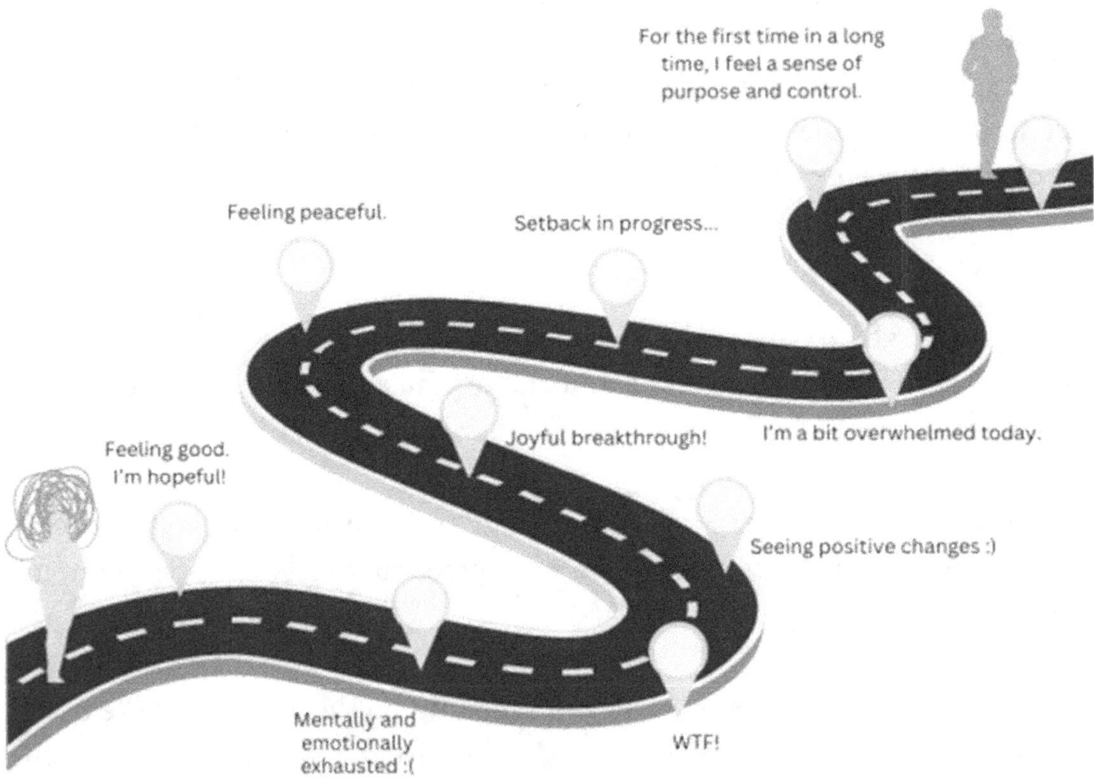

Living with Intention

Living with intention entails making conscious decisions. Life doesn't just happen to us. We have tremendous power and influence over what happens in our lives. So, I ask you now to set your intention, whether that's as simple as, "I intend to finish one chapter a day and do at least one of the exercises in this book" to more profound goals such as, "I intend to embrace this journey, including all its ups and downs, and take proactive steps towards managing my anxiety."

Please set your intention:

You Matter.

Throughout this journey, please remember that you matter. Your experiences, feelings, and struggles are valid. And your desire for anxiety relief and a better life isn't just important; it's your right.

Also, you're not alone. I have walked a similar path. So, know that YOU HAVE IT IN YOU to manage your anxiety—and transform. Remember, too, to celebrate your progress, no matter how small, because each tiny win is exactly that—a win!

Ava Watters

Amazon Bestselling Author
Acceptance Therapy Advocate

Part 1: Understanding Anxiety

"It is very hard to explain to people who have never known severe depression or anxiety the sheer continuous intensity of it. There is no off switch." – Matt Haig

Chapter 1. What is Anxiety?

Anxiety is a feeling of worry or fear about what *might* happen in the future. It's like your brain is always looking for danger, even when no real danger is around.

Everyone feels anxious sometimes, like before a big interview or project or when trying something new. But if you often feel anxious, and it hinders you from doing things you want or need to do, then it becomes a problem.

Anxiety can make your heart race, your palms sweat, and your stomach feel upset. It can also make you feel restless, tired, or unable to concentrate. It's like an alarm system in your body that's a bit too sensitive, going off even when there's no real threat.

Chapter 2. Anxiety and the Brain

What most people don't understand about anxiety is that it's not just something you *feel*; it affects how the brain works, especially in regions that handle threat response and stress management. When anxiety kicks in, it can cause some areas of the brain to become hyperactive while slowing down others. Here's a basic description of how this all happens.

- The **amygdala** acts as the brain's alarm system and emotion hub. When you sense a threat, it kicks into high gear, triggering feelings of anxiety. For people with anxiety disorders, the amygdala can be overly sensitive, reacting to situations that aren't truly dangerous or even present. This over-activity can lead to intense fear and anxiety, even in non-threatening situations. (Amygdala: "Ooh, threat. Danger! Danger!")

- The **hypothalamus** acts as a command center, managing your body's response to stress. So, when the amygdala detects a threat, it alerts the hypothalamus. The hypothalamus then activates the fight-or-flight response, releasing stress hormones like adrenaline and cortisol. These hormones prepare your body to react to the threat. (Hypothalamus: "There's danger? Pump out the stress hormones!")

- The **prefrontal cortex** is crucial for decision-making, attention, and emotion regulation. However, when anxiety levels are high, this part of the brain can struggle, making it difficult to think clearly, make decisions, and keep emotions in check.

  This can make anxiety feel overwhelming and difficult to manage. (Other people's prefrontal cortex: "Okay, I've checked. There's no real threat. Calm down." Anxious person's prefrontal cortex: "OH.MY.GOD! What's going on? What should I do? What should I not do? Argh!!!!")

- The **hippocampus** helps with forming memories and regulating emotions. Long-term or chronic anxiety can affect the hippocampus, leading to problems with memory and emotional regulation. This disruption can make it challenging to differentiate between real and imagined threats, worsening anxiety. (Hippocampus: "Wait, is this a real danger or just my imagination? I'm not sure, but let's stay on high alert just in case.")

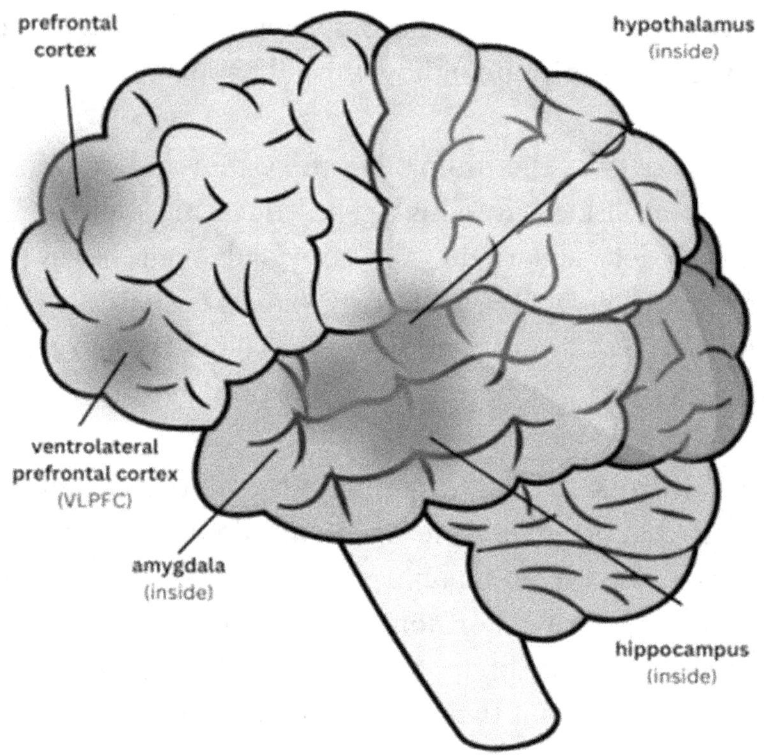

Disclaimer: *The brain anatomy image provided is for reference purposes only. It's a simplified representation and doesn't include all anatomical details or variations. Please refer to a medical practitioner or reliable educational sites for precise and comprehensive medical information.*

Anxiety is an internal distraction. It usually comes as lightning-fast, unconscious thoughts and emotions that *hijack* your state of mind and focus.

The great thing is that the human brain can be effectively trained! The key lies in that part of our brains called the ventrolateral prefrontal cortex (VLPFC). Think of it as a control center that helps you manage your thoughts and behaviors, especially when feeling anxious.

Key Functions of the VLPFC

- **Decision Making**: Helps you make choices, especially when you need to weigh different options.
- **Emotion Regulation**: Helps control your emotions, keeping them in check.
- **Attention and Focus**: Helps you concentrate on tasks and ignore distractions.
- **Inhibitory Control**: Helps you stop yourself from doing something impulsive.

Example: Imagine you're at a social gathering and feeling anxious about meeting new people. Your VLPFC helps you decide to introduce yourself instead of retreating to a corner (*decision-making*), calm your nerves by reminding yourself that it's okay to feel nervous (*emotion regulation*), focus on the conversation at hand rather than worrying about what others think (*attention and focus*), and resist the urge to leave early (*inhibitory control*).

So, how do you train your VLPFC? Mindfulness is the key. Remember, anxiety is an internal distraction that hijacks your state of mind and focus. So when intrusive anxious thoughts arise, it's important to have the skill to gently redirect your attention to the present moment (back to reality). (See Chapter 4: Mindfulness for a deeper dive into cultivating mindfulness.)

Important: It's important to note that anxiety not only affects the brain, but it can physically change the brain's structure and function over time.[85] If anxiety remains unaddressed, the amygdala (the brain's alarm system and emotion center) may grow larger, making it even more sensitive to perceived threats.

Conversely, the prefrontal cortex (responsible for focusing and decision-making) and the hippocampus (involved in emotion regulation and memory) may shrink, weakening their ability to manage stress and regulate emotions effectively.

Basically, the longer anxiety is not addressed, the more these changes can become entrenched, making it harder to break the cycle of anxiety and restore normal brain function.

Important: Untreated anxiety can also lead to the development of other conditions, such as insomnia[86], obesity[87 , 88], chronic pain[89], depression[90,91], heart disease[92,93], and more. Bottom line: the sooner you address anxiety, the better.

Chapter 3. What Type of Anxiety Do You Have?

Anxiety is the most common mental health condition, and reports indicate that it affects nearly 30% of US adults at some point throughout their lives.[94] Globally, anxiety affects nearly 300 million people.[95] It also comes in various shapes and sizes. I had Generalized Anxiety Disorder or GAD.

Please read below and see which one best describes your current situation. Having an idea of what type of anxiety you have will guide you better moving forward. If you think you might be dealing with any of the types of anxiety mentioned below, please don't hesitate to speak with your doctor.

1. **Generalized Anxiety Disorder (GAD)**: Excessive, uncontrollable worry about everyday things such as health, work, or social interactions. This worry is often out of proportion to the actual situation.

   Symptoms: Restlessness, fatigue, difficulty concentrating, irritability, muscle tension, and sleep disturbances.

2. **Panic Disorder**: Recurrent and unexpected panic attacks, which are sudden periods of intense fear that may include feelings of impending doom.

   Symptoms: Rapid heart rate, sweating, trembling, shortness of breath, feelings of choking, chest pain, nausea, dizziness, and fear of losing control or dying.

3. **Social Anxiety Disorder (SAD, or Social Phobia)**: Intense fear of social situations where one may be judged, embarrassed, or humiliated. SAD has been increasing in recent years.[96] The increasing use of social media, which drastically decreased the need for face-to-face interactions contributed to this. The COVID-19 pandemic also exacerbated social phobia because of the prolonged social isolation we all had to go through.[97]

Symptoms: Fear of speaking in public, avoiding social gatherings, extreme self-consciousness, and worry about being judged.

4. **Specific Phobias:** Intense, irrational fear of specific objects or situations, such as heights, animals, or flying. The fear is usually out of proportion to the actual danger posed.

   Symptoms: Immediate anxiety response when exposed to the phobic object or situation, avoidance behavior, and sometimes physical symptoms like sweating or trembling.

5. **Agoraphobia**: Fear of being in situations where escape might be difficult or help prove to be unavailable if panic-like symptoms occur.

   Symptoms: Avoidance of certain places, feeling trapped or helpless, and experiencing panic-like symptoms when in feared situations.

6. **Separation Anxiety Disorder**: Excessive fear or anxiety about being separated from attachment figures, such as parents or loved ones. This is more common in children but can also occur in adults.

   Symptoms: Excessive distress when anticipating or experiencing separation, worry about losing attachment figures, refusal to go out due to fear of separation, and physical symptoms like headaches or stomachaches when separation occurs.

7. **Selective Mutism**: Consistent inability to speak in certain social situations where speaking is expected despite speaking in other situations. This is often seen in children.

   Symptoms: Inability to speak in specific settings (e.g., school), speaking normally in comfortable settings (e.g., home), and avoiding speaking-related situations.

8. **Health Anxiety (Hypochondriasis)**: Excessive worry about having a serious illness despite medical reassurance and lack of significant symptoms.

   Symptoms: Constantly checking for signs of illness, frequent doctor visits, and avoiding activities due to fear of health problems.

9. **Substance/Medication-Induced Anxiety Disorder**: Anxiety symptoms that are directly caused by substance use, withdrawal, or exposure to medication.

   Symptoms: Intense anxiety or panic attacks, restlessness, difficulty concentrating, and physical symptoms like rapid heart rate or sweating, occurring during or shortly after substance use or withdrawal.

10. **Anxiety Disorder Due to Another Medical Condition**: Significant anxiety symptoms that are the direct result of a medical condition. For example, conditions like hyperthyroidism, heart disease, chronic pain, etc., can cause anxiety symptoms.[98]

    Symptoms: Excessive worry, panic attacks, or other anxiety symptoms directly linked to the medical condition, often alongside symptoms of the underlying medical issue.

A note about Post-Traumatic Stress Disorder (PTSD):
PTSD used to be classified as an anxiety disorder because it involves symptoms like intense fear, panic attacks, and extreme anxiety. However, in 2013, the American Psychiatric Association (APA) re-categorized it in the updated Diagnostic and Statistical Manual of Mental Disorders (DSM-5) under "Trauma- and Stressor-Related Disorders." This is to reflect PTSD's direct connection to traumatic experiences.

A note about Obsessive-Compulsive Disorder (OCD):
Just like PTSD, OCD was re-classified in 2013 in the updated DSM-5 under "Obsessive-Compulsive and Related Disorders." This is to reflect OCD's unique

features, which are the presence of obsessions (repeated, persistent, and unwanted thoughts, urges, or images that cause distress or anxiety) and compulsions (repetitive behaviors or mental acts one feels driven to perform in response to an obsession).

Body Dysmorphic Disorder (BDD), often thought of as an anxiety disorder, is also classified under "Obsessive-Compulsive and Related Disorders." This is to highlight BDD's primary characteristics of *obsessive thoughts* about perceived flaws and the *compulsive behaviors* performed to address these thoughts.

Important: Although PTSD, OCD, and BDD are not categorized as an anxiety disorder, anxiety IS a key characteristic of these disorders. As such, the skills you'll learn in this book will greatly benefit you if you suffer from these problems. In particular, you'll learn how to survive or tolerate moments of high stress and anxiety associated with these symptoms (Chapters 6) and how to manage the unhelpful thoughts that characterize these disorders (Chapters 7 and 8).

Worksheet 1:   Anxiety Self-Assessment Questionnaire

Still unsure about what type of anxiety you may have? While there isn't a single simple test that can definitively diagnose anxiety disorders, there are screening tools that can help you understand if you might have an anxiety disorder and its severity. One widely used tool is the Generalized Anxiety Disorder 7 (GAD-7).[99] Here's how it works:

For each question below, rate how often you have been bothered by the following problems over the <u>past two weeks</u>. Use the following scale:

0 = Not at all
1 = Several days
2 = More than half the days
3 = Nearly every day

How often have you been bothered by the following problems?	Not at all	Several days	More than half the days	Nearly every day
Feeling nervous, anxious, or on edge	0	1	2	3
Not being able to stop or control worrying	0	1	2	3
Worrying too much about different things	0	1	2	3
Trouble relaxing	0	1	2	3
Being so restless that it is hard to sit still	0	1	2	3
Becoming easily annoyed or irritable	0	1	2	3
Feeling afraid as if something awful might happen	0	1	2	3

Scoring:
0-4: Minimal anxiety
5-9: Mild anxiety
10-14: Moderate anxiety
15-21: Severe anxiety

What to Do Next: Scoring in the 0-4 range indicates you likely have minimal anxiety. It's still a good idea to practice the techniques in this book to prevent its escalation. For scores 5-9 and above, please try the ACT strategies outlined in this book. If at any point you feel overwhelmed, please don't hesitate to reach out to a mental health professional.

Disclaimer: Please note that the GAD-7 is just a screening tool and not a substitute for a professional diagnosis. If you want an accurate assessment, please talk to a healthcare provider who can provide a more comprehensive evaluation and recommend appropriate treatment options.

Chapter 4. What's Causing Your Anxiety?

Anxiety can be caused by a variety of factors, often a combination of them. Following is a quick table of the most common causes. Can you pinpoint the reason(s) for your anxiety?

WHAT CAUSES ANXIETY?				
Genetic	Biological	Psychological	Environmental	Lifestyle
Family history of anxiety	Brain chemistry *(Imbalances in neurotransmitters, such as serotonin, dopamine, and norepinephrine, can affect mood regulation and contribute to anxiety.)*	Negative thinking patterns, cognitive distortions, mind traps, etc.	Work and financial stress	Lack of physical activity
Genetic predisposition	Hormonal imbalances *(Fluctuations in hormones, particularly during puberty, pregnancy, menopause, or thyroid issues, can influence anxiety levels.)*	Traumatic experiences	Unstable home environment *(e.g., abuse, neglect, etc.)*	Poor diet *(Lack of essential nutrients like magnesium, zinc, and omega-3 fatty acids can contribute to anxiety.)*
	Chronic illness or medical	Stressful life events *(e.g., loss,*	Social environment *(e.g., difficult*	Substance abuse

		WHAT CAUSES ANXIETY?		
Genetic	Biological	Psychological	Environmental	Lifestyle
	conditions	*divorce, illness, injury, conflict, etc.)*	*relationships, social isolation, academic pressure, tech overload, etc.)*	
		Changing values *(Shifting values or living an inauthentic life can lead to internal conflict, identity crisis, negative self-judgment, etc.)*	Urban living *(Noise pollution, overcrowding, and fast-paced living can increase stress and anxiety.)*	Excessive caffeine or alcohol intake
				Sleep deprivation, excessive caffeine or alcohol intake

STRESS

Many of the causes of anxiety listed above highlight stress as a significant underlying factor. However, it's essential to understand that experiencing stress doesn't necessarily equate to having an anxiety disorder.

Stress is your body's natural response to any demand or challenge. It can be caused by everyday pressures such as work, school, relationships, or major life changes. Stress triggers a "fight or flight" response, releasing hormones like adrenaline and cortisol, which prepare your body to deal with the challenge. Also, stress is caused by circumstance, and when the "cause" is addressed or has passed, stress ends as well.

Anxiety, on the other hand, is an ongoing feeling of worry, nervousness, or unease about something with an uncertain outcome. Now, occasional anxiety is a natural reaction to stress. However, when anxiety becomes excessive, prolonged, and interferes with daily life, it can develop into an anxiety disorder. At this stage, anxiety is continuous, regardless of circumstances.

So, stress is not the same as an anxiety disorder. However, when stress is constant and unrelenting, your body stays in a heightened state of alert. Over time, this can exhaust your body and mind, leading to anxiety symptoms.

We live in very stressful times, so it's unsurprising to be unaware of how stressed you are, which is unhealthy. In fact, many people sort of "slide" into an anxiety disorder because they're NOT fully aware of just how much stress they're carrying! So, even if you did the Anxiety Self-Assessment Questionnaire and got a good score, please still do the following exercise.

Worksheet 2: Perceived Stress Scale (PSS)

The Perceived Stress Scale (PSS) is a psychological tool that assesses how various situations affect our emotions and perceived stress.[100] Following is an adapted version of the PSS for anxiety.

For each question below, rate your feelings and thoughts during the <u>last month</u> using the following scale:

0 = Never
1 = Almost Never
2 = Sometimes
3 = Fairly Often
4 = Very Often

1. In the last month, how often have you been upset because of something that happened unexpectedly?
   [ ] Never
   [ ] Almost Never
   [ ] Sometimes
   [ ] Fairly Often
   [ ] Very Often

2. In the last month, how often have you felt you could not control the important things in your life?
   [ ] Never
   [ ] Almost Never
   [ ] Sometimes
   [ ] Fairly Often
   [ ] Very Often

3. In the last month, how often have you felt nervous and "stressed"?
   [ ] Never
   [ ] Almost Never
   [ ] Sometimes
   [ ] Fairly Often

[ ] Very Often

4. In the last month, how often have you felt confident about your ability to handle your personal problems?
   [ ] Never
   [ ] Almost Never
   [ ] Sometimes
   [ ] Fairly Often
   [ ] Very Often

5. In the last month, how often have you felt that things were going your way?
   [ ] Never
   [ ] Almost Never
   [ ] Sometimes
   [ ] Fairly Often
   [ ] Very Often

6. In the last month, how often have you found that you could not cope with everything you had to do?
   [ ] Never
   [ ] Almost Never
   [ ] Sometimes
   [ ] Fairly Often
   [ ] Very Often

7. In the last month, how often have you been able to control irritations in your life?
   [ ] Never
   [ ] Almost Never
   [ ] Sometimes
   [ ] Fairly Often
   [ ] Very Often

8. In the last month, how often have you felt that you were on top of things?
   [ ] Never

[ ] Almost Never
[ ] Sometimes
[ ] Fairly Often
[ ] Very Often

9. In the last month, how often have you been angered because of things outside your control?
[ ] Never
[ ] Almost Never
[ ] Sometimes
[ ] Fairly Often
[ ] Very Often

10. In the last month, how often have you felt difficulties were piling up so high that you could not overcome them?
[ ] Never
[ ] Almost Never
[ ] Sometimes
[ ] Fairly Often
[ ] Very Often

Scoring:

Questions 4, 5, 7, and 8 are negative questions. That is, they are phrased so that a lower frequency of these experiences indicates higher stress levels. When scoring these questions, you will need to reverse their scores. For example, if you rated yourself a 4 (Very Often) on these questions, it should be scored as a 0; if you rated yourself a 0 (Never), it should be scored as a 4. For the rest of the questions, normal scoring applies.

Tally your score for all 10 questions. Typically, scores are interpreted as follows:

0-13: Low stress
14-26: Moderate stress
27-40: High stress

Disclaimer: Please note that the PSS is just a screening tool, not a professional diagnosis substitute. If you want an accurate assessment, please talk to a healthcare provider who can comprehensively evaluate your stress levels.

Anxiety in Women

Research shows that women are more likely than men to experience anxiety disorders [101,102,103] due to the following unique aspects:

"M" is for Multitasking

Women often juggle multiple roles, such as work, caregiving, and household responsibilities, which can contribute to higher stress and anxiety levels. (Somehow, we have equated the word "woman" to "multi-tasking!") In addition, external pressures and expectations around appearance, behavior, and success can add to anxiety.

"M" is for Menopause

Menopause marks the end of a woman's reproductive years, typically occurring between ages 45 and 55. This transition involves SIGNIFICANT hormonal changes, particularly a decrease in estrogen and progesterone, which can affect mental health.[104,105]

In addition to hormonal changes, there are also physical symptoms such as hot flashes, night sweats, and sleep disturbances. And let's not forget the psychological impact, too. The transition to menopause can bring about concerns related to aging, body image, and changes in identity, which can exacerbate anxiety.

Anxiety in Men

While anxiety disorders are more commonly diagnosed in women, men also experience significant levels of anxiety. It's just that men are less likely to seek help due to societal expectations and the stigma surrounding mental health.[106,107]

Many years ago, I was watching an episode of Oprah. I don't remember what the topic was exactly and who the male guests were. However, at one point, one of them said something like, "It's just the pressure, the pressure of knowing that it's all up to you to provide. And it's not like you can just call your buddies and vent."

After that episode, I looked at my dad a bit differently. I realized that I just never truly considered and appreciated the fact that he was the sole breadwinner in our home, and I KNEW there were times when money was tight. (By the way, my mom's an amazing homemaker; she and Dad have a great relationship. Still, I can't help but sometimes wonder what my Dad felt during those times.)

In addition to the stigma that discourages men from expressing vulnerability or seeking mental health support, they usually don't even recognize anxiety symptoms! Men are more likely to attribute mental health symptoms to physical health issues instead.

Worksheet 3: Specific Anxiety Triggers

Now that you have a clearer understanding of anxiety and its potential causes, it's important to identify your *specific triggers*. Knowing what (or who) sets off your anxiety will help you tailor the ACT skills you'll learn in the succeeding chapters to your unique needs and experiences. For now, just focus on this exercise to help you determine what sets off or triggers your anxiety.

Step 1. Daily Reflection. For TWO WEEKS, take a few minutes each day to reflect on moments when you felt anxious. Don't overthink, analyze, or evaluate anything yet. Just record the event as requested below. (If you need more space, please grab a few sheets of paper or use a notebook or journal.)

Situation: Describe what was happening when you felt anxious.
Example: I was window shopping for some summer clothes.

Location: Where were you?
Example: At the mall.

People Involved: Who were you with?

Example: I was alone.

Thoughts: What were you thinking?

Example: I realized that it was usually with my mom whenever I went window shopping. I was also shocked to realize that I didn't have to stop for food at her favorite place because she was no longer here.

Feelings: Describe your emotions.

Example: I felt loss, grief, sadness, loneliness.

Physical Reactions: Note any physical symptoms.

Example: heart racing, sweating, fast breathing

Step 2. Identify Patterns. After two weeks, look back at your daily reflections to see if common situations, thoughts, or people are associated with your anxiety.

Example: My anxiety seems to be triggered by thoughts of my mother, who passed away recently.

Step 3. Dissect the Trigger. Once you identify a potential trigger, break it down into specific elements to understand why it causes anxiety.

What's the trigger?
Example: Thoughts about my mother.

Why do you think it's triggering anxiety?

Example: I suddenly feel completely alone and lost in this world, like I lost my anchor. I think I also lost part of my sense of purpose because, for a long time, I was my mother's caregiver.

Step 4. Record Your Reactions. Note your physical, emotional, and behavioral reactions to the trigger. (This helps recognize the full impact of the trigger.)

Physical Reaction	Emotional Reaction	Behavioral Reaction
Example: My heart races, and I start sweating.	*Example: I start to feel lost and scared.*	*Example: I avoid eye contact and try to leave the situation or area. "Get out of here" is what I want to do.*

It's possible to have more than just one anxiety trigger, so do this exercise as long and as often as you need. As you go through the following chapters and learn various ACT skills and coping techniques, keep track of new triggers you identify. This ongoing awareness will help you apply what you learn more effectively, ensuring that you address all the factors contributing to your anxiety.

Important: It's extremely helpful to determine the cause of your anxiety. However, note that it's NOT necessary to know its cause to find relief. You can still use all of the techniques in this book to manage and reduce your anxiety because they focus on symptom management and building mental and emotional flexibility. These strategies can help you achieve significant anxiety relief and improve your quality of life, regardless of whether you know the exact cause of your anxiety or not.

Chapter 5. How Anxiety Hurts You

Unaddressed anxiety can have a wide range of negative effects in life. I know because I think I've experienced pretty much most of the things you'll read below. Are you experiencing any of the following?

Emotional Health

- **Increased irritability.** Anxiety is often associated with internal turmoil and feelings of inadequacy, but did you know that it can manifest as anger?[108,109] Anxiety often makes you more prone to irritability and mood swings, and small issues may trigger disproportionate emotional responses. Impact: This can strain your relationships with family, friends, and coworkers, creating a cycle of frustration and misunderstanding.

- **Persistent worry and fear.** Untreated anxiety can lead to feelings of being overwhelmed and a persistent sense of dread. Impact: You might find it difficult to enjoy life, even its simplest pleasures.

- **Low self-esteem.** Anxiety can make you doubt your abilities and worth, leading to negative self-perception and reduced confidence. Impact: This can hinder your personal and professional growth and discourage you from pursuing new opportunities.

- **Emotional exhaustion.** Chronic anxiety can drain you emotionally, leading to feelings of exhaustion and burnout. Impact: This can reduce your ability to cope with daily stresses and responsibilities, further exacerbating anxiety symptoms.

- **Feelings of hopelessness.** Persistent anxiety can lead to feelings of hopelessness and helplessness because you feel trapped in your anxious thoughts and unable to find relief. Impact: This can increase your risk of depression and decrease your motivation to seek help or make positive changes.

- **Social withdrawal.** Anxiety can make social interactions feel overwhelming, leading individuals to withdraw from social activities and isolate themselves. Impact: Social isolation can lead to loneliness, further deteriorating emotional health and reducing support networks.

- **Difficulty experiencing pleasure.** Unaddressed anxiety may make it hard to enjoy activities you once found pleasurable due to constant worry and tension. Impact: This can reduce overall life satisfaction and contribute to *anhedonia*, a core symptom of depression.

Physical Health

- **Chronic health problems.** Persistent anxiety can contribute to the development or worsening of chronic health conditions such as heart disease, hypertension, and gastrointestinal issues.

- **Weakened immune system.** Ongoing anxiety can weaken the immune system, making the body more susceptible to infections and illnesses.

- **Sleep disturbances.** Anxiety often leads to difficulty falling asleep or staying asleep, resulting in poor sleep quality and chronic fatigue.

- **Muscle tension and pain.** Constant anxiety can cause muscle tension, leading to headaches, back pain, and other musculoskeletal issues.

Mental Health

- **Depression.** Unaddressed anxiety can lead to or exacerbate depression, creating a cycle of worsening mental health.

- **Substance abuse.** Some individuals may turn to alcohol, drugs, or other substances to cope with anxiety, which can lead to substance abuse and addiction.

- **Cognitive impairment.** Chronic anxiety can affect concentration, memory, and decision-making abilities, impacting daily tasks and overall cognitive function.

Daily Functioning

- **Work performance.** Anxiety can impair job performance by causing difficulties in concentration, decision-making, and maintaining productivity. It may also lead to increased absenteeism.

- **Academic challenges.** For students, anxiety can impact academic performance by affecting concentration, test performance, and participation in school activities.

Long-Term Consequences

- **Decreased quality of life.** Chronic anxiety can significantly diminish one's overall quality of life, limiting opportunities and experiences.

- **Ruined relationships.** Anxiety can make you physically and emotionally absent. Missing out on important events, neglecting responsibilities, or being unable to provide the support and presence important people in your life need can strain relationships to the point of breaking.

- **Development of comorbid conditions**. Untreated anxiety can lead to the development of other mental health conditions, such as depression, obsessive-compulsive disorder (OCD) or post-traumatic stress disorder (PTSD).

- **Increased risk of self-harm.** Severe, untreated anxiety can increase the risk of self-harm and suicidal thoughts and behaviors, particularly if it coexists with depression.

I know that this may all seem daunting. However, I can tell you from experience that inaction is the last thing you should do. Relief IS possible. Here's my tip: just take this ACT journey with me, *one page at a time*.

Part 2: Acceptance and Commitment Therapy and How It Can Bring Anxiety Relief

"Sometimes the smallest step in the right direction ends up being the biggest step of your life. Tiptoe if you must, but take the step." – Naeem Callaway

Acceptance and Commitment Therapy (ACT) was developed in the 1980s by prominent psychologist Steven C. Hayes[110], and his personal and professional experiences influenced it.

You see, long before he became a psychologist, Hayes struggled with panic disorder. So, his personal experience with anxiety and panic attacks played a significant role in shaping his approach to therapy.

Professionally, Hayes and his colleagues would be working with people struggling with psychological problems such as anxiety and depression. And, well, he just thought that there's got to be a better way to help people struggling with these issues, so ACT was born.

As with many forms of psychotherapy, ACT is influenced by other therapies. It draws from:

- **Behaviorism** emphasizes the influence of our environment and learning experiences on our behavior.

  For example, imagine you touched a hot stove as a child and got burned. Because of that painful experience, you learned to avoid touching hot stoves. This is behaviorism in action: your behavior (avoiding hot stoves) is shaped by your past experience (getting burned).

- **Relational Frame Theory (RFT)** is about how our minds connect words, thoughts, and experiences in ways that can sometimes cause stress or anxiety.

For example, suppose that you had to make a school project presentation as a teen. You were nervous, so you stuttered and said something incorrect. Your classmates laughed, and you were made fun of for weeks. After that, whenever you hear the word "presentation," you feel nervous and anxious. This happens because your brain has linked the word "presentation" with the memory of failing and the feelings of stress from that experience.

- **Cognitive Behavioral Therapy (CBT) and Behavioral Therapy** focus on modifying maladaptive or unhelpful behavior.

For example, suppose you experience tremendous stress before work deadlines. In CBT, you might work on changing your thoughts from "I'll NEVER finish on time!" to "I've prepared enough. This should help to finish on time." Meanwhile, in Behavioral Therapy, you might practice relaxation techniques, like deep breathing or progressive muscle relaxation, to reduce anxiety before the looming deadline.

In addition to the above influences, ACT incorporates acceptance- and mindfulness-based strategies and values-based living to help develop *psychological flexibility.*

Psychological flexibility is about resilience or your "bounce-back ability." It's your capability to come back from setbacks, adjust to changing circumstances, and thrive despite your anxiety.

You see, ACT acknowledges that life is full of ups and downs. The secret is enjoying the ups and developing the flexibility and resilience to navigate the downs. One thing that's very important to realize is that when you work on yourself, your mental and emotional resilience improves! This means that something that triggers your anxiety today might not have the same impact on you tomorrow. Now, isn't that thought a relief in itself?

So, how do you develop psychological flexibility?

Chapter 6. ACT: Original Hexaflex Model

Psychological flexibility can be developed by practicing these skills: *Acceptance*, *Mindfulness*, *Cognitive Defusion*, *Self as Context*, *Values Clarification*, and *Committed Action*.

Chapter 7. ACT: My Expanded Model

Before discussing the six core principles of ACT, I'd like to include a skill I learned in DBT: **Willingness**.

When I started my healing journey, I found myself... *resisting*. I think that after years of ignoring my anxiety, something inside me was avoiding dealing with it head-on.

Call it fear, call it ignorance, call it bullheadedness... whatever it was, I needed to get over it. Why? Because whatever I was doing up to that point was clearly NOT working. (Otherwise, I wouldn't have ended up experiencing anxiety-induced burnout and a breakdown.)

As I talked to more people, I realized many face the same issue. Oh, we WANT to get better, but for many of us, there's some reluctance we need to overcome first. Otherwise, no amount of information and skills training will be effective. So, I'd like to expand on the ACT framework to this:

Disclaimer: Please note that this expansion is based on my personal experiences and the insights I've gained from others who have shared similar journeys. While I believe this additional focus on Willingness is vital, it's not part of the original ACT framework. Also, I want to clarify that I'm not a licensed mental health professional; the information I share is meant to complement, not replace, professional advice or treatment.

Note: ACT core principles are interconnected, working together to promote psychological flexibility. Although I highly encourage you to go over them in the order presented in this book, you don't necessarily have to do them in sequence. Depending on what feels most relevant to your journey, you can focus on one principle more than others at different times. The key is to integrate these principles into your life in a natural and supportive way.

Gentle reminder: The best way to benefit from the ACT skills in this book is to continuously practice the exercises *before* you need them. Doing so will make you more prepared to apply them whenever anxiety arises.

Chapter 8. Willingness

"Willingness is the key to transformation. It's the first step towards the life you desire." — Unknown

Willingness is openness to experience thoughts and emotions without avoidance. It's a commitment to engage with life as it is, even when it involves doubt, discomfort, or fear. Resistance or unwillingness can be due to various reasons, including:

- **Emotional pain.** Healing often requires facing painful emotions or experiences. This can lead to resistance, especially if you prefer to stay in your comfort zone rather than confront difficult feelings. <u>Mindset change</u>: Discomfort is a natural part of healing. No bruise ever got better without going through some form of pain.

- **Fear of change.** Change can be intimidating, and you may fear the unknown that comes with confronting your anxiety. <u>Mindset change</u>: If you don't take the step to change, you'll stay exactly where you are right now.

- **Fear of vulnerability.** No one likes feeling vulnerable. This was my personal roadblock. I HATED showing any sign of weakness because then people might discover that I was struggling inside. But then I told myself, "Well, you ARE struggling, Ava. How much more are you willing to punish yourself?" <u>Mindset change</u>: Sometimes, we need to be weak and vulnerable to be strong.

- **Doubt in effectiveness.** You may question whether what you learn in this book will help you or whether it's worth your time and effort. <u>Mindset change</u>: Everyone's path to healing is unique, and you won't know what works for you... until you try something that might work for you.

- **Perceived stigma.** There's STILL stigma around prioritizing one's self and seeking help. <u>Mindset change</u>: Seeking help for your anxiety is a sign of strength, not weakness. It's okay to prioritize your mental health and well-being, just as you would for any physical ailment.

- **Unrealistic expectations**. You might expect quick fixes or immediate results. You might even tell yourself, "Well, if I don't feel anything different in the next day or so, this is not for me." Pre-setting unrealistic results is a clear sign of unwillingness. It means you're not 100% open to whatever may happen in your journey. <u>Mindset change</u>: There's no time limit or "deadline" for managing and overcoming anxiety. Think of yourself as a wonderful flowering plant. Just nourish it. It will bloom when it's ready.

- **Fear of hope.** When it comes to mental health healing, I believe most of us are afraid to hope because hope can feel like a double-edged sword. Hoping means you risk feeling disappointed. To quote Finnick Odair, one of my favorite characters in the film The Hunger Games, "It takes ten times as long to put yourself back together as it does to fall apart."

However, I've learned that giving in to "fear of hope" means we become unwilling to take risks. And risk is the only way to potentially achieve change. <u>Mindset change</u>: Don't be afraid of hope; rather, be wearier of staying in place. Don't underestimate yourself. Better days are possible, but only if you're willing to pursue them.

So, willingness is crucial to healing, but HOW do you cultivate it? What do you do? Following are various exercises specifically crafted to help you embrace a greater sense of willingness in your journey.

Worksheet 4: Willing Hands

Willing Hands is a perfect example of the mind-body connection in action. By focusing on your hands, you can influence your mind to be more open and willing.

Step 1. Find a comfortable position. Sit or stand in a quiet place where you won't be disturbed. Ensure your back is straight and your feet are flat on the ground.

Step 2. Relax your hands on your thighs with palms facing upward. Let your fingers naturally curl in a relaxed position.

Step 3. Take a few deep breaths, inhaling through your nose and exhaling through your mouth.

Step 4. On your next inhale, **slowly close your hands.** Don't make a tight fist. Just gently close them. As you exhale, **slowly open your hands and palms** and relax your fingers. **Tip**: Include a positive, willing-focused thought as you open your hands. For example, you can say, "I'm open to new," "I'm willing," "I'm ready for change," or "I'm willing to discover [your name] 2.0."

Step 5. If you're still feeling any resistance, do step 4 above a few more times until you feel tension or resistance fade.

Worksheet 5: Vulnerability

As mentioned, fear of vulnerability is one of the main reasons why we might be unwilling to do anything new or different. This exercise aims to help you practice vulnerability by gradually opening up about your feelings, thoughts, and experiences in a safe and controlled manner.

Step 1. Reflect on what vulnerability means to you. Consider why you might be afraid or don't want to feel vulnerable by completing the sentence below. (Write as many reasons you can think of.)

I don't like feeling vulnerable because:

Example: I don't want others to see my struggles and judge me.

Step 2. Write a brief paragraph about how practicing vulnerability might help you.

Example: Maybe if I can be vulnerable, I can RELAX in my relationships because I'm not always "on guard."

Step 3. Identify your "safe people." Name a few trusted individuals with whom you feel comfortable sharing your feelings. These could be close friends, family members, or a therapist.

Example: Rose. I trust my wife more than anyone. Also, I know she's been worried about me lately. Next to her would be Martin, my best friend since grade school. Although it's so tough to "share" with guys, I trust Martin.

Step 4. Share minor vulnerabilities. There's no need to rush this process and have a "big reveal" (unless that's what you want). So start by sharing something small but personal with one of your trusted individuals. This could be a minor worry or a recent disappointment.

Example: Babe, I get really anxious in the morning during breakfast; just the RUSH of it all. I feel overwhelmed, and sort of can't think straight. I worry about whether I'm eating the right thing, if I'll have enough time, if I'll be late for work... it's a whirlwind of thoughts that makes starting my day really tough.

Important: It's a BIG step on your part to decide to share something. However, if the other person has no clue about your anxiety, please be patient and don't feel bad if they don't react the way you want them to. The most important thing here is your decision to share something and allow yourself to be vulnerable.

At the same time, be prepared for questions. If the person to which you opened up asks you how they can help, let them know.

What help do you need?

Example: I'd appreciate a bit more routine to our mornings so I don't start the day overwhelmed.

On the other hand, if you just want to share, that's okay too. You can say, "I'm just sharing for now so you understand how I feel and what's happening with me. I'm not ready yet to dive into this topic further. Please be patient."

Step 5. Gradually share more significant experiences. As you become more comfortable, gradually share more significant thoughts and feelings. This could involve discussing deeper fears, past experiences, or ongoing struggles.

Step 6. Be kind to yourself. Practice self-compassion, especially if you feel exposed or uncomfortable after being vulnerable. It would help if you have a self-compassionate statement you can read to yourself regularly. Here are a few examples:

[ ] It's good to share my feelings.
[ ] It's okay to feel vulnerable. I'm taking steps to improve my well-being.
[ ] Vulnerability is a strength, not a weakness.

[ ] It's normal to feel anxious sometimes. I'm allowed to experience my thoughts and emotions without judgment.
[ ] I'm doing my best, and that's enough. Every step I take is part of my healing journey.

Step 7. Share with a wider circle. Once you're comfortable with your trusted individuals, consider expanding your circle of vulnerability. This might include sharing in support groups, at work, or in social settings when appropriate.

Step 8. Reflect and adjust. Continuously reflect on your experiences with vulnerability. Note what works well and what doesn't. Adjust your approach as needed. **Tip**: Keep a vulnerability journal where you document your journey, progress, and insights.

Step 9. Acknowledge your growth! Celebrate your efforts and progress in practicing vulnerability. Acknowledge the courage it takes to open up and the positive changes you've experienced.

Worksheet 6: Switching the Struggle OFF

An unwilling person is a struggling person. For example, it might be that something inside you doubts the efficacy of ACT to give you anxiety relief. This doubt is causing your unwillingness to learn the skills in this book, or it might make you do the activities here half-heartedly.

This exercise aims to help you recognize and reduce any internal resistance to engaging with the skills presented in this book. By "switching off the struggle," you can open yourself to learning and applying ACT effectively.

Step 1. Identify your doubts. Take a moment to reflect on any doubts or concerns you have about using ACT to help with your anxiety. Write down any thoughts that come to mind.

Your Doubts:

Examples:
I don't think this will work for me.
I've tried other things before, and they didn't help, so why would this one?
This may be too complicated for me.

Step 2. Acknowledge your feelings. Recognize that it's okay to feel uncertain or skeptical. Write down how these doubts make you feel physically and emotionally.

Your Feelings:

Examples:
I feel unsure.
I feel worried that nothing will help me.

Step 3. What else? Think about what life can be like if you surrender to the process for just a minute.

What else could happen?

Examples:
I could get some relief from my anxiety.
I could finally take that trip I've always wanted but never could due to my anxiety.
I could be happier.

Step 4. Switch off the struggle. Keeping your answers in the previous step in mind, visualize any doubts and resistance as a switch you can turn off. Picture yourself physically flipping the switch down to "OFF." As you do this, take a deep breath and allow the tension of those doubts to fade away. Write down how you feel after "switching off" those thoughts.

After switching off the struggle...

Example: I know my worries are still there but I'm entertaining the potential positive outcomes more now.

Just sharing: I also like imagining my unwillingness as words, sentences, or even a poster inside a room with me. I then imagine flipping the lights in the room to "OFF," getting out of the room, and closing the door. Kind of like leaving my unwillingness behind.

Step 5. Write a commitment statement to yourself, emphasizing your willingness to engage with the skills in this book. Remind yourself why you want to work on your anxiety.

Example:
I commit to embracing the skills outlined in this book to help manage my anxiety. I want to feel more in control of my thoughts and emotions, improve my relationships, and live a fulfilling life. I'm willing to face discomfort and uncertainty to find relief and build a more resilient self. I commit to showing up for myself and taking the steps necessary to create positive change in my life.

Your Commitment Statement:

Chapter 9. Mindfulness

"The greatest gift you can give yourself is a little bit of your own attention." — Anthony J. D'Angelo

Mindfulness is living in NOW, which is often against anxiety. How? An anxious mind often lives in the past or the future.

Myra[2] has suffered from anxiety ever since she can remember, which has made her a very meticulous planner. From a young age, she mapped out every aspect of her life. She kept a calendar filled with reminders, to-do lists, and goals—nearly every minute of her day accounted for.

Despite her efforts, Myra frequently felt overwhelmed. Instead of feeling confident in her plans, she often worries about forgetting to include something important on her lists. This anxiety would lead her to repeatedly check her lists, and even after reassuring herself that she had written everything down, she would begin to fret about whether she had enough time to complete it all.

As each year passed, Myra's anxiety grew, and so did her lists. She would laugh when her sister would say, "Myra, your lists have lists!" but deep inside, she was hurting deeply.

Because of the constant "jokes" about her lists, she started withdrawing socially. She eventually quit her job as a Team Leader in a data processing company (she couldn't handle the stress of being responsible for a project and the anxiety of dealing with people) and took freelance data entry jobs at home. This, of course, shrunk her social circle even more.

---

[2] *Name changed for privacy.*

"At one point, I just noticed that I was sort of "stuck." I wanted to have conversations, but I get anxious just thinking about talking to people. I was lonely, but I didn't want to go out.

When family members visit (and they MUST schedule it with me first!), I would be anxious the minute the visit was set, terrified while they were here, and I couldn't sleep properly for days because I would relive every moment of the visit in my mind. I was stuck between loneliness and the discomfort of any form of connection."

One day, as she sat at her desk scrolling through social media, Myra stumbled upon a quote from the Dalai Lama that goes something like this, "The past is already gone. The future is not yet here. There's only one moment for you to live" and "Man is so anxious about the future that he does not enjoy the present, the result being that he never lives in the present."

"For some reason, those quotes really got to me. In one crystal clear moment, I saw myself as someone never living in the present, and maybe that meant I wasn't really "living" at all."

Myra wondered if she could truly just "live in the moment." Intrigued, she decided to give mindfulness a try. She started with just five minutes each morning. She would wake up, sit in bed, close her eyes, and focus on her breath.

"Believe it or not, my "list habit" helped. I scheduled those five minutes, so in my mind, I had to do them. So, getting started was not a problem, but it felt hard and awkward. So many thoughts flooded my mind. My schedule... did I check that I have what I need for breakfast last night... what if the phone rings? I found it very challenging to quiet my mind and let go of my worries."

Myra realized she needed something to focus on during those five minutes, so she turned to Breath Counting. She would inhale and say

"1", exhale and say "2", inhale again and say "3," etc. The goal was to get to 20 mindfully. If she lost count, she had to start all over again at "1". She would do this until her five minutes were up. Gradually, Myra started to notice a shift in her attention.

"At the start, it was about the focus on the counting. But at one point, I began to notice the gentle rhythm of my breath. When I inhaled, I didn't just count anymore; I also felt the cool air enter my nostrils and the warm air leave my mouth as I exhaled. I learned to invite a sense of calm with each inhale, and with each exhale, I tried to let go of any tension I physically felt. I got excited. Is this mindfulness? Am I capable of being "in the moment" now?

Pretty soon, the five minutes turned to 10, which turned to 15 on a thick towel on the flower. The mindfulness turned to yoga, which gave me this intense desire to buy a yoga mat... but not online. For the first time in a very long time, I called my sister to see if she wanted to go out and buy a yoga mat with me. She was shocked and so happy for me. Her reaction made me cry. I didn't know how much I had missed that connection until that moment.

I have a long way to go. I know that. But I have some fragile sense of peace now that I don't think I've ever felt. I still have anxiety. I know that, too. But my mind doesn't rush like a runaway train in the mornings so much anymore. I'm hopeful all this positive change will continue to grow and spread."

Yes, mindfulness is being present, but it's not just about existing in the moment. It's about creating that gateway to *true awareness*. If you notice, Myra started with mindful breath counting, but it took a while for her to be fully aware of HOW she was breathing, to actually feel and experience how air entered and exited her body,

Mindful awareness is a crucial starting point to anxiety relief because you can't accept your anxiety, be compassionate about it, and address it if you haven't first fully recognized its presence—and effects—in your life.

I think of mindfulness as a valuable tool for managing anxiety both in the short term and in the long term.

Short-term. When anxious, you enter "automatic" or "knee-jerk reaction" mode. Something happens (trigger), you get anxious (emotion), and you react (behavior)—all in seconds or minutes. Mindfulness gives you the time, space, and opportunity to *think before you act.*

For example, suppose you have Social Anxiety Disorder (SAD). But, determined to face your fears, you finally agree to join a friend for coffee. You worry that you'll be late, so you arrive early. You sit down, and now you're worried if your friend will even arrive.

Your friend arrives (whew!), but they're not alone. This is NOT what you agreed to, and your anxiety skyrockets. You feel a rush of panic and start feeling cornered and overwhelmed.

Your friend and their companion reach your table, but before they can even sit, you stand up, mumble an excuse, grab your things, and rush out of the coffee shop. Later that night, you torment yourself and drown in a mix of embarrassment and frustration. You realize that your knee-jerk reaction was driven by your intense anxiety, causing you to flee without considering the situation fully. That is where mindfulness helps you in the short term.

When a trigger occurs, mindfulness enables you to take a mental step back and be in the moment (present awareness) so you can assess the situation fully and objectively. This helps prevent you from making knee-jerk reactions that might worsen the situation.

Long-term. At the same time, something amazing happens when you keep practicing mindfulness even when you don't need it. You start developing that *psychological flexibility.* It's like gaining "mental muscle." The more you exercise mindfulness, the better you become at handling moments of stress and anxiety. And that's not just theory; science shows that with *continued practice,* mindfulness:

- Reduces stress.[111,112] Mindfulness helps you stop dwelling on worries, like constantly replaying a stressful conversation or fearing what might go wrong in the future. By focusing on the present moment, you train yourself to acknowledge and let go of anxious thoughts faster, reducing the overall feeling of stress.

- Improves focus.[113,114] When you struggle with anxiety, your mind can feel scattered, jumping from one worry to another. Practicing mindfulness, specifically Focused-Attention (FA) meditation, trains your mind to concentrate on one task at a time. (See Candle Meditation.)

  For example, suppose you get anxious when talking to people you just met. If you have improved focus, you can fully engage in a conversation with them instead of worrying about saying something "wrong" or overthinking your responses. This allows you to listen actively, respond genuinely, and build connections rather than being trapped in your anxious thoughts.

- Enhances emotional regulation.[115 , 116] Mindfulness allows you to acknowledge and accept your emotions *without judgment.* For example, when you feel anxious before a big presentation, instead of trying to push those feelings away, mindfulness teaches you to recognize that anxious thoughts and feelings are just that—thoughts and feelings. By accepting that you are having them in the moment, you can better manage your reaction to them.

Ready to be more mindful? The following exercise will help you achieve just that.

Worksheet 7: Mindful Breathing for Stress Relief

This exercise is designed to help you manage stress and anxiety using the power of deep breathing and visualization.

Step 1. Sit or lie down in a comfortable position. Ensure your back is straight but not rigid to allow for deep breathing.

Step 2. Gently place one hand on your heart and the other on your belly. This simple gesture creates a sense of warmth and safety in your mind and body. If you feel comfortable, close your eyes to help you focus inward.

Step 3. Inhale slowly and deeply through your nose. Feel your chest and abdomen expand as you fill your lungs with air. Feel your hands ride that gentle up-and-down wave as you inhale slowly and exhale deeply.

Step 4. Pause briefly. Hold your breath for a moment at the top of the inhale. Notice the stillness and fullness in your lungs.

Step 5. Exhale slowly and completely through your mouth. Feel your body release tension with each out-breath. **Tip**: Say "Go" as you exhale, signifying the release of the stress you're experiencing.

Step 6. Repeat the breathing cycle. Continue this breathing pattern: inhale deeply through your nose, hold for a moment, and exhale slowly through your mouth. Repeat for several minutes.

Step 7. Focus on the sensation. As you breathe, focus on the sensation of your hand on your heart. Feel the warmth and gentle pressure. Silently remind yourself that it's okay to feel stressed. Affirm to yourself that you are safe and capable of handling your emotions.

Step 8. Visualize your stress. In your mind, assign a color, shape, or texture to your stress. For example, imagine your stress as a crumpled sheet of red paper. Keep this image in your mind's eye. As you breathe out, visualize this crumpled paper slowly smoothing out and untangling with each exhale. Imagine that this is your stress leaving your body.

Step 9. Practice self-compassion. If negative thoughts or strong emotions arise, acknowledge them without judgment. Use self-compassionate statements such as, "It's okay to feel stressed. I'm here for myself now" or "I'm allowed to take this time to care for myself."

Step 10. Continue this mindful breathing practice for 5-10 minutes or as long as needed. Gradually increase the duration as you become more comfortable with the exercise. When you're ready, gently open your eyes. Take a moment to notice how you feel and reflect on any changes in your stress or anxiety levels.

Worksheet 8: Grounding for Anxiety Release

When we're anxious, it often feels like we're being pulled in different directions. We might be thinking about something that happened (past) or worrying about something that might happen (future). This exercise aims to help you manage anxiety by helping you ground yourself in the present moment (now).

Step 1. Find a quiet place to sit comfortably on a chair without distractions.

Step 2. Set a time for this exercise using a timer, your watch, or your mobile phone. Start with 5-10 minutes and gradually increase the time as you become more comfortable.

Step 3. Ground yourself. Begin by grounding yourself in the present moment. Place your feet flat on the floor and feel the connection with the ground. Take a few deep breaths, inhaling through your nose and exhaling through your mouth.

Step 4. Close your eyes and bring your attention to your body. Start with your feet and slowly move your attention upward, noticing tension or discomfort. As you scan each part of your body, try to release any tension. For example, if you notice tension in your toes, consciously relax them.

Step 5. Focus on your breath. Shift your focus to your breath. Notice the sensation of the air entering your nostrils, filling your lungs, and then leaving your body. Pay attention to the rhythm of your breath without trying to change it. Simply observe it as it is.

Step 6. Count your breaths. To help maintain focus, count each breath. Inhale and mentally count "one," exhale and count "two," and continue up to ten. Then start over at one. If your mind wanders, gently bring your attention back to your breath and start counting again.

Step 7. Acknowledge and release thoughts. It's normal for thoughts to arise. When they do, simply acknowledge them without judgment. For example, when a thought arises, imagine it as a stress balloon, and you're holding its string in your hand. When you exhale, imagine releasing your hold on the string. The balloon gently flies away, carrying your worries with it.

Step 8. If it helps, you can **anchor your attention using a calming phrase or mantra**. For example, silently repeat "I am calm" or "This too shall pass" with each breath. Match the mantra to your breathing pattern for added focus.

Step 9. Engage all your senses. To deepen your mindfulness, briefly shift your attention to your senses and notice:

- FIVE things you can see;
- FOUR things you can hear;
- THREE things you can touch or feel;
- TWO things you can smell and
- ONE thing you can taste.

Spend a few moments on each sense, then return your focus to your breath.

Step 10. Practice self-compassion. Be kind to yourself throughout this exercise. If you find it difficult to stay focused or if your anxiety persists, remind yourself that it's okay. Mindfulness is a practice, and it's normal to have challenges. Silently offer yourself phrases of self-compassion, such as "May I be kind to myself," "It's okay to feel this way," or "I will be patient with myself."

Step 11. Gradually end your practice. Take a few deep breaths when your timer goes off or you feel ready to end the exercise. Slowly bring your awareness back to your surroundings. Open your eyes and take a moment to notice how you feel.

Worksheet 9: Candle Meditation

This Focused-Attention exercise is a powerful technique that can help alleviate anxiety by training your mind to concentrate on a single focus point. This practice helps reduce the scattered, overwhelming thoughts that often accompany anxiety, promoting a sense of calm and control.

Step 1. Select a candle that you find pleasant. It can be scented or unscented. Place it in a safe, stable holder.

Step 2. Choose a quiet, comfortable place where you won't be disturbed. Dim the lights to create a calming atmosphere.

Step 3. Set the candle at eye level, about two feet before you. Sit in a comfortable position, either on a chair or on the floor with a cushion.

Step 4. Light the candle and take a moment to get settled in your position. Take a few deep breaths to relax your body and mind.

Step 5. Gently direct your gaze to the flame of the candle. Observe the flame's colors, shapes, and movements without straining your eyes.

Step 6. Start deep breathing. Begin to take slow, deep breaths. Inhale through your nose for a count of four, hold for a count of four, and exhale through your mouth for a count of four. Continue this square breathing pattern throughout the meditation.

Step 7. Observe your thoughts. As you focus on the flame, you may notice thoughts arising in your mind. Simply observe these thoughts without judgment and gently bring your attention to the candle flame.

Step 8. Engage your senses. Notice any scents from the candle if it is scented. Feel the warmth of the flame if you hold your hand near it (but not too close to avoid burns).

Step 9. Anchor yourself in the present. If your mind wanders, gently guide it back to the present moment by focusing on the flame and your breath. Remind yourself that it's normal for the mind to wander and that the practice is in gently returning to the focus point.

Step 10. Maintain your focus. Continue observing the flame and maintaining your breathing pattern for 5-10 minutes. As you become more comfortable with the practice, you can gradually increase the duration to 15 minutes or longer.

Step 11. Slowly close your focused meditation. When you're ready to end the meditation, slowly bring your attention away from the flame. Take a few deep breaths, close your eyes, and bring your focus inward. Reflect on how you feel after the meditation and notice any changes in your body or mind.

Worksheet 10: Mindful Walking

Mindful walking is a simple yet powerful practice combining mindfulness' benefits with physical activity. By focusing on the present moment as you walk, you ground yourself to "now," providing a break from anxious thoughts.

Step 1. Choose a peaceful location. Find a quiet, safe place where you can walk without interruptions. This could be a park, a quiet street, a community garden, or even your backyard.

Step 2. Stand still and breathe deeply. Before you start walking, take a moment to stand still. Take a few deep breaths. Inhale through your nose, letting your abdomen expand, and exhale through your mouth, releasing any tension.

Step 3. Set an intention. Set a positive intention for your walk. It could be to clear your mind, connect with nature, or simply enjoy the movement.

Step 4. Start walking at a slow and steady pace. Pay attention to the sensation of your feet touching the ground. Do your feet land flat on the ground or roll from heel to toe? Notice the surface texture beneath your feet and how it feels with each step.

Step 5. Focus on your breath. As you walk, bring your attention to your breath. Notice the rhythm of your inhales and exhales. Try to synchronize your steps with your breathing. For example, inhale for two steps and exhale for two steps.

Step 6. Engage your senses. Become aware of your surroundings. Notice the sights, sounds, smells, and even the feel of the air on your skin. This sensory engagement helps anchor you in the present moment.

Step 7. Observe your body. Pay attention to how your body moves. Notice the sensation of your muscles working, your arms swing, and your spine's position. Be mindful of any areas of tension.

Step 8. Visualize your anxiety. If you notice anxious thoughts arising, visualize them as a tangible object in your environment. For instance, imagine your anxiety as a branch or leaf on a tree along your path. As you continue walking and pass the tree, focus on the feeling that you are literally leaving your anxiety behind, moving further away from it with each step.

Step 9. Practice self-compassion. If you find your mind wandering or become distracted, gently bring your attention back to your walking. Use self-compassionate statements like, "It's okay to get distracted. I'll just gently bring my focus back."

Step 10. Conclude your walk with gratitude. After your walk, take a moment to give thanks for the experience. Appreciate the time you dedicated to your well-being and the calmness you've cultivated. Reflect on the sensations you felt, the sights you saw, the images or scenes you've encountered, etc. This gratitude practice can enhance the positive effects of your mindful walk, leaving you with a greater sense of peace and fulfillment.

Worksheet 11: NeuroAffective Touching

NeuroAffective Touching (NAT) is a therapeutic technique that combines mindfulness with gentle physical touch to help alleviate anxiety. By engaging the mind and body, NAT can promote safety, reduce stress, and bring calmness.

Step 1. Find a quiet, comfortable space. Sit or lie down in a place where you won't be disturbed. Ensure your environment is calm and peaceful.

Step 2. Take a few deep breaths to center yourself. Close your eyes if you feel comfortable, and bring your awareness to your body.

Step 3. Choose a focus area. Select an area of your body where you feel tension or discomfort. Common areas include the chest, abdomen, or shoulders.

Step 4. Apply gentle touch. Place your hand gently on the chosen area. Use a light, comforting touch as if you were reassuring a loved one.

Step 5. Focus on the sensation. Direct your attention to the feeling of your hand on your body. Notice its warmth, pressure, and any other physical sensations.

Step 6. Visualize calming energy. The human body is made of energy.[117] As such, imagine a warm, soothing light emanating from your hand, calming that part of your body, feeling stress, anxiety, tension, or discomfort. Visualize this light, spreading warmth and goodwill through your body.

Step 7. Breathe mindfully. Inhale slowly through your nose, feeling your chest or abdomen rise under your hand. Exhale gently through your mouth, noticing the release of tension.

Step 8. Acknowledge your emotions. If strong emotions arise, acknowledge them without judgment. Allow yourself to feel and process these emotions as part of the healing process.

Step 9. Switch focus areas. If you feel the need, move your hand to another area of your body that requires attention. Repeat the process of gentle touch and mindful breathing for each body part that needs it.

Step 10. Gradually end the session. When you feel ready, slowly bring your awareness back to the room. Open your eyes, gently move your hand away, and take a few deep breaths.

Chapter 10. Acceptance

"Acceptance doesn't mean resignation; it means understanding that something is what it is and that there's got to be a way through it." — Michael J. Fox

Acceptance means actively embracing your thoughts, feelings, and experiences without trying to deny, avoid, change, or judge them. It involves opening up to the reality of your inner experiences and allowing them to exist AS IS, even when they are uncomfortable or painful.

I know that it's hard to accept anxiety. For the longest time, I truly didn't want to accept it. I thought that to accept anxiety meant I was "weak," that anxiety won over me somehow, and that by accepting it, I had sealed my faith, and so all hope was gone. I was so wrong! I learned that the secret was NOT to focus on anxiety itself but to relearn what "acceptance" truly means.

Acceptance is NOT being "okay" with anxiety. You are just acknowledging the fact that it currently exists in your life.

Acceptance is NOT surrendering, giving up, or giving in to anxiety. You cannot accept something in the future. So, accepting anxiety means accepting its presence in your life now. It doesn't mean you don't want to get relief from it and change your circumstances moving forward.

Acceptance is NOT about downplaying anxiety's impact. Acceptance only acknowledges. It doesn't under- or overestimate, or under- or overvalue anything.

Acceptance is NOT a sign of weakness. Acceptance builds resilience. When you accept your anxiety, you also accept your amazing capacity to manage it. This builds inner strength and resilience, empowering you to face anxiety with confidence and a sense of control.

Acceptance is NOT shutting yourself off from the world because of your anxiety. Many people mistakenly believe that accepting anxiety means limiting yourself to it, as though you've "sealed your fate." In truth, it's the opposite. Acceptance unlocks the door of anxiety's cage, freeing you to engage with the world without letting anxiety hold you back.

Acceptance is NOT inaction. On the contrary, acceptance creates space for action. By accepting anxiety, you stop fighting against it and instead start focusing on what you can do to improve your situation. This shift from resistance to action leads to "better" and "change."

Acceptance is NOT self-criticism. Acceptance fosters self-compassion. Recognizing, without judgment, that anxiety is a part of your experience helps you treat yourself with kindness and understanding. Remember, anxiety does NOT make you "less."

As I learned the true meaning of acceptance, I realized I was struggling with it because I was overcomplicating it! Acceptance is simple, and a concept I learned in Dialectical Behavior Therapy (DBT) captures it perfectly: Radical Acceptance.

Radical means "complete" or "all-encompassing." No ifs or buts, no desires or regrets, no exceptions, and no conditions. And so, to radically accept means to accept reality AS IS.

Radical Acceptance

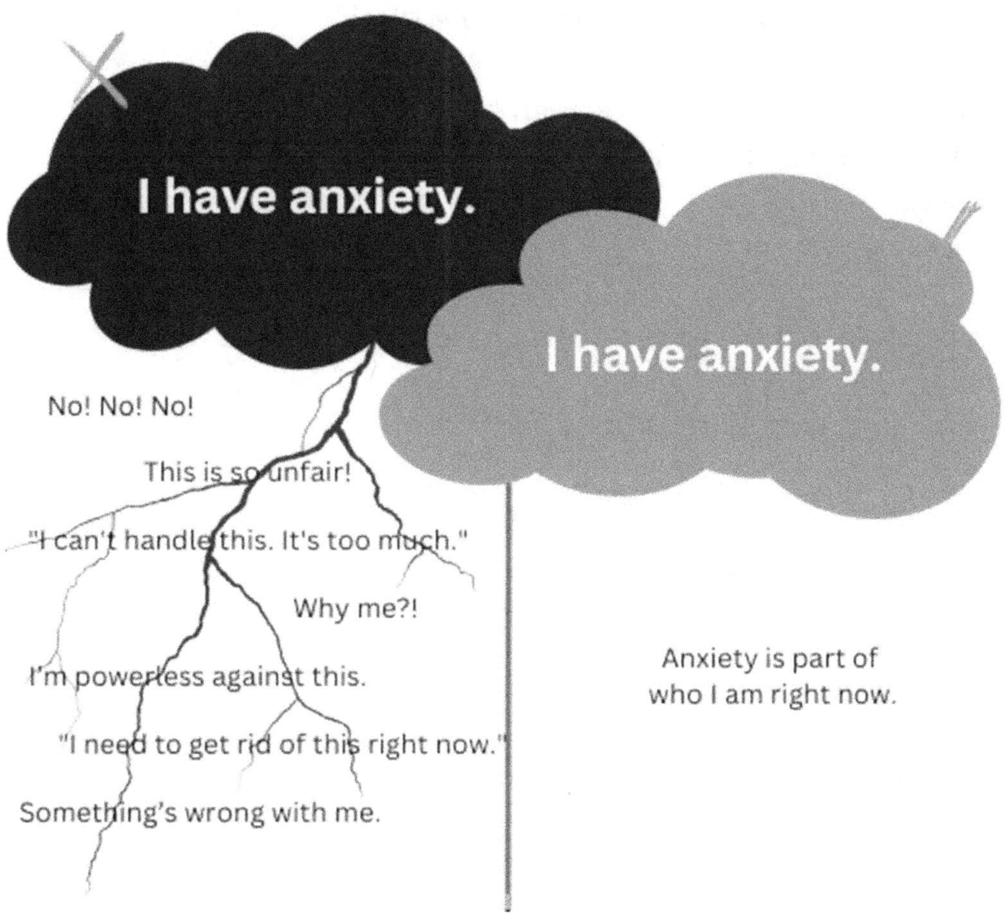

So, what happens when you DON'T accept anxiety's presence and impact on your life? It usually means four things: you're denying, resisting, avoiding, or unaware.

- **Denying** is when you refuse to acknowledge the presence of anxiety, convincing yourself that it doesn't exist or isn't affecting you. (*Who? Me? I don't have anxiety. What are you talking about?*)

- **Avoiding** is when you try to escape or steer clear of situations that trigger anxiety, often leading to avoidance behaviors that can exacerbate the problem. (*I don't like taking elevators. Why? Oh, uh... just because.*)

- **Resisting** is when you fight against the anxiety, which can create additional stress and make the anxiety worse. (*I can push through this. I don't need help from anything or anyone.*)

- **Unaware** is when you're not giving anxiety signs and symptoms the attention they deserve. It's like ignoring the check engine light on your car. You keep driving as if everything is fine until the car breaks down unexpectedly one day.

Unfortunately, here's the problem of doing any of the above:

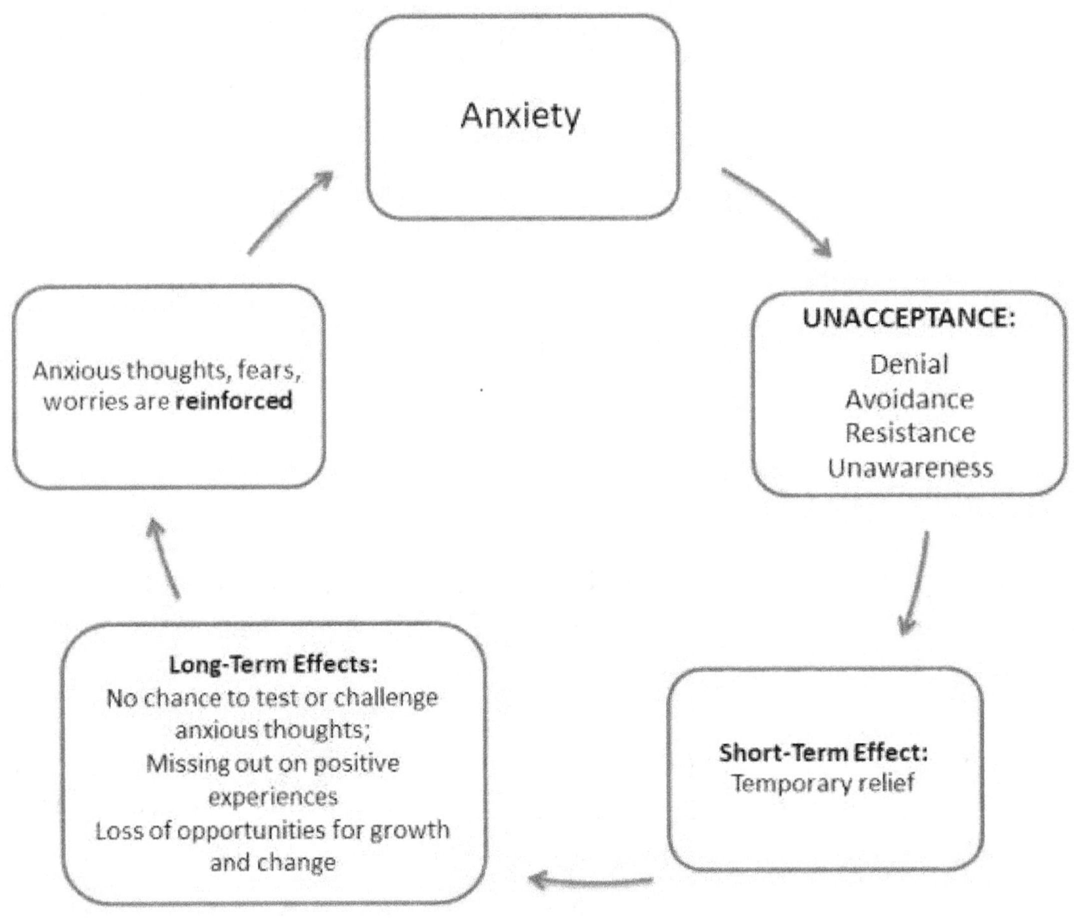

Worksheet 12: Acceptance Moments

If acceptance is unusual for you, this exercise will help it become more of a habit. It calls for intentionally creating moments of acceptance throughout the day.

Step 1. Morning reflection. As soon as you wake up, take a few minutes to set an intention for the day. Use acceptance statements to ground yourself. For example, "Today, I accept whatever emotions come my way and will approach them with kindness."

Step 2. Acceptance check-ins. Set reminders on your phone or calendar to pause and check in with yourself at least thrice daily (e.g., morning, midday, evening). When the reminder goes off, take a moment to pause and practice deep breathing while scanning your body for tension or discomfort.

Acknowledge any emotions or thoughts that are present. Use acceptance statements to acknowledge them without judgment. For example, "I notice I'm feeling anxious right now. It's okay to feel this way. I have a right to this emotion. But, you know what? I'm going to be okay," or "I'm feeling calm. I'm grateful for this feeling."

Step 3. Acceptance journaling. At the end of each day, take 5-10 minutes to write about your experiences. Reflect on moments when you felt anxious, angry, stressed, happy, or any other strong emotion. Here are a few journal prompts:

- *What emotions did I experience today?*
- *How did I respond to these emotions?*
- *What can I accept about my experience today?*

Example journal entry: Today, I felt really anxious before my meeting. I accept that this anxiety is part of my experience. I handled it by taking deep breaths, washing my face with cold water, and reminding myself it's okay to feel this way.

Step 4. Acceptance in action. Throughout the day, practice acceptance during various activities (e.g., during a commute, while eating, or during a break). Practice mindfulness by deliberately pausing, observing, and noting your thoughts and emotions. And whatever arises, accept them without judgment.

For example, while drinking your morning coffee, take a moment to notice its warmth, scent, and taste. Acknowledge any thoughts about the day ahead and remind yourself, "Whatever comes up, I'll be okay."

Step 5. Evening wind-down. Before bed, take a few minutes to "reflect and release" your day. **Important**: Try not to overthink or ruminate. Just go over the day and quickly acknowledge any unresolved emotions or thoughts. If it helps, use a mantra to help release any lingering stress.

Example: I did my best today. I accept what I accomplished and what I didn't. It's okay to let go and rest now.

Worksheet 13: Anxiety Acceptance Affirmations

This exercise involves creating and repeating statements that foster an attitude of acceptance toward your anxiety.

Step 1. Write down a few acceptance statements. Here are a few ideas:

[ ] I accept myself, including my anxious thoughts and feelings.
[ ] I accept that I am feeling anxious right now.
[ ] It's okay to feel this way at this moment.
[ ] I'm struggling. I accept that this is due to my anxiety.
[ ] I accept that my anxiety is part of my current experience, and that's okay.
[ ] My anxiety doesn't define me; it's just a part of what I'm experiencing right now.
[ ] It's okay to be anxious and uncertain and to not have all the answers right now.

Step 2. Repeat your acceptance statements to yourself daily, especially during anxious moments.

Step 3. Use soothing gestures like placing your hand on your heart or giving yourself a one-armed hug (i.e., place one hand over the opposite shoulder) while repeating your acceptance statements to reinforce the message.

Step 4. Practice this exercise for a few minutes daily and during heightened anxiety.

Worksheet 14: Using Acceptance to Handle Difficult Situations

This exercise aims to help you develop and practice acceptance in handling difficult situations, which can reduce their impact and help you respond more effectively.

Step 1. Identify a difficult situation. Think of a recent situation that caused you distress or discomfort, and write down a brief description.

Example: I never felt comfortable with my brother-in-law. I just feel he's always judging me. He lives overseas but was on vacation here, so my husband invited him for dinner. As soon as I found out, I couldn't sleep properly. I went into "hyper mode," obsessively planning and changing the food menu, thinking of how to rearrange the furniture, and worrying about making a fool of myself. My mind kept racing with anxious thoughts, and I felt a constant knot in my stomach. I was overwhelmed with the need to make everything perfect, fearing his judgment every step of the way.

Step 2. Observe your thoughts and feelings. Sit comfortably in a quiet place and close your eyes. Take a few deep breaths to center yourself. Recall the difficult situation you described above, and notice any changes in your body and the thoughts and feelings that arise NOW. Write them down AS IS. Don't censor yourself or analyze anything.

Example: I feel my heart racing and my palms sweating as I think about the event. I notice I'm slightly clenching my jaw. I'm getting anxious again.

Step 3. Acknowledge and accept your reactions without trying to change or judge them.

Examples:
- I accept that thinking about the situation is making me anxious right now.
- I think that whatever I did was still not enough. I accept this thought.
- I'm noticing that I'm afraid of being judged. I accept this fear as part of my current experience.

Step 4. Use mindfulness to <u>stay present</u>. Practice a short mindfulness meditation to stay present. Focus on your breath or use a guided mindfulness app (e.g., Headspace, Calm, etc.). When your mind wanders to a difficult situation, gently bring it back to the present moment. Do this for 5-10 minutes.

Step 5. After the mindfulness exercise, **take a few minutes to reflect** on the experience. Write down any insights or changes in perspective you noticed.

Example: After the mindfulness exercise, I felt calmer and more detached from the situation and my anxious thoughts. I accept that the situation is in the PAST and that I have no control over it anymore; I cannot change it, so I'll let it go with each deep exhale.

Step 6. Create an action plan. If this reflective exercise helped you identify a trigger, think of practical steps you can take the next time you face a similar difficult situation. Write down these steps and how you will use acceptance to handle the situation. (If you didn't identify any trigger, that's okay too.)

Example: I think I've always known deep inside that my brother-in-law is one of my anxiety triggers. I accept this fully now. I don't have an "action plan" for this yet, but my first step is to talk to my husband. I'll communicate that I prefer to limit contact with my brother-in-law as I go through my anxiety relief journey. I want to be better at managing my anxiety in general before addressing my brother-in-law.

Step 7. Celebrate yourself for facing and accepting your difficult emotions with simple, positive gestures. For example, engage in a favorite activity, treat yourself to a favorite snack or beverage, etc.

Chapter 11. Cognitive Defusion

"You don't have to control your thoughts. You just have to stop letting them control you." – Dan Millman

Do you remember the <u>What Causes Anxiety</u> table in Chapter 4? Although there is no exact data available, it's widely believed that **psychological factors** such as cognitive distortions (e.g., negative thinking patterns, mind traps, etc.) contribute significantly to many of today's mental health issues, including anxiety. (Correcting or modifying cognitive distortions is the main focus of CBT).

I don't know about you, but I don't recall a single positive thought whenever I experience anxiety. Most anxious thoughts are negative or, at the very least, unhelpful. They often involve worrying about potential dangers, failures, or negative outcomes, which leads to predominantly negative thinking patterns.

Here are just some of the most common beliefs or thinking patterns that people with anxiety disorders have:

Generalized Anxiety Disorder (GAD)	Specific Phobias (e.g., fear of heights, animals, flying, etc.)
I'm not good enough. *I'm unlovable.* *I'm always going to fail.* *I'm a burden to others.* *I'm weak.* *I'm not deserving of happiness.* *I'm a disappointment.* *I'm going to embarrass myself.* *I'm going to mess everything up.*	*If I encounter [the phobic object or situation], something terrible will happen.* *I won't be able to handle it if I face [the phobic object or situation].* *I need to avoid [phobic object or situation] because it's extremely dangerous, and I will get hurt or even die.* *I will LOSE IT if I'm near [the phobic object or situation].*

I'm broken.	*No one understands how frightening [the phobic object or situation] is to me.*
Social Anxiety Disorder (SAD, or Social Phobia)	**Panic Disorder**
Everyone is judging me. *I will embarrass myself.* *People will think I'm weird or awkward.* *I will say something stupid.* *I cannot handle social situations at all.*	*I'm losing control.* *I'm going crazy.* *I'm going to die during a panic attack.* *I can't breathe.* *I'm having a heart attack.*
Agoraphobia	**Separation Anxiety Disorder**
I won't be able to escape if something goes wrong. *Help won't be available if I need it.* *I'll lose control in public.* *No place is safe.* *Crowded places are dangerous.*	*Something bad will happen if I'm not with my loved one.* *I can't handle being alone.* *I'm going to be alone because I deserve it.* *I'll never see them again if they leave.* *They're going to leave me. They're going to leave me. They're going to leave me.* *They won't come back.*
Selective Mutism	**Health Anxiety (Hypochondriasis)**
People will judge me if I speak. *I never find the right words.* *It's safer to stay quiet.* *I will embarrass myself if I speak*	*I'm going to die from this.* *Doctors are missing something.* *Every symptom means something is wrong.*

up. No one in this world wants to hear what I have to say.	I need constant reassurance about my health. I have a serious illness.
Substance/Medication-Induced Anxiety Disorder	**Anxiety Disorder Due to Another Medical Condition (e.g., heart disease, chronic pain, etc.)**
This substance is making me anxious. Withdrawal symptoms will never go away. I can't control my anxiety without medication. My anxiety will get worse if I stop using. I'm not normal without my meds.	I'm terrified I won't be able to work anymore because of my illness. What if I never get better? I'm in pain. I'll always be in pain. I can't manage. I'm scared. Always scared. What if there's no cure? What if I use up all my savings? What if I end up alone with no one to care for me?

Our thoughts are very powerful. Science proves that how we think and feel colors our entire experience of physical reality.[118,119,120]

In CBT, the relationship between our thoughts, our emotions, and our behaviors is emphasized. This concept is called the *cognitive triangle*. More specifically, it aims to explain how our thoughts influence how we feel, which subsequently influences how we act, which then influences (or rather reinforces) our thoughts. On and on it goes...

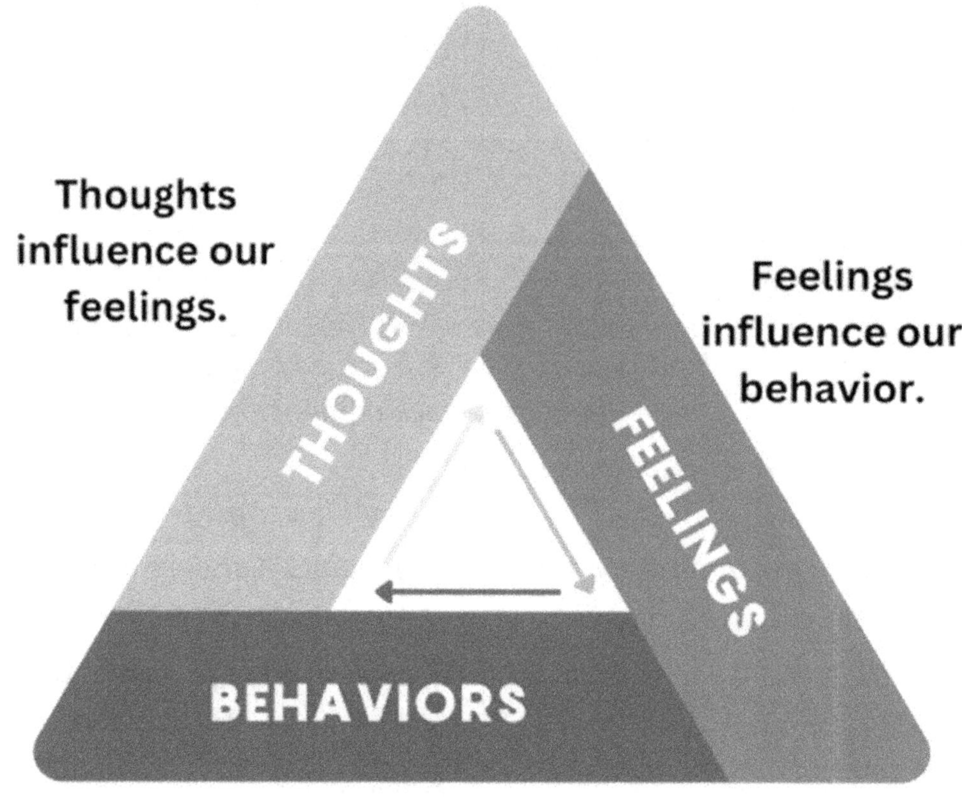

As you can see in the above image, anxiety is like a self-fulfilling prophesy. That's why, when it comes to anxiety, it's important to remember this: don't believe your thoughts. Why not? Because anxiety is generally considered to be an emotional response, not a logical one.

Now, as I always say, your emotions are valid. Nothing and no one should discredit your feelings. But... what if your *thoughts* are invalid? What if they're somehow distorted or misaligned from reality? THIS is the point of Cognitive Defusion.

Cognitive Defusion encourages you to detach, unglue, or unhook yourself from negative, unhelpful, unproductive, and unverified thoughts. By doing this, you break the cycle of the *cognitive triangle*, opening the door to new or alternative emotions and subsequent behaviors, ultimately leading to anxiety relief.

Further, cognitive defusion focuses on distancing yourself from your anxious thoughts and seeing them for what they are—JUST THOUGHTS (not reality). Besides, just because you have a thought doesn't mean you need to think about it.

Thoughts vs. Thinking

Thoughts are random ideas or images that pop into your mind (i.e., internal mental distractions). You don't have much control over them; they appear and disappear.

Thinking is a *process* of consciously engaging with your thoughts. It's deliberate and purposeful, involving reasoning and reflection. And because it's deliberate, you have more control over thinking because it involves active effort and focus.

So, bottom-line, thoughts are like clouds that drift into your mind without you doing anything. Thinking is deciding to shape those clouds into something meaningful.

When it comes to anxiety relief, it's important to understand this difference because now you know that not every anxiety-driven thought needs to be acted upon.

It takes practice to see your thoughts as just thoughts or uninvited mental events. The following exercises are designed to help you with this.

Worksheet 15: Cognitive Defusion Gameboard

Create psychological distance between your thoughts and yourself using the Cognitive Defusion Gameboard below. By using an interactive exercise, you can make the practice of *defusion* more engaging and enjoyable.

Now, keep an open mind, okay? Some activities may come across as "quirky," but just try them. As I often say, you'll never know what works until you try one that might.

Step 1. Gameboard. Print the gameboard image below or draw a similar one on a piece of paper or digital drawing tool.

Step 2. Game pieces. Get a small token to move around the board (a coin, a button, a chess piece, or any small object). You will also need a die to decide which technique to do and how many spaces to move.

Step 3. Instructions.

- Place your token on the starting point of the gameboard.
- Roll the die to determine how many spaces to move your token. Move the token accordingly.
- Based on the space you land on, practice the cognitive defusion technique mentioned on it.
- After practicing the defusion technique, take a moment to reflect on how you feel. Notice any changes in your anxiety levels or your perspective on the thought.
- IF you're still anxious, roll the die again and move your token to the next technique. Repeat the process of practicing the technique and reflecting on your experience until you feel relief.

START 1	2 Labeling Thoughts	3 Metaphors	4 Silly Voices	5 Thank Your Mind
10 Repetition	9 Thoughts ON Objects	8 Breathing with Thoughts	7 Objectify the Thought I	6 Writing & Observing
11 Objectify the Thought II	12 Musical Thoughts	13 **CHOOSE!** Do whatever technique you want today.	14 Mindful Acknowledgment	15 Storytelling
20 Labeling Thoughts	19 Metaphors	18 Silly Voices	17 Thank Your Mind	16 Repetition
21 Thoughts ON Objects	22 Breathing with Thoughts	23 Objectify the Thought I	24 Writing & Observing	25 Objectify the Thought II
26 Musical Thoughts	27 Mindful Acknowledgment	28 Storytelling	**FINISH** Go and celebrate. You deserve it!	

- **Labeling Thoughts.** When a negative thought arises, label it as a thought rather than a fact. For example, instead of "I'm going to die," say, "I'm having the THOUGHT that I'm going to die."

- **Metaphors.** Visualize your thoughts in a way that helps you see them as separate from yourself. For example, imagine your thoughts as leaves floating down a stream or clouds passing by in the sky.

- **Silly Voices.** Say your negative thoughts out loud in a silly or exaggerated voice. For example, repeat "I'm a failure" in the voice of a cartoon character. This can make the thought seem less serious and impactful. (*Just sharing: I like doing this using a Minion-type voice.*)

- **Thank Your Mind.** Acknowledge your thoughts without letting them control you. For example, when a negative thought arises, say, "Thanks, mind. That's an interesting thought."

- **Repetition.** Repeat the thought out loud or in your head until it loses meaning and becomes just a series of sounds. For example, repeat "I'm going to get trapped in an elevator" repeatedly until it feels like a nonsensical string of words.

- **Thoughts ON Objects.** Imagine placing your thoughts on various objects and watching them move away. For example, picture an anxious thought as a balloon drifting into the sky, a car driving away, or your pet cat running away from you.

- **Writing and Observing.** Write down your thoughts and observe them as if you were an outsider. For example, write "Everyone is looking at me and judging me" on a piece of paper. Look at the paper and remind yourself that it's just a thought, not a fact. Next, crumple the paper and throw it in the trash can.

- **Breathing with Thoughts.** Use your breath to help create distance from your thoughts. For example, practice Mindful Breathing.

- **Objectify the Thought I.** Turn the thought into an object. Visualize your thought as a physical object, like a rock or a pen. Name it (or not), see it as separate from yourself, and then move on.

Just sharing: Peanut butter. I swear I don't know where it came from. I was having anxious thoughts, and the words "peanut butter" popped into my head. I didn't question or analyze it; I just went with it. So, whenever anxiety would start, I'd say something like, "Well, "peanut butter" entered my mind again" or "Hmmm, peanut butter" or "Hi peanut butter". I wouldn't voice out or explain the thought; I just called it peanut butter. And for some weird reason, the grip of my anxious thought would loosen.

- **Objectify the Thought II.** Turn the thought into an object. Visualize your thoughts as a physical object, like a rock or a coffee mug. Look at it, examine it, and see it as separate from yourself.

Maxene[2], a close friend of mine whose anxiety went from bad to worse after going through divorce trauma, has this to share.

"I was blindsided by my divorce. On my side, I thought we were A-Okay. And then, one day, he just sat me down and... left. I already had GAD, but it was manageable. After the divorce, I spiraled. That was three years, countless therapy and counseling sessions, and a round of anti-anxiety meds that gave me severe withdrawal symptoms ago.

Anyway... when I learned about objectifying thoughts, I bought a goldfish for this very purpose. Whenever I sensed anxiety looming, I would look at that goldfish and imagine it as my anxiety. (I didn't name it, so it remained detached from me.) I don't know why, but it worked. Physically seeing the goldfish helped me objectify my anxious thoughts, making them seem external and manageable rather than an internal and overwhelming part of myself."

- **Musical Thoughts.** Sing your negative thoughts to the tune of a familiar song. For example, sing "I can't do this. I'm going to fail" to the tune of "Twinkle, Twinkle Little Star."

- **Mindful Acknowledgment.** Recognize the thought without trying to change or judge it. For example, when you think a negative thought such as "Everyone is belittling me," say to yourself, "I notice I'm having the thought that..."

- **Storytelling.** Turn your negative thoughts into a story with a beginning, middle, and end. This will help you see your negative thoughts as just ONE possible interpretation. (Note: This technique might take some time, but you don't have to finish your story in one go. It can be a work in progress as long as doing so provides relief.)

Here's a sample short story based on the anxious thought, "I don't feel safe in this world."

--- *The Beginning* ---

Emily had always felt a creeping sense of danger lurking around every corner. Every news story about a crime or disaster seemed to confirm her fears: the world is a dangerous place. This anxiety kept her indoors, far away from the unknown variables of the outside world.

--- *The Middle* ---

One day, a power outage struck her neighborhood. Emily was struck with anxiety, but she didn't go out. After all, she ensured she had enough supplies for at least a week. However, the lack of power meant Emily couldn't get online by Day 3 (she had already exhausted all her devices' power). By the end of the week, Emily was starting to feel loneliness like she never felt before.

By the end of the following week, Emily forced herself out of her apartment in search of light, warmth, water, and any contact. She ventured to a nearby community center where neighbors gathered with candles and flashlights. There, Emily met Alex, a volunteer who noticed her discomfort and started a gentle conversation. Alex shared stories about his travels around the world, describing not just the challenges but the incredible kindness of strangers he'd encountered.

As Alex talked about his tales, Emily began to think, "How can this man be so OUT there and feel so safe and happy? He doesn't look fearful in the least of the unknown." Emily questioned whether the world might hold more safety than she had realized.

--- *The End* ---

Over time, Emily decided to challenge her fears. She started small, visiting the library and nearby local parks because they were quiet and peaceful. She then visited a small coffee shop about a block from where she lived, where Emily discovered peaceful moments, a few friendly faces, and the most amazing croissant sandwich she had ever eaten! (Part of her was thinking, "I've been missing this?!")

Each positive experience built her confidence, slowly reshaping her belief about the world's dangers. Emily and Alex kept in touch, and two years later, she joined him on a volunteer trip abroad, finding a sense of safety not in isolation but in the shared humanity and kindness of the people she met. Emily also realized that the world hadn't changed, but her interpretation of it had transformed.

Worksheet 16: Deal with Real

Did you know our brains can't distinguish between what's real and what's not? Studies show that our brains often respond to real and imagined scenarios with the same intensity.[121,122,123] This is why, even when we logically understand that our fears or worries might not happen, we still tend to react to them (in both emotion and behavior) as if they're real.

Does this mean we're all just walking around, incapable of knowing what's real and what's not? No. Humans have a sort of built-in "reality threshold." If a signal or stimulus crosses this threshold, the brain logs it as "real;" if it doesn't, it files it under "imagined."[124]

The "reality threshold" usually works because most imagined signals are faint. Unfortunately, this is not the case for those who suffer from anxiety. Our imagined signals are so intense they *cross* the reality threshold, making us mistake them for reality.

This following exercise aims to help you successfully detach or defuse from anxious thoughts and get you to focus on facts or what's real.

Step 1. Identify your anxious thoughts. Sit in a quiet place with a pen and notebook. Close your eyes and take a few deep breaths to calm yourself. Next, write down the thoughts that are causing your anxiety. Be as specific as you can.

Example: I'm consumed with financial worries. I'm afraid I'm going to go bankrupt and end up homeless.

Step 2. Emotion check-in. On a scale of 1 to 10 (1 being the lowest and 10 being the highest), how intense is your anxiety right now? Encircle your answer.

1	2	3	4	5	6	7	8	9	10

Step 3. Label your anxious thoughts. Read the thoughts you wrote down, and then say any of the following to yourself:

[ ] This is a thought, not a fact.
[ ] This is a passing thought. It doesn't need mental energy or intention.
[ ] I'm having a THOUGHT. I don't need to think about it.
[ ] This is just a thought I'm having. It doesn't define me.
[ ] This is a thought, a mental event. It's not my current reality.
[ ] This is an uninvited thought. I don't need to have a conversation with it.

Step 4. Visualize the thought as an object. Choose an object representing your thought (e.g., rock, leaf, cup, etc.). Imagine holding the object in your hand, examining it from all angles. This step helps you look at the thought with detached curiosity.

Step 5. Examine the evidence. Next, you will differentiate between thoughts and facts by examining the evidence. Write down as much evidence as possible *for* and *against* each thought.

Anxious Thoughts	What evidence *supports* this thought?	What evidence *contradicts* this thought?
Example: I'm going to go bankrupt.	*Example: I don't have any savings.*	*Example:* *- I have a stable job with a regular income.* *- I have a friend good with finances and can help give me budgeting tips.*

Anxious Thoughts	What evidence *supports* this thought?	What evidence *contradicts* this thought?

Step 6. Emotion check-in. Do your emotions match the *facts* of the situation, or do they match your *assumptions* of the situation? Encircle your answer.

FACTS	ASSUMPTIONS

On a scale of 1 to 10 (1 being the lowest and 10 being the highest), how intense is your anxiety right now? Encircle your answer.

1	2	3	4	5	6	7	8	9	10

Hopefully, you can feel less intense emotions by taking a step back and writing down evidence for and against your anxious thoughts. If not, that's okay too. Remember, your emotions are always valid.

Step 7. Reframe. Replace each negative and unhelpful thought with a more balanced, fact-based perspective.

Anxious Thought	Is this thought helpful? Why or why not?	What's a more realistic, fact-based way to look at this situation?
Example: I'm going to go bankrupt.	*Example: NO. I just get more anxious when I think about this.*	*Example: I may not have any savings now, but having a stable job means I can tighten my belt and put away a little something starting my next paycheck.*

Anxious Thought	Is this thought helpful? Why or why not?	What's a more realistic, fact-based way to look at this situation?

Step 8. Take a little break to focus on the present moment. Practice mindfulness by focusing on your current surroundings. Use your senses to notice:

- FIVE things you can see,
- FOUR things you can hear,
- THREE things you can touch or feel,
- TWO things you can smell and
- ONE thing you can taste.

Step 9. Create an action plan. When we're anxious, we get stuck in a place of worry. Shifting your mind from "worry" to "solution" helps break the anxiety cycle and empowers you to take control of the situation. So, identify specific steps you can take to address the issue or mitigate its impact. This proactive approach reduces anxiety and fosters a sense of accomplishment and confidence!

Anxious Thought	What can I do right now?	What can I do in the near future?
Example: I'm going to go bankrupt.	*Example:* *- Sit down and create a*	*Example:* *- Look for additional*

Anxious Thought	What can I do right now?	What can I do in the near future?
	budget. *- Go through my stuff and identify at least three things I can sell online or to family and friends.*	*sources of income.* *- Consult a financial advisor.*

Important: If you can't fill this table out just yet, that's okay. You might find that the best thing you can do right now is to simply process steps 1-6 above or talk to someone for help or advice. The important thing is to start training your mind to focus on present facts and reality.

Chapter 12. Self as Context

"It is the mark of an educated mind to be able to entertain
a thought without accepting it." – Aristotle

Self as Context is a skill that helps you see yourself separate from your thoughts, feelings, and experiences. It's about understanding that **you're MORE than the anxious contents of your mind**.

Cognitive Defusion vs. Self as Context

Many are confused by these two core skills in ACT, so let me quickly differentiate them here.

Cognitive defusion involves distancing yourself from your thoughts to see them as just thoughts, not truths. Self as context refers to the perspective of viewing yourself as the observer of your experiences rather than being defined by them.

Cognitive Defusion

Consumed by anxiety.

Hmmm, I'm noticing that I'm having anxious thoughts.

Self as Context

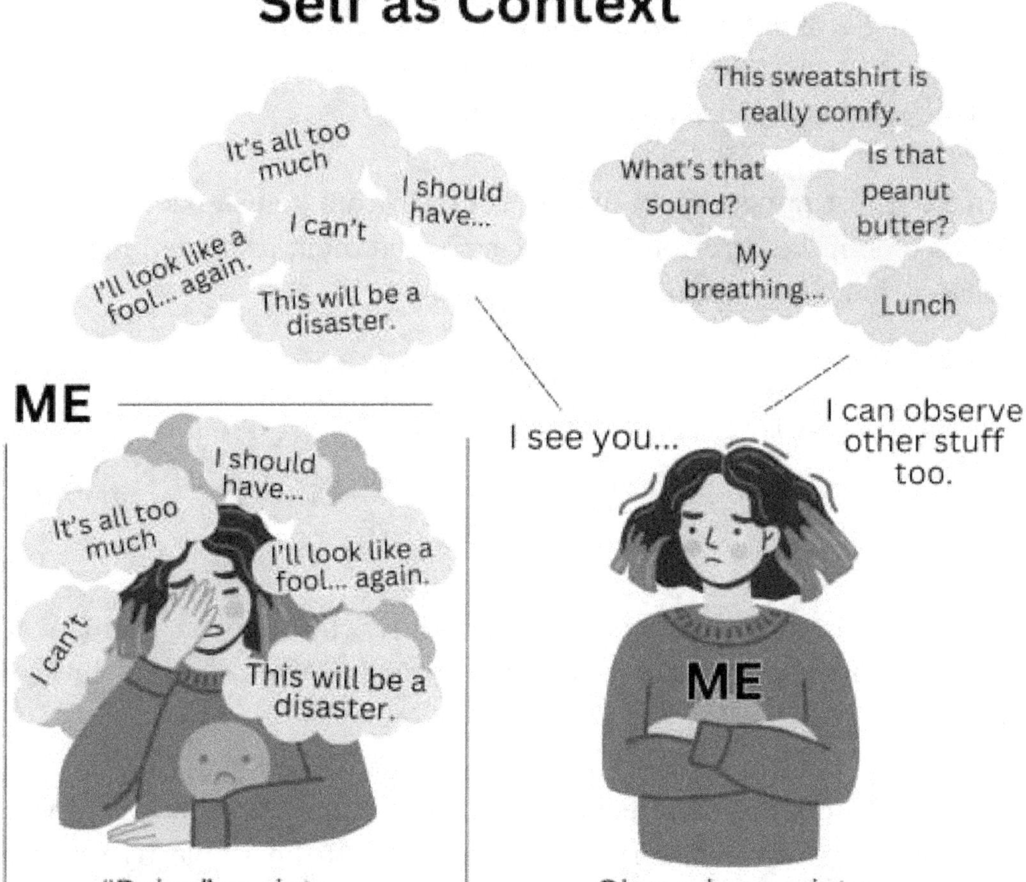

"Being" anxiety.

Observing anxiety.

Separating one's self from one's own thoughts isn't easy, all the more so for people with anxiety. For one, anxious thoughts can feel like warnings of danger, making it hard to ignore or detach from them. They also often come with a high "emotional charge," which makes the thought feel more intense and thus harder to let go. Lastly, anxiety is not a one-time event. We often experience the same thought patterns over and over, creating a cycle that's hard to break.

But as you know by now, beliefs and thoughts rooted in anxiety can be damaging in the long run. Remember, you're NOT your thoughts, but think of them long enough, and they can be.

For instance, if you think you are unlovable, you might start to view yourself as terrible or disgusting. Similarly, if your thoughts constantly revolve around "getting sick," you might begin to see yourself as an "ill person" and even start to exhibit symptoms of the illness you fear. (This is similar to the *nocebo effect*, where negative expectations can lead to negative health outcomes, much like the opposite of the placebo effect.)

So, it's not just important to unglue yourself from your anxious thoughts and feelings (*cognitive defusion*) but to clearly see them as something completely separate from your person.

You have thoughts. You are NOT your thoughts.
You experience emotions. You are NOT your emotions.

If you're NOT your thoughts and emotions, who are you then? You're an **observer** of them. It's the "you" that's noticing what's going through your mind.

Now, your thoughts and feelings change frequently. However, "you," the observer (Observer Self) remains consistent. It's the stable part of you that experiences all your mental and emotional states.

It's important to identify as the "Observer Self" so that you realize that your anxious thoughts and feelings are separate from who you are as a person. So, instead of saying or thinking, "I'm invisible," you can say or think, "I notice that I'm feeling invisible." This shift helps you see anxiety as something that you're experiencing, not something that defines you.

Also, something amazing happens when you identify as the "Observer Self." You start to see anxiety as something you can manage better because it's "separate" from you. And because they're separate, they become less overwhelming. You might even become curious about it! For example, suppose you're overwhelmed and start thinking, "I cannot handle this!"

Without Self as Context, you might feel completely engulfed by this thought, believing it fully and thus exacerbating your anxiety.

With Self as Context, you go, "Hmmm, I'm having the thought I can't handle this." This acknowledgment helps you see the thought as a temporary experience. You realize that while the thought is present, it doesn't define your capability or who you are. Observer Self remains calm and detached, enabling you to consider ways to manage anxiety without being overwhelmed by it.

The following exercises are all designed to help you see yourself as the Observer Self whenever you experience anxiety.

Worksheet 17: The Movie in My Mind

Step 1. Find a comfortable place to sit where you won't be disturbed. Take a few deep, calming breaths to center yourself.

Step 2. Close your eyes and **notice your thoughts** as they come and go.

Step 3. Shift to the Observer Self by imagining sitting in a movie theater, watching your thoughts play out on the screen. You are the observer, <u>not</u> the actor.

Step 4. After a few minutes, open your eyes and **reflect** on the experience. Notice how you could observe your thoughts without being caught up in them.

Step 5. Journal (optional). Write down your thoughts during the exercise and describe how observing it from a distance felt.

Example: I thought about how alone I feel since the divorce. I always think of the phrase, "I don't see a future anymore." However, observing my thoughts like a movie made me realize that while my feelings of loneliness and despair are real, it doesn't define my entire existence. In my "movie," I saw my 11-year-old daughter and remembered that I still have meaningful connections. This helped me feel less overwhelmed and more hopeful about building a new chapter in my life.

Worksheet 18: The Lighthouse

Imagine that you're a lighthouse standing tall and firm on the shore. It remains steady and strong despite the changing weather and turbulent waves around it. Your thoughts and feelings are like the weather and waves—they come and go, but you, as the lighthouse, remain constant.

Step 1. Find a quiet place where you can sit comfortably without distractions. Take a few deep breaths to center yourself and prepare for the visualization.

Step 2. Create a vivid mental image of the lighthouse. Close your eyes and picture a lighthouse standing tall on the shore. Visualize its strong foundation, tall structure, and the bright light it emits to guide ships safely through the storm. Imagine the waves crashing against the lighthouse and the weather changing, but the lighthouse stands firm and unaffected.

Step 3. Identify and accept your anxious thoughts and feelings. Think about your current anxieties and worries. What thoughts and feelings are causing you distress? Write them down or mentally note them.

Example: I am worried about my job security.

Step 4. Connect your thoughts and feelings to the weather and waves. Imagine each of your anxious thoughts and feelings as different weather conditions or waves crashing against the lighthouse. For example, your worries could be represented by a stormy sky. Acknowledge these thoughts and feelings without judgment, just as the lighthouse acknowledges the weather and waves without being affected by them.

Step 5. Internalize the perspective of being the lighthouse. Remind yourself that you are the lighthouse—steady, strong, and constant. Your anxious thoughts and feelings are temporary and external, like the weather and waves. Say to yourself, "I am the lighthouse. My thoughts and feelings are like the weather and waves—they come and go, but I remain steady and strong."

Step 6. When you're ready, open your eyes and take a few moments to reflect on how the visualization made you feel. Write down any insights or feelings of calmness and strength that you experienced.

Example: I felt less overwhelmed by my worries. The lighthouse visualization helped me see my thoughts and feelings as temporary and external.

Whenever you feel overwhelmed by anxiety, take a moment to visualize the lighthouse. Remember that you are the lighthouse; your thoughts and feelings are like the weather and waves—*they will pass.*

Worksheet 19: The Chessboard

Imagine your mind as a chessboard; chess pieces are your thoughts and feelings. The pieces can be black or white, representing negative and positive thoughts and feelings. Just like playing chess in real life, remember that the chessboard holds all these pieces but is not affected by the game itself. It simply provides the space for the game to unfold.

Step 1. Find a quiet place where you can sit comfortably without distractions. Take a few deep breaths to center yourself and prepare for the visualization.

Step 2. Recognize and categorize your thoughts and feelings as chess pieces. Think about any recent (or current) anxious thoughts and feelings. Write them down. Label each thought or feeling as either a black piece (negative) or a white piece (positive). (This step alone helps with anxiety because it makes you realize that negative AND positive thoughts and emotions exist.)

Example:
I'm scared of failing (black piece).
I felt proud of my work yesterday (white piece).

Step 3. Visualize your thoughts and feelings as pieces on a chessboard. On a piece of paper, draw a simple chessboard or imagine one in your mind. Place each thought or feeling on the chessboard. See them as separate pieces on the board. Visualize the black and white pieces moving around, sometimes in conflict, sometimes in harmony.

Here's an example:

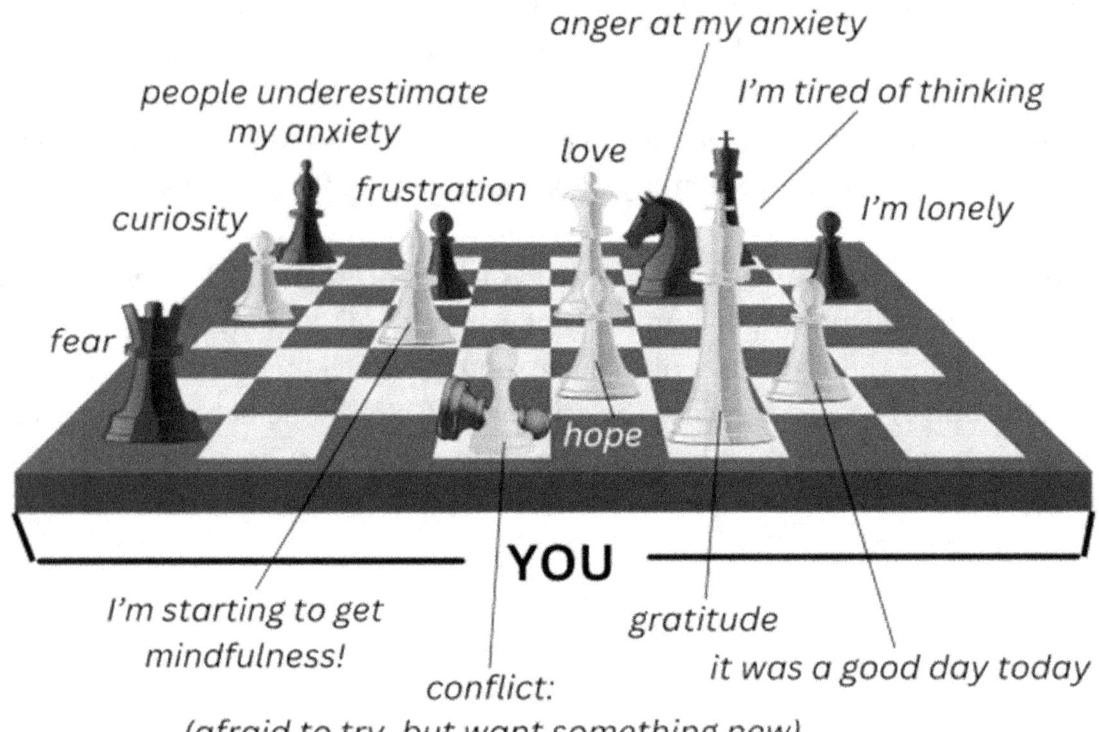

Step 4. Recognize that the chessboard is you (your mind). Realize that you, as the observer of your thoughts and feelings, are like the chessboard. You hold all these thoughts and feelings (chess pieces), but they DO NOT define you. Say to yourself, "I am the chessboard. I can hold all my thoughts and feelings without being controlled by them."

Step 5. Observe without judging. Whenever an anxious thought or feeling arises, just place it on the chessboard in your mind. Watch it without judgment. Remember, the pieces may move, be added, or disappear... but the chessboard remains steady and unaffected.

Worksheet 20: Self as Context Journal

Step 1. Create a dedicated space for your Self as Context journal. You can use a notebook, journal, digital document, etc. Divide each page into two columns: "Observed Thoughts and Feelings" and "Observing Self."

Step 2. Set aside 10-15 minutes to reflect at the end of each day. In the "Observed Thoughts and Feelings" column, write down any anxious thoughts or feelings you experienced during the day. In the "Observing Self" column, write about your experience of having these thoughts and feelings.

Observed Thoughts and Feelings	Observing Self
Example: *I felt a panic attack come on as my partner was leaving this morning.*	*Example:* *I noticed that I had a lot of worries about them cheating or being abandoned as they were leaving. I observed this worry and felt it in my chest. I also felt my jaw clenching. I then took a deep breath and told myself, "I am not my worry; I am the one noticing it. I am having an uninvited mental event. This is not my reality."*

Observed Thoughts and Feelings	Observing Self

Step 3. Observe without judging. As you write in your journal, practice observing your thoughts and feelings without judging them as good or bad. Simply note their presence and your experience of observing them.

Step 4. Reflect on any patterns and insights. At the end of each week, review your journal entries. Look for patterns in your anxious thoughts and feelings and how your Observing Self responded to them. Write a summary of any insights or patterns you noticed.

Example: This week, I observed that my anxiety often spikes in the morning. It begins when my partner gets ready for work and intensifies when they leave. I realized that maybe it's because I'm the one literally being left behind that triggers my anxiety. Now that I'm noticing this pattern, I think maybe I should shift to going to the gym most mornings. Maybe "getting ready" and "leaving" at the same time helps.

Step 5. Continue and express gratitude. Review your journal and reflect on your progress at the end of each month. Write a note of appreciation to yourself for the effort you've put into managing your anxiety.

Example: I'm proud of consistently journaling and observing my thoughts and feelings. I can see how this practice is helping me feel more in control and less defined by my anxiety.

Worksheet 21: Me, Them, and The Observer

This exercise will help you get anxiety relief by encouraging a sense of detachment through examining your anxious thoughts and sensations from multiple perspectives or viewpoints. The goal is to realize that your thoughts or what you fear are not the only possible outcomes in real life.

Step 1. Create a dedicated space for your Perspective-Taking exercise. You can use a notebook, journal, digital document, etc. Divide each page into three columns: "Me," "Them," and "Observer."

Step 2. Recall a recent event that caused anxiety, and then describe this event from the following points of view:

- **Me**: Describe the situation from your own perspective.
- **Them**: Describe the same situation from the perspective of someone else involved. This could be a friend, family member, or even a stranger present during the event. Write down what you imagine their thoughts, feelings, and reactions might have been.
- **Observer**: Describe the same situation from the perspective of an impartial observer, someone outside looking in and watching the event unfold. This observer has no emotional attachment to the situation. Write down what this person might see and think.

Event/Situation: *Team building weekend with colleagues.*		
Me	**Them**	**Observer**
Example: I woke up really anxious that Saturday. I just felt that something really bad was going to happen.	*Example: When I arrived at work, my colleague Ben joined me in the elevator.*	*Example: The Observer saw two people walk into an elevator...*
But I went anyway.	*He seemed calm and talked about how good this weekend would be*	*One was quiet. The other was talking animatedly about a*

Otherwise, thoughts of losing my job would consume me over the weekend.	*for the team, that we all deserved to have fun, etc. He didn't seem to notice my anxiety at all.*	*team-building activity. The Observer thought, "That might be fun."*
At work, I took the elevator to the 17th floor, but in my head, I was thinking…		
I'd probably say something wrong and embarrass myself in front of everyone. What if I can't participate in the activities? I'll be humiliated, and no one will take me seriously at work!		

Event/Situation:

Me	Them	Observer

Step 3. Reflect on the different perspectives. Read through each section of your writing. Reflect on how each perspective provides a different view of the same event. Next, consider how anxiety might influence your perspective while the other perspectives provide a more balanced view.

Example: Reading through the "Them" and "Observer" sections, I realize that my intense fear was not shared by my colleague or noticed by the observer.

Whenever you feel anxious about a situation, pause and try to view it from the perspectives of "Me," "Them," and "Observer." This practice will help you detach from your immediate anxious reaction and see the situation more clearly.

Chapter 13. Values Clarification

"When your values are clear to you, making decisions becomes easier." - Roy E. Disney

Values clarification is identifying and understanding what is most important to you. Your values guide your actions, reflect what you stand for, and give your life meaning and purpose.

I've come to realize that time really does pass quickly. When I experienced my burnout and breakdown, I was a 30-something someone. The weird part was recognizing that I wasn't *deliberate* about who I became. It was like life "just happened," and I woke up one day as "Ava." I know I'm not alone in this.

As children, we often adopt our parents' values as our own. When we venture out into the world, we tend to live by the values imposed by society. In relationships, we frequently prioritize other people's expectations and desires above our own. And what about the values imposed on us by cultural norms, educational institutions, or workplace environments? All of these make it challenging to discern what truly matters to us as individuals.

Important: This is not about assigning blame to others or judging ourselves for being influenced by external values. Instead, it's about recognizing how these influences shape us and taking the proactive step to identify and embrace our own values. Now is the time to look *inward* and figure out what values YOU consider important at this stage in your life.

What does clarifying your values have to do with anxiety?! If you don't know what's important to you, it can cause or feed your anxiety because:

- **You lack direction and purpose.** Without clear values, you might feel aimless or directionless, unsure of what you want to achieve or where to go. This lack of direction can create a sense of uncertainty and instability, which fuels anxiety. When you don't know what you stand for or what you're working towards, every decision can feel overwhelming.

- **You often feel stressed and conflicted.** Values help guide your decisions and actions. Without them, you might find yourself in situations that conflict with your innate subconscious beliefs or desires. This internal conflict can lead to stress and anxiety as you struggle to reconcile your actions with your undefined values. For example, you might take on a job or relationship that doesn't align with your true self, leading to chronic dissatisfaction and anxiety.

- **You find it difficult to make decisions.** Clear values provide a framework for making decisions. When you don't know your values, even small decisions can become paralyzing. This constant indecision and second-guessing can increase anxiety because you might always be worried about making the wrong choice and its potential consequences.

- **You're not living authentically.** Living according to others' expectations rather than your own values can create an inauthentic life. This can lead to anxiety because you feel a disconnect or mismatch between your true self and the life you are living. Over time, this can result in feelings of emptiness and anxiety.

- **You may develop low self-esteem and self-worth.** When your actions and life path don't align with your values, it can affect how you view yourself. This misalignment can lead to feelings of inadequacy and low self-worth, which are closely linked to anxiety. You might feel like you're not living up to your potential or being true to yourself.

- **Avoidance behavior might become your norm.** Without clear values, you might avoid situations that require you to confront your true desires and beliefs. This avoidance can lead to increased anxiety over time because you're not addressing the root causes of your discomfort. Avoiding difficult decisions or conversations prevents personal growth and perpetuates a cycle of anxiety.

So, HOW do you clarify your values?

Firstly, I find that it's futile to keep looking at the past and trying to figure out where things went "wrong." It's a waste of time. Yes, reflecting on past mistakes and experiences and learning from them is beneficial. However, ruminating about the past and constantly wondering "what if" isn't helpful. (Remember, you cannot undo the past.) So, when clarifying your values, focus on who you are NOW and what you hope to achieve in the future. The exercises in this chapter are designed to help you do just that.

Important: Approach the following exercises with curiosity. Don't see them as tasks or responsibilities. View them as an exciting journey into self-discovery!

Worksheet 22: Discovering Values Using Values Cards

Step 1. Print. Print out the Values Cards table below and cut out each value. Please feel free to add more if you want to.

ACCEPTANCE embracing oneself and others as they are, without judgment	**ACCOUNTABILITY** taking responsibility for one's actions and decisions	**AUTHENTICITY** being true to oneself and living in alignment with one's values, beliefs, and identity
BALANCE finding equilibrium between work, relationships, and self-care	**CALMNESS** maintaining a state of tranquility and peace of mind	**CARING** showing kindness and concern for others
COMMITMENT dedication to pursuing one's goals and values	**COMPASSION** showing empathy and understanding towards others	**CONFIDENCE** believing in one's abilities and self-worth
CONNECTION building and maintaining meaningful relationships	**CONSISTENCY** acting in a reliable and predictable manner	**CONTENTMENT** finding satisfaction and happiness in the present moment
COURAGE facing challenges and fears with bravery	**CREATIVITY** using imagination and innovation to express oneself	**DEPENDABILITY** being reliable and trustworthy

DETERMINATION persistently pursuing one's goals despite obstacles	**EMPATHY** understanding and sharing the feelings of others	**ENCOURAGEMENT** supporting and uplifting yourself and others
FAIRNESS treating others with equity and justice	**FLEXIBILITY** adapting to new circumstances and situations	**FORGIVENESS** letting go of resentment and freeing yourself from negative thoughts and emotions
GRATITUDE recognizing and appreciating the positives in life	**GROWTH** striving for personal development and self-improvement	**HARMONY** creating a peaceful and balanced environment
HEALTH maintaining physical and mental well-being	**HONESTY** being truthful and transparent in actions and words	**HUMILITY** valuing modesty and acknowledging one's limitations
INDEPENDENCE relying on oneself and making decisions autonomously	**INNER PEACE** achieving a state of mental and emotional tranquility	**INTEGRITY** upholding moral principles and honesty
KINDNESS showing generosity and consideration towards others	**LEARNING** continuously seeking knowledge and personal growth	**LOYALTY** being faithful and supportive to others

MINDFULNESS being present and fully engaged in the moment	**OPEN-MINDEDNESS** being receptive to new ideas and different perspectives	**PATIENCE** remaining calm and tolerant in challenging situations
PERSEVERANCE persisting in the face of difficulties	**POSITIVITY** maintaining an optimistic and hopeful attitude	**PURPOSE** living with intention and direction
RELIABILITY being dependable and consistent in actions	**RESILIENCE** bouncing back from adversity and maintaining strength	**RESPECT** valuing and honoring others
SELF-ACCEPTANCE embracing one's own worth and abilities	**SELF-CARE** prioritizing one's own well-being and health	**SELF-COMPASSION** treating oneself with kindness and understanding
SELF-DISCIPLINE exercising control over one's actions and impulses	**STABILITY** a sense of security, predictability, and steadiness in one's environment and life	**SIMPLICITY** seeing and appreciating the simple things in life
SUPPORTIVENESS providing help and encouragement to others	**TOLERANCE** accepting and respecting differences in others	**TRUST** believing in the reliability and integrity of others

<table>
<tr>
<td>WISDOM

applying knowledge and experience to make sound decisions</td>
<td>Add another value you want here...</td>
<td>Add another value you want here...</td>
</tr>
</table>

Step 2. Reflect. Take time to read each value and consider what it means to you personally. Reflect on how each value has played a role in your life and how it might help you manage anxiety.

Step 3. Sort. Sort the cards into three piles:

- **Very Important**: Values that resonate deeply with you and feel essential to your life.
- **Somewhat Important**: Values that matter to you but are not as crucial as the "Very Important" ones.
- **Less Important:** Values that are nice to cultivate but aren't critical to your sense of self or well-being.

Step 4. Prioritize. From the "Very Important" pile, choose your Top 5-10 values. These will be the core values that you can focus on to guide your actions and decisions.

Of course, you're "Somewhat Important" and "Less Important" values are also critical. But just focus on your "Very Important" values for now so that you don't get overwhelmed.

Step 5. Explore. Consider how each of your top values can help you manage your anxiety.

Example:
Mindfulness: Practicing mindfulness can help me stay present and hopefully reduce worries about the future.

Step 6. Accomplish. For each of your top values, write down at least three simple but specific actions to put the value into practice. For example:

Example: Mindfulness
- *Set aside 10 minutes each morning for mindfulness meditation.*
- *Do **Mindful Walking** every Saturday morning.*
- *List 3 things I'm grateful for at the end of each day.*

Step 7. Integrate. Make a conscious effort to incorporate your top values into your daily routines and decision-making processes. This alignment can help reduce anxiety by providing a sense of direction and purpose.

Step 8. Review and adjust. Every now and then, review your values and how they're influencing your life. Reflect on any changes and adjust your action plans to align with your core values.

Worksheet 23: Uncovering Values

Even though you might not have taken a moment to deeply reflect and identify your values (like what you did in the previous exercise), it doesn't mean you've never lived according to at least some of them. This exercise aims to "open your eyes" to values you may have already prioritized by reflecting on past events that have helped alleviate your anxiety.

Step 1. Reflect on past moments of anxiety relief. Think about a time when you felt relief from anxiety and experienced a sense of peace or fulfillment. What were you doing? What values do you think you were honoring in that moment?

Example: I remember feeling a sense of calm when I spent time gardening. The quiet and connection to nature eased my anxiety.

Step 2. Recall "decision points." Remember when you were faced with a decision during an anxious period. What guided you to make the choice you did? What values were at play?

*Example: I once chose between attending a high-stress social event (a colleague's gender reveal party) or staying home and reading a book about my anxiety disorder. I chose to stay home, valuing **self-care, growth,** and **peace** over social obligations. I think this is also about **authenticity** because I knew if I attended, I wouldn't just be anxious; I'd be "faking it" for hours for people I barely knew.*

Step 3. Envision your ideal self or your ideal life in an alternate universe. What are the most important things to you in that vision? What values do those things represent, especially in the context of managing anxiety?

Example: I see myself working in a peaceful environment, perhaps as a yoga instructor. This vision represents my values of tranquility, health, mindfulness, and balance.

Step 4. Optional: Think about your role models. If you want more insight, consider people you admire. What qualities do they have that you respect and want to emulate?

Example:
*My grandfather is my role model. To me, he was always a picture of **kindness**, **calmness**, **patience**, and **family**.*

Step 5. Optional: Consider what makes you anxious. If you want more insight, reflect on the past month. Reflect on situations that made you anxious. Often, anxiety arises when our values are violated or when you're not living in alignment with them.

Example:
Situation*: I suffered an anxiety attack when I was told that I had to participate in a competitive work event designed to foster "team spirit" through a series of high-pressure games. I was in distress for weeks, anxious about performing well under stress and the social dynamics involved.*
Reflection*: Thinking about it now, I realize that my anxiety hinted that I was straying from my deeper values of calmness and inner peace. Also, I'm so not an extrovert so participating in the event and being "game" was making me feel like a fraud.*
Values Identified*: calmness, inner peace, personal authenticity*

Situation:	
Reflection:	
Values Identified:	

Step 6. Identify common themes. Reflect on your answers from the previous steps and look for common themes or patterns. These can give you clues about your personal values related to anxiety relief.

Example: I've noticed that most of my anxiety revolves around work (e.g., work performance, interaction with colleagues, social work events, etc.). I mostly get triggered there and bring the resulting anxiety with me everywhere throughout the day.

Step 7. Prioritize the values you've identified. Based on what feels most authentic and important, consider which values you want to prioritize in your daily life and decision-making, particularly in managing anxiety.

*Example: I realize that I want to prioritize **inner peace**. Looking back, I seek daily opportunities to create calm environments and practice relaxation techniques.*

Tip: Repeat this exercise to uncover more personal values.

Important: Prioritizing your values doesn't necessarily mean you need to overhaul your life (unless this is what you want to do). Focusing on your values can also mean making daily decisions, even small ones, according to these values. For example, if you value inner peace, you might create a quiet corner in your home for relaxation and mindfulness practices. You can level up later by integrating more substantial changes, like adopting a daily meditation routine.

Values vs. Goals

It's important to note that values are not the same as goals. Values are enduring principles that guide your behavior and give your life meaning. They're ongoing, continuous, and lived rather than achieved. For example, valuing *honesty* means striving to be authentic and truthful in ALL your interactions, regardless of the outcome. If you stop being honest, you no longer live by that value.

Conversely, goals are specific, achievable outcomes or targets you can "cross off." They're concrete and measurable; once achieved, you set new goals. So, a value is like a compass guiding your way; a goal is like a landmark you aim to reach as you follow that direction.

Although values and goals are different, they complement each other. Values provide direction and motivation, ensuring that your goals are meaningful and aligned with what truly matters to you. Goals give you tangible milestones to strive for, helping you to make progress and measure your success as you live according to your values.

If you feel that your current life goals aren't in alignment with your values, the following exercises will help you refine your objectives and ensure they truly reflect what's important to you.

Worksheet 24: Ikigai

Ikigai is a Japanese concept that means "reason for being." It's a philosophy that will help you find purpose and meaning in your life by identifying the intersection of four key elements: *what you love, what you are good at, what the world needs,* and *what you can be paid for.* When these elements align, they clarify your values and help you align your daily activities with your deeper purpose, reducing anxiety and uncertainty.

Step 1. Find a quiet place and sit comfortably. Take a few deep breaths to center yourself.

Step 2. Write down the things that you love doing. Think about activities that bring you joy and make you lose track of time. For example, "I love painting, spending time with my family, and helping others."

Step 3. Write down the things that you're good at. List your skills and strengths and where you excel, whether through natural talent or acquired skills. For example, "I'm good at art, creative thinking, and listening to others."

Step 4. Write down what you believe the world needs. This could be anything from more kindness and creativity to better mental health awareness. For example, "The world needs more empathy, less judgmental behavior, and better mental health support."

Step 5. Write down what you can be paid for. Consider your professional skills and how they can translate into a career or side project. For example, "I can be paid for art classes for kids and adults, art workshops, and maybe even designing websites."

Step 6. Find the intersection! Look for the overlaps among the four lists. Identify where your passions, skills, societal needs, and potential for income align. This is your Ikigai. For example, "My Ikigai seems to point to creating therapeutic art programs that help people manage anxiety through creative expression."

Step 7. Examine how your Ikigai aligns with your core values. Ask yourself if your Ikigai reflects what you believe in and what fulfills you. For example, "My core values of empathy, creativity, and mental health are reflected in my Ikigai of providing therapeutic art programs."

Step 8. Create a plan to integrate your Ikigai into your daily life. Set small, achievable goals that align with your Ikigai and help manage your anxiety. For example, "I will start by offering free weekly art therapy sessions in my community, gradually building up to a sustainable program."

Note: If you discover that your Ikigia, or life's purpose, doesn't align with your core values, it's time for some introspection and adjustment.

- **Reevaluate your Ikigai.** Sometimes, what you think is your Ikigai might be influenced by external pressures like societal expectations, family traditions, or financial needs rather than what truly brings us joy and fulfillment. Take time to reassess whether what you've identified in the previous steps truly resonates with what you want from life.

- **Modify your approach.** If your Ikigai is something you're passionate about but clashes with your values, consider ways to modify how you engage with this passion. For example, if you love your job but find that the competitive environment conflicts with your value of *calmness and inner peace*, look for ways to foster teamwork and community within your workplace. You can also seek other job opportunities where the atmosphere is not so cut-throat.

- **Seek balance!** Your life's purpose doesn't have to fulfill every aspect of your values. Find balance by integrating activities that reflect your values into your daily life, even if they are outside your primary Ikigai.

For example, suppose your Ikigai revolves around a high-pressure, demanding career in finance, which provides personal satisfaction through achievements and financial success. However, it doesn't fulfill other core values such as *service, supportiveness,* and *connection.* To achieve balance, you could integrate these values into your life by volunteering at local community centers on weekends or joining a group that organizes social events for underprivileged communities.

Worksheet 25: Value-Action Alignment

This exercise aims to help you identify your core values and ensure your daily actions align with these values.

Step 1. Reflect on what truly matters. Spend a few minutes reflecting on what is most important to you in different areas of your life (e.g., self, family, relationships, career, health, etc.). Think about moments when you felt truly fulfilled and content. What values were you honoring during those times?

Step 2. Review the <u>Discovering Values</u> exercise. Select the Top 3 values that resonate most with you in each life category. Next to each value, write down why that value is important to you.

Example:
Life Aspect: Self
Value #1: Authenticity. I want to be "myself." I think it will make me feel grounded and reduce the anxiety I feel from trying to be someone I'm not.
Value #2: Calmness. If I prioritize calmness, I can think more clearly and make better decisions, reducing the overall stress in my life.
Value #3: Growth. I'm anxious about the future. So, I think continuous personal growth will keep me motivated and help build my resilience and confidence.

Step 3. Action-value alignment. Rate how well your daily actions align with each value on a scale of 1 to 10 (with 1 being the lowest and 10 being the highest).

Life Aspect: Self									
Value: Authenticity									
Rating:									
1	2	3	4	5	6	7	8	9	10

Life Aspect: Self									
Value #1:									
Rating:									
1	2	3	4	5	6	7	8	9	10
Value #2:									
Rating:									
1	2	3	4	5	6	7	8	9	10
Value #3:									
Rating:									
1	2	3	4	5	6	7	8	9	10

Life Aspect: Family									
Value #1:									
Rating:									
1	2	3	4	5	6	7	8	9	10
Value #2:									
Rating:									
1	2	3	4	5	6	7	8	9	10
Value #3:									
Rating:									
1	2	3	4	5	6	7	8	9	10

Life Aspect: Work/Career									
Value #1:									
Rating:									
1	2	3	4	5	6	7	8	9	10

Value #2:									
Rating:									
1	2	3	4	5	6	7	8	9	10
Value #3:									
Rating:									
1	2	3	4	5	6	7	8	9	10

Note: Feel free to add more life aspects to your list and what values you want to rate.

Step 4. Identify gaps. Are you seeing gaps between your values and your actions?

Example: Yes. I rated the value of Authenticity as "2".

What specific actions are not in alignment?

Example: I still say "Yes" too often even though I don't want to, making me feel like a loser and a fraud often.

Step 5. Set goals. Write down specific, achievable goals to align your actions with your values. Write down at least one goal for each value.

Example: To be more authentic, I will say "No" to the first invitation I REALLY don't want to attend, no matter how hard the other person tries to persuade me.

Step 6. Develop an action plan. For each goal you listed above, write down the steps you must take to achieve it. Include resources or support you need, potential obstacles, and how you will overcome them.

Example: How to say "No."
- *I need to learn at least three ways to say "No" because saying a direct "No" is hard for me right now. For example, maybe I can sort of say "No" by offering an alternative? Something like, "I can't go with you guys to a bar tonight, but maybe next week?"*
- *Start with simple, low-stakes stuff like saying "No" when my corner barista offers to upgrade my order.*
- *Potential obstacle? My sister. We're close, and she means well, but she doesn't understand my anxiety about going home late. I need to be open (authentic!) and tell her about my anxiety over this.*

Conflicting Values

Real-life talk: I think some of my values are in conflict. Is that possible? It can definitely feel that way. For me, one of the values that I thought were in conflict was *independence* and *connection*.

I value my independence and like making my own decisions, but I also value the deep connection I have with my husband. So, at first, I was a bit conflicted about it. However, I realized I can balance these values by identifying which aspects I want to exert my independence on and which I need to prioritize connection.

First, I discussed this with my husband, so healthy communication was definitely important in this case. Ultimately, we agreed that for my *independence*, I should be free as a bird to pursue my hobbies and make personal decisions about my career. For *connection*, we have date night every Tuesday (yes, Tuesday), where we focus on each other without distractions. Further, we must discuss and mutually agree (no independent decisions) on matters that affect us both.

If the previous exercises showed that you're having what seems like conflicting values, please do the following exercise to achieve balance and clarity.

Worksheet 26: Balancing Conflicting Values

Step 1. Identify the conflict. Write down the values that seem to be in conflict and reflect on why each value is important to you.

Example: Stability vs. Growth

Stability: I prefer routines, predictability, and safe environments because they help me manage my anxiety.

Growth: I want to explore new places and try new activities. I think trying to step out of my comfort zone and learning new things will help me.

Step 2. Communicate openly. Discuss your thoughts and feelings if other people are involved with keeping these values. You might also just want input from trusted friends or family members about your desire to balance these values. Share your concerns and aspirations and see what they think.

Step 3. Find common ground. Explore areas where the values can coexist.

Example: Stability vs. Growth

- *I'll start with small, manageable adventures that don't completely disrupt my routine.*
- *I ALWAYS stay home on Saturdays, so maybe I'll start by going out with a friend for breakfast or brunch on Saturday. This way, I can still go back to what I usually do when I return home.*

Step 4. Set boundaries. Establish limits on how much change you can handle, ensuring you can try new experiences while maintaining constancy.

Example: Stability vs. Growth
I'll only plan new activities during weekends to maintain a stable weekday routine.

Step 5. Small steps. Allow yourself to grow in small, manageable ways.

Example: I'll explore new things or visit new places WITHIN my city before planning any bigger trips. This way, my sense of stability is not threatened.

Step 6. Reflect and adjust. Regularly assess how well you're balancing these values. Make adjustments as needed to ensure both values are being honored.

Chapter 14. Committed Action

"It's not intentions that matter. It's actions. We are what we do and say, not what we intend to." – Anonymous

Committed Action is about taking concrete steps guided by your values, even in the face of difficult thoughts, feelings, or circumstances. It's about committing to behave in ways that align with your core values and sustain those behaviors over time despite challenges.

This ACT skill is important because you can identify your values and make plans to live by them, but if you don't continuously act on those plans, they remain intentions. **Committed action bridges the gap between understanding your values and living according to them.** It turns abstract values into concrete actions.

Key Components of Committed Action

- **Values-Guided.** Your behavior (actions) is constantly and purposefully driven by your personal values. For example, if you value health and well-being, you might commit to regular exercise and healthy eating, even when your anxiety tells you to stay in bed or reach for comfort food.

- **Flexibility.** Committed action involves being adaptable and flexible in your approach. It's about trying to live according to your values but not in a way that's resistant to change or the unexpected. For example, suppose you planned to attend a social event (value: connection) but felt overwhelmed with anxiety on the day. Instead of forcing yourself to go, you might decide to have a one-on-one coffee date with a close friend instead. This way, you still honor your value but adapt to your current emotional state.

- **Persistence.** Committed action requires perseverance and resilience. You must continuously take values-based action even when faced with obstacles or setbacks. For example, suppose you value *growth* in your work life or career. In this case, you might continue applying for new job opportunities despite experiencing anxiety over interviews or potential rejection. Each action taken, despite anxiety, demonstrates persistence toward your career goals.

- **Behavioral Change.** Committed action is *active*. It focuses on actual changes in behavior, not just changes in thoughts or feelings. It's about doing, not just thinking. For example, suppose you value *creativity*. Instead of just thinking about starting a new art project, you set aside time each day to paint or draw. Even if anxiety makes it hard to start, you focus on the *action* of creating art, leading to real behavioral change.

The following exercises are all designed to help you take committed steps to live and act according your core values—even in the face of internal resistance and life challenges.

Worksheet 27: WOOP!

WOOP stands for **W**ish, **O**utcome, **O**bstacle, and **P**lan. It's a goal-setting technique created by German psychologist Gabriele Oettingen.[125] It helps you visualize your goals, anticipate potential challenges, and create effective strategies to overcome them.

WOOP can be particularly useful for managing anxiety, as it allows you to structure your thoughts and actions constructively. Linking it to your core values ensures that your actions are aligned with what truly matters to you.

Step 1. Identify your core values. Reflect on what's most important to you concerning your wish.

Step 2. Wish. Identify a meaningful and challenging goal related to your situation. This should be something that excites you, is important for your personal growth, and is aligned with your core values.

Step 3. Outcome. Visualize the best possible outcome if you achieve this goal. Think about how you would feel, what benefits you would gain, and how it would positively impact your life.

Step 4. Obstacle. Identify the main obstacles that might prevent you from achieving your goal. These could be internal (e.g., fears, habits, cognitive distortions, etc.) or external (e.g., finances, time constraints, knowledge, etc.).

Step 5. Plan. Develop a specific plan to overcome these obstacles. Create "if-then" statements to prepare for potential challenges.

RELATED VALUES:	*Example: self-care, connection, calmness, adaptability*
WISH	**My wish is to...**

Example:

Smoothly transition to my new city and establish a sense of comfort and routine ASAP (preferably within three months). As I relocate, I want to maintain self-care activities. I'm also anxious about being "uprooted," so I wish to build meaningful connections in my new place soon. Everything will be new to me, which scares me, so I wish for calmness inside me and to demonstrate adaptability in my new surroundings.

OUTCOME

The best outcome for me is...

Example: A successful relocation. Achieving this will make me feel confident and happy. It also means I end up with a cozy home, a new social circle, and a good understanding of my new city.

<table>
<tr><td></td><td></td></tr>
<tr><td>OBSTACLE</td><td>

The potential obstacles are...

Example: my anxiety, feeling homesick, struggling to make new friends, and dealing with the unfamiliarity of my new environment

</td></tr>
<tr><td>PLAN</td><td>

If... Then I will...

Examples:

Anxiety: If I experience anxiety, then I will practice deep breathing exercises, take a short walk to clear my mind, or use a grounding technique to bring myself back to the present moment.

Self-Care: If I feel homesick, I will schedule regular video calls with my family and friends back home to maintain my emotional well-being.

</td></tr>
</table>

Connection: If I struggle to make new friends at work, I will join local clubs or groups that interest me. Maybe a book club, a sports team, or a Meetup group.

Adaptability: If I feel overwhelmed by my new environment, I will dedicate time each week to explore just ONE part of the city and familiarize myself with it.

Worksheet 28: Willingness Dial

Do this exercise whenever you are unwilling to act or accomplish a goal related to your values.

Step 1. Identify the challenging task or situation. Think about a task, goal, or situation you find challenging or currently avoiding. Also, identify why not doing this task goes against one of your core values.

Example:
Situation: Calling my parents to discuss my anxiety.
Violated Value: Authenticity

Step 2. Visualize a willingness dial. Close your eyes and take a few deep breaths to center yourself. Picture a dial in your mind, similar to a volume knob, labeled from 0 to 10, with 0 representing no willingness, while 10 represents full willingness to engage in the task or situation.

Ask yourself, "On a scale from 0 to 10, where is my current willingness to engage in this task?" Be honest with yourself and assign a number to your current level of willingness. For example, you might feel your willingness is at a "3."

Step 3. Explore the reasons behind your current willingness level. What thoughts, emotions, or physical sensations are influencing your willingness?

Example: I feel anxious about calling my parents and finally talking to them about my anxiety. I fear their disappointment and rejection; maybe they won't even believe me. I'm afraid to feel that vulnerable.

Step 4. Identify small steps to increase your willingness. Think about small, manageable steps that could increase your willingness by one or two points. These steps should be specific and doable.

Example: I can...
Practice mindfulness before the call, and prepare a script for the phone call.

Step 5. Commit to taking one small step. Choose one of the small steps you listed and commit to doing it. Write it down or say it out loud to reinforce your commitment. For example, "I will write a short script to guide my phone call and read it twice before dialing."

Step 6. Visualize moving the willingness dial. Close your eyes again and visualize moving the dial from your current number to one or two points higher. Imagine yourself feeling more willing and ready to engage in the task. Picture yourself taking the small step you committed to and experiencing success.

Step 7. Take action. With the increased willingness you've just visualized, immediately dive into the task or situation without delay.

Worksheet 29: Acceptance and Commitment

This exercise will help you accept difficult emotions that might prevent you from doing value-driven actions.

Step 1. Identify the issue and related core value(s). Write down the specific issue you're dealing with and the affected value.

Example:
Issue: Thoughts like "I'm not good enough."
Affected value: self-care

Step 2. Write down any difficult emotions you're experiencing related to the issue. Be mindful and recognize your feelings without judgment.

Example: When thoughts like "I'm not good enough" enter my mind, I feel depressed and overwhelmed because I feel like they're preventing me from practicing self-care.

Step 3. Accept your emotions AS IS. Practice accepting your emotions instead of trying to avoid or suppress them. Understand that it's okay to feel this way and emotions are a natural part of life.

Example: I accept that feeling sadness and anxiety due to "I'm not good enough" thoughts are normal. It's okay to feel this way. I don't need to fight these feelings.

Step 4. Define value-driven actions. After accepting your difficult emotions, determine actions that align with your core values as best as possible.

Examples:
- If thoughts of not being good enough enter my mind, I'll practice mindfulness and the __STOP__ exercise.
- I will practice self-compassion by writing three positive things about myself every morning.
- I will dedicate 30 minutes each day to an activity that I enjoy, and that relaxes me, like reading a book or walking in nature.

Step 5. Commit to action. Plan when and how to carry out the actions you listed in the previous step.

Example:
Action: I will dedicate 30 minutes each day to an activity that I enjoy and relaxes me, like reading a book or walking in nature.
Commitment: I will schedule this time as a non-negotiable appointment on my calendar.

Worksheet 30: Behavioral Activation

Committed action is "values in motion." This exercise will help you focus on activities that promote living according to your values.

Step 1. List one core value, specify a goal related to this value, and outline activities you can do within one week to achieve this goal.

Example:
Values: initiative
Goal: Be the one to reach out to others and not wait for others to contact me first.
Activities: Call a friend or family member to catch up. Ask a colleague or acquaintance to plan a coffee or lunch meeting.

Step 2. Schedule activities. Plan when and how you will engage in these activities. Schedule them realistically within your week to ensure you can commit to them.

Example:
Monday: Call a friend in the evening.
Tuesday: Email a colleague to arrange a coffee meeting.
Wednesday: Text a family member to check in and chat.
Thursday: Send a message to an old friend to reconnect.
Friday: Approach a coworker and ask if they want to have lunch together.

Important: Please DO NOT be discouraged if you receive a "No" or if things don't go as you hoped or planned. The important thing is to start and continue your efforts!

Step 3. Reflect. After completing each activity, take some time to reflect on how it impacted your mood and how it aligned with your values. Write down your thoughts and feelings.

Example: Calling a friend on Monday made me feel happy and less alone.

Worksheet 31: FEAR

Committed action involves taking effective action guided by your values, even in the presence of difficult thoughts and emotions. The FEAR exercise (Fusion, Excessive goals, Avoidance of discomfort, and Remoteness from values) helps you break free from patterns that might be preventing you from living a life aligned with your values.

Step 1. Identify a core value and related goal you're finding hard to live by.

Example:
Value: Health
Goal: Start and stick to a regular exercise routine to improve my physical and mental well-being.

Step 2. Recognize FEAR patterns. Complete the FEAR table below to identify the thoughts, goals, behaviors, and beliefs that might prevent you from committing to your core values.

- **<u>F</u>usion:** When you become entangled (fused) with your negative thinking patterns and believe them as absolute truths.
- **<u>E</u>xcessive goals:** When your objectives are too high or unachievable given your present circumstances or resources.
- **<u>A</u>voidance of discomfort:** When you steer clear of situations that cause anxiety or stress.
- **<u>R</u>emoteness from values:** When you lose touch with WHY this core value is important to you.

Value:	*Example: Health*
Goal:	*Example: Start and stick to a regular exercise routine to improve my physical and mental well-being.*
Fusion	**What thoughts are making you think your goal is unachievable?** *Example: I'm too out of shape to even start exercising. I've tried before, and I'll probably fail again.*
Excessive goals	**What goal(s) might be "too much" or exceeding your current resources (e.g., skills, time, money, etc.)?** *Example: I want to work out for one solid hour daily, or it's*

	not worth it. This may be unrealistic because I'm just starting, and my workload is currently high.
Avoidance of discomfort	**What discomfort are you avoiding?** *Example: I think I'm avoiding exercising because it's too physically uncomfortable and tiring. Also, time-wise, one hour of exercising out of my schedule is inconvenient.*
Remoteness	**Are you perhaps losing touch with or forgetting**

from values	**what is important or meaningful about this goal?**
	Example: I guess I'm too focused on how hard this goal is, and I forget why prioritizing my well-being matters.

Worksheet 32: Reflection and Recommitment

Challenges, obstacles, setbacks... they're all part of life. So, it's possible that despite your best efforts, you find yourself "veering off track" of your outlined committed actions to live a value-based life. This exercise will help you understand why you deviated from your plans and how to recommit to them.

Step 1. Find a quiet place where you can reflect without distractions. Take a few deep breaths to center yourself.

Step 2. Reflect on your day and identify moments when you failed to live according to your values.

What happened today that made you feel you failed to live by your values?

Example: Today, I was short, grumpy, and dismissive with a colleague when they asked for help. This behavior goes against my values of being supportive and kind.

How did you feel during those moments?

Example: I felt frustrated and impatient, which made me snap at them. Afterward, I felt guilty and disappointed in myself for not being more understanding.

Step 3. Identify triggers. Think about what triggered you to act in a way that wasn't aligned with your values.

What specific events or emotions led to your actions?

Example: I was feeling overwhelmed with my own workload. When my colleague interrupted me, it triggered feelings of stress and impatience.

Were there any external pressures or internal thoughts that influenced your behavior?

Example: The external pressure of looming deadlines contributed to my stress. Internally, I thought I didn't have time to help others, making me react negatively.

Step 4. Consider the impact of your actions on yourself and others.

How did acting against your values affect your mood, stress levels, and relationships?

Example: Acting against my values increased my stress because I was dwelling on my reaction. It also strained my relationship with my colleague, making me worry about how they perceive me.

What consequences did you notice?

Example: My colleague seemed annoyed and less willing to approach me afterward, which could lead to a breakdown in our teamwork. Additionally, I felt more stressed and guilty, which affected my focus for the rest of the day.

Step 5. Recommit to your values. Write down your core values and why they are important to you. Make a commitment to realign your actions with your values moving forward.

List at least three core values, and why do they matter to you?

Example:

Kindness*: Being kind is important to me because it fosters positive relationships and a supportive environment.*

Patience*: Patience helps me respond thoughtfully rather than react impulsively, which is essential for maintaining balance and harmony in my interactions.*

Integrity*: Acting with integrity ensures I stay true to my principles, even in challenging situations.*

How can you ensure your actions align with these values tomorrow?

Example: Tomorrow, I will remind myself to take a deep breath before responding to anyone, ensuring I approach them with kindness and patience. I'll also prioritize my tasks to avoid feeling overwhelmed and maintain my integrity by being honest about my availability.

Step 6. Set specific actions. Identify specific actions you can take tomorrow to live according to your values. Remember, a plan without action is just *intention*.

What specific steps will you take <u>tomorrow</u> to honor your values?

Example:
I will set aside time in the morning to plan my day, ensuring I have a clear idea of what needs to be done.
I'll practice mindfulness during my breaks to keep my stress levels in check.
I'll approach my colleague first thing in the morning to apologize and offer my help when I'm less busy.

How will you handle similar triggers or situations differently?

Example: If I feel overwhelmed again, I'll take a moment to breathe and assess the situation calmly before responding (mindfulness!). I'll remind myself that being supportive and kind is more important than the immediate task, and I can find a balance between helping others and managing my responsibilities.

Conclusion

Anxiety. I've suffered from it for years, so I have a pretty good idea of just how much pain you're carrying right now. However, I realized I can lighten the mental, emotional, and often physical load I carry. I can get better and experience anxiety relief. Contrary to popular belief, though, it's not as simple as deciding to put down that "load." (If only it was THAT easy!)

The door to anxiety relief starts to open when you realize and decide you need help. Your decision to get this book marks the beginning of your journey, but it's the consistent and committed actions that will truly make a difference!

Acceptance and Commitment Therapy (ACT) teaches you that rather than battling anxiety, you can accept its presence without letting it dictate your life. By practicing the skills in this book and developing *psychological flexibility*, you can slowly but surely loosen the grip that anxiety has on you.

Remember, relief doesn't come from eliminating anxiety entirely but from changing your relationship with it. It's about learning to carry your load in a way that feels lighter, even on the toughest days.

So, take that first step, then another, and keep moving forward. Relief is possible, and it starts with acceptance, commitment, and the courage to live a life true to your values.

Don't Forget Your Gift!

Download and print our free
**15-Day Mindfulness and Acceptance
(Planner + Journal)!** Just go to
https://life-zen.com to get your gift, or
scan the QR code on this page.

A Little Help?

Dear Reader,

I hope this **ACT Therapy Workbook Toolbox (3 Books in 1)** has positively influenced your mental and emotional healing journey. When I was suffering from burnout and a breakdown, "help" was a distant concept, and I felt lost in a maze of overwhelming emotions. But through the principles of Radical Acceptance and ACT, I found a guiding light, and I hope you have too.

Many people don't realize how hard it is to get reviews and how much they help us authors. So, I would be incredibly grateful if you could take just a few seconds to write a short review about this 3-in-1 book on Amazon, even if it's just a few words.

What to do: Please leave a review on Amazon here:
https://amazon.com/review/create-review?&asin=B0DQ89WNJS
Or scan the QR code on this page.

Note: If you're from outside the US, please update your Amazon link from amazon.<u>com</u> to your country code (e.g., amazon.<u>co.uk</u>, amazon.<u>ca</u>, etc.).

If you're reading on a Kindle or an e-reader, scroll to the bottom of the book and swipe up to prompt the Review page.

THANK YOU FOR YOUR HELP!

Ava Watters

Further Reading

About the Author

Ava Walters is the founder of LifeZen Publications. Coming from a family with a history of mental health issues, her journey began as a personal quest to find balance, inner peace, and what we all desire—happiness. This pursuit has led her to explore traditional psychotherapeutic methods and diverse holistic practices.

She has an MBA with a specialization in International Project Management (IPM). However, her trajectory took a significant turn after experiencing "a burnout and a breakdown." She then returned to her first love—writing, complementing it with her deep passion for psychology. This transformation marked the beginning of her new journey. One focused on unraveling the intricate connections between human behavior and mental healing.

When she's not writing, Ava can be found on her yoga mat, taking long nature walks with her husband, or in the kitchen, constantly experimenting with new recipes to her husband's delight.

Learn more about Ava and LifeZen Publications here:
https://life-zen.com/

References

BOOK 1 REFERENCES

[1] Linehan, M. (2015). *DBT Skills Training Manual.* Guilford Press.

[2] Killingsworth, M. A., & Gilbert, D. T. (2010). A wandering mind is an unhappy mind. *Science, 330*(6006), 932–932. https://doi.org/10.1126/science.1192439

[3] Figueiredo, T., Lima, G., Erthal, P., Martins, R., Corção, P., Leonel, M., Ayrão, V., Fortes, D., & Mattos, P. (2020). Mind-wandering, depression, anxiety and ADHD: Disentangling the relationship. *Psychiatry Research, 285,* 112798. https://doi.org/10.1016/j.psychres.2020.112798

[4] Ray, J. (2022, June 28). *World Unhappier, more stressed out than ever.* Gallup.com. https://news.gallup.com/poll/394025/world-unhappier-stressed-ever.aspx

[5] Desai, R. (2020, August 28). *Stress has made us shallow breathers. here's what it does to our bodies.* The Swaddle. https://www.theswaddle.com/stress-has-made-us-shallow-breathers-heres-what-it-does-to-our-bodies

[6] *Deep vs shallow breathing - causes, dangers, benefits, exercises.* Buteyko Clinic International. (2020, December 9). https://buteykoclinic.com/deep-vs-shallow-breathing-causes-dangers-benefits-exercises/

[7] Zaccaro, A., Piarulli, A., Laurino, M., Garbella, E., Menicucci, D., Neri, B., & Gemignani, A. (2018). How breath-control can change your life: A systematic review on psycho-physiological correlates of slow breathing. *Frontiers in Human Neuroscience, 12.* https://doi.org/10.3389/fnhum.2018.00353

[8] Langshur, E., & Klemp, N. J. (2018). *Start here: Master the lifelong habit of Wellbeing.* Gallery Books.

[9] Brownlee, D. (2020, January 15). *Doing this at least 10 minutes a day could transform your productivity*. Forbes. https://www.forbes.com/sites/danabrownlee/2020/01/15/doing-this-at-least-10-minutes-a-day-could-transform-your-productivity/

[10] Knox, R. (2018, April 6). *Harvard study: Clearing your mind affects your genes and can lower your blood pressure*. WBUR News. https://www.wbur.org/news/2018/04/06/harvard-study-relax-genes

[11] Khoury, B., Lecomte, T., Fortin, G., Masse, M., Therien, P., Bouchard, V., Chapleau, M.-A., Paquin, K., & Hofmann, S. G. (2013). Mindfulness-based therapy: A comprehensive meta-analysis. *Clinical Psychology Review, 33*(6), 763–771. https://doi.org/10.1016/j.cpr.2013.05.005

[12] Black, D. S., & Slavich, G. M. (2016). Mindfulness meditation and the immune system: A systematic review of randomized controlled trials. *Annals of the New York Academy of Sciences, 1373*(1), 13–24. https://doi.org/10.1111/nyas.12998

[13] Carrière, K., Khoury, B., Günak, M. M., & Knäuper, B. (2017). Mindfulness-based interventions for weight loss: A systematic review and meta-analysis. *Obesity Reviews, 19*(2), 164–177. https://doi.org/10.1111/obr.12623

[14] Rusch, H. L., Rosario, M., Levison, L. M., Olivera, A., Livingston, W. S., Wu, T., & Gill, J. M. (2018). The effect of mindfulness meditation on sleep quality: A systematic review and meta-analysis of randomized controlled trials. *Annals of the New York Academy of Sciences, 1445*(1), 5–16. https://doi.org/10.1111/nyas.13996

[15] Zeidan, F., Johnson, S. K., Diamond, B. J., David, Z., & Goolkasian, P. (2010). Mindfulness meditation improves cognition: Evidence of brief mental training. *Consciousness and Cognition, 19*(2), 597–605. https://doi.org/10.1016/j.concog.2010.03.014

[16] Schertz, K. E., & Berman, M. G. (2019). Understanding nature and its cognitive benefits. *Current Directions in Psychological Science, 28*(5), 496–502. https://doi.org/10.1177/0963721419854100

[17] Robbins, J. (2020, January 9). *Ecopsychology: How immersion in nature benefits your health.* Yale E360. https://e360.yale.edu/features/ecopsychology-how-immersion-in-nature-benefits-your-health

[18] Jimenez, M. P., DeVille, N. V., Elliott, E. G., Schiff, J. E., Wilt, G. E., Hart, J. E., & James, P. (2021). Associations between Nature Exposure and Health: A review of the evidence. *International Journal of Environmental Research and Public Health, 18*(9), 4790. https://doi.org/10.3390/ijerph18094790

[19] Lerner, J. S., Li, Y., Valdesolo, P., & Kassam, K. S. (2015). Emotion and decision making. *Annual Review of Psychology, 66*(1), 799–823. https://doi.org/10.1146/annurev-psych-010213-115043

[20] Sifferlin, A. (2014, August 6). *Trustworthiness: Your brain makes a judgment in milliseconds.* Time. https://time.com/3083667/brain-trustworthiness/

[21] Forsythe, F. (2019, February 20). *Why judging others is our natural instinct, Harvard Psychologist explains.* Learning Mind. https://www.learning-mind.com/judging-others/

[22] Ortet, G., Pinazo, D., Walker, D., Gallego, S., Mezquita, L., & Ibáñez, M. I. (2020). Personality and nonjudging make you happier: Contribution of the five-factor model, mindfulness facets and a mindfulness intervention to subjective well-being. *PLOS ONE, 15*(2). https://doi.org/10.1371/journal.pone.0228655

[23] Shahar, G. (2017, August 9). *The hazards of self-criticism.* Psychology Today. https://www.psychologytoday.com/us/blog/stress-self-and-health/201708/the-hazards-self-criticism

[24] McIntyre, R., Smith, P., & Rimes, K. A. (2018). The role of self-criticism in common mental health difficulties in students: A systematic review of prospective studies. *Mental Health & Prevention, 10*, 13–27. https://doi.org/10.1016/j.mhp.2018.02.003

[25] Warren, R., Smeets, E., & Neff, K. (2016, December). *Self-criticism and self-compassion: Risk and resilience.* Self-Compassion. https://self-compassion.org/wp-content/uploads/2016/12/Self-Criticism.pdf

[26] Doan, T., Ha, V., Strazdins, L., & Chateau, D. (2022). Healthy minds live in healthy bodies – effect of physical health on Mental Health: Evidence from Australian Longitudinal Data. *Current Psychology, 42*(22), 18702–18713. https://doi.org/10.1007/s12144-022-03053-7

[27] Mahindru, A., Patil, P., & Agrawal, V. (2023). Role of physical activity on mental health and well-being: A Review. *Cureus.* https://doi.org/10.7759/cureus.33475

[28] John, S. N. (2013). *The Book of Afformations: Discovering the Missing Piece to Abundant Health, Wealth, Love, and Happiness.* Hay House.

[29] Childs, J. H., & Stoeber, J. (2012). Do you want me to be perfect? Two longitudinal studies on socially prescribed perfectionism, stress and burnout in the Workplace. *Work and Stress, 26*(4), 347–364. https://doi.org/10.1080/02678373.2012.737547

[30] Smith, M. M., Sherry, S. B., McLarnon, M. E., Flett, G. L., Hewitt, P. L., Saklofske, D. H., & Etherson, M. E. (2018). Why does socially prescribed perfectionism place people at risk for depression? A five-month, two-wave longitudinal study of the perfectionism social disconnection model. *Personality and Individual Differences, 134*, 49–54. https://doi.org/10.1016/j.paid.2018.05.040

[31] *Embracing body positivity linked to a happier life, Global Study reveals.* Mind Help. (2023, September 5). https://mind.help/news/mental-health-and-happiness

[32] Nummenmaa, L., Glerean, E., Hari, R., & Hietanen, J. K. (2013). Bodily maps of emotions. *Proceedings of the National Academy of Sciences, 111*(2), 646–651. https://doi.org/10.1073/pnas.1321664111

[33] Kaleja, L. (2021, January 6). *Self-forgiveness for most people is harder than to forgive others.* Medium. https://medium.com/better-

advice/self-forgiveness-for-most-people-is-harder-than-to-forgive-others-6419537d42d2

[34] Macaskill, A. (2012). Differentiating dispositional self-forgiveness from other-forgiveness: Associations with mental health and life satisfaction. *Journal of Social and Clinical Psychology, 31*(1), 28–50. https://doi.org/10.1521/jscp.2012.31.1.28

[35] Gendlin, E. T. (2007). *Focusing.* Bantam.

[36] Guilfoyle, J. R., Struthers, C. W., van Monsjou, E., & Shoikhedbrod, A. (2019). Sorry is the hardest word to say: The role of self-control in apologizing. *Basic and Applied Social Psychology, 41*(1), 72–90. https://doi.org/10.1080/01973533.2018.1553715

[37] Northwestern Medicine. (2021, September). *5 benefits of healthy relationships.* https://www.nm.org/healthbeat/healthy-tips/5-benefits-of-healthy-relationships

[38] Firth, J., Torous, J., Stubbs, B., Firth, J. A., Steiner, G. Z., Smith, L., Alvarez-Jimenez, M., Gleeson, J., Vancampfort, D., Armitage, C. J., & Sarris, J. (2019). The "Online Brain" How the internet may be changing our cognition. *World Psychiatry, 18*(2), 119–129. https://doi.org/10.1002/wps.20617

[39] Thomas, S. (2023, July 4). *How social media changes our perception of reality.* Insight Digital Magazine. https://www.thechicagoschool.edu/insight\from-the-magazine/a-virtual-life/

[40] *The importance of learning and growing your knowledge - beautiful minds.* Beautiful Minds®. (2022, October 12). https://beautifulminds.com.au/the-importance-of-learning-and-growing-your-knowledge/

[41] Brower, T. (2021, October 17). *Learning is a sure path to happiness: Science proves it.* Forbes. https://www.forbes.com/sites/tracybrower/2021/10/17/learning-is-a-sure-path-to-happiness-science-proves-it/

[42] Otake, K., Shimai, S., Tanaka-Matsumi, J., Otsui, K., & Fredrickson, B. L. (2006). Happy people become happier through kindness: A counting kindnesses intervention. *Journal of Happiness Studies, 7*(3), 361–375. https://doi.org/10.1007/s10902-005-3650-z

[43] Emmons, R. A., & McCullough, M. E. (2003). Counting blessings versus burdens: An experimental investigation of gratitude and subjective well-being in daily life. *Journal of Personality and Social Psychology, 84*(2), 377–389. https://doi.org/10.1037/0022-3514.84.2.377

BOOK 2 REFERENCES

[44] Wikimedia Foundation. (2023, September 8). *Steven C. Hayes.* Wikipedia. https://en.wikipedia.org/wiki/Steven_C._Hayes

[45] Öhman, A., & Mineka, S. (2001). Fears, phobias, and preparedness: Toward an evolved module of fear and Fear Learning. *Psychological Review, 108*(3), 483–522. https://doi.org/10.1037/0033-295x.108.3.483

[46] Hasheminasab, M., Babapour Kheiroddin, J., Mahmood Aliloo, M., & Fakhari, A. (2015). Acceptance and Commitment Therapy (ACT) For Generalized Anxiety Disorder. Iranian journal of public health, 44(5), 718–719.

[47] Eifert, G. H., Forsyth, J. P., Arch, J., Espejo, E., Keller, M., & Langer, D. (2009). Acceptance and commitment therapy for anxiety disorders: Three case studies exemplifying A unified treatment protocol. *Cognitive and Behavioral Practice, 16*(4), 368–385. https://doi.org/10.1016/j.cbpra.2009.06.001

[48] Beygi, Z., Tighband Jangali, R., Derakhshan, N., Alidadi, M., Javanbakhsh, F., & Mahboobizadeh, M. (2023). An overview of reviews on the effects of acceptance and commitment therapy (ACT) on depression and anxiety. *Iranian Journal of Psychiatry.* https://doi.org/10.18502/ijps.v18i2.12373

[49] Pohar, R., & Argáez, C. (2017, August 28). Acceptance and Commitment Therapy for Post-Traumatic Stress Disorder, Anxiety, and Depression: A

Review of Clinical Effectiveness. Ottawa (ON): Canadian Agency for Drugs and Technologies in Health. Retrieved from https://www.ncbi.nlm.nih.gov/books/NBK525684/

[50] Kelly, M. M., Reilly, E. D., Ameral, V., Richter, S., & Fukuda, S. (2022). A randomized pilot study of acceptance and commitment therapy to improve social support for veterans with PTSD. *Journal of Clinical Medicine, 11*(12), 3482. https://doi.org/10.3390/jcm11123482

[51] Vakili, Y., & Gharraee, B. (2014). The effectiveness of acceptance and commitment therapy in treating a case of obsessive compulsive disorder. Iranian journal of psychiatry, 9(2), 115–117.

[52] Soondrum, T., Wang, X., Gao, F., Liu, Q., Fan, J., & Zhu, X. (2022). The applicability of acceptance and commitment therapy for obsessive-compulsive disorder: A systematic review and meta-analysis. *Brain Sciences, 12*(5), 656. https://doi.org/10.3390/brainsci12050656

[53] Osaji, J., Ojimba, C., & Ahmed, S. (2020). The use of acceptance and commitment therapy in Substance Use Disorders: A review of literature. *Journal of Clinical Medicine Research, 12*(10), 629–633. https://doi.org/10.14740/jocmr4311

[54] Mosel, S. (2022, October 21). *Acceptance and commitment therapy (ACT) for substance abuse.* American Addiction Centers. https://americanaddictioncenters.org/therapy-treatment/act Reviewed by: Kristen Fuller, MD

[55] Eklund, M., Kiritsis, C., Livheim, F., & Ghaderi, A. (2023). ACT-based self-help for perceived stress and its mental health implications without therapist support: A randomized controlled trial. *Journal of Contextual Behavioral Science, 27,* 98–106. https://doi.org/10.1016/j.jcbs.2023.01.003

[56] Wersebe, H., Lieb, R., Meyer, A. H., Hofer, P., & Gloster, A. T. (2018). The link between stress, well-being, and psychological flexibility during an acceptance and commitment therapy self-help intervention. *International Journal of Clinical and Health Psychology, 18*(1), 60–68. https://doi.org/10.1016/j.ijchp.2017.09.002

[57] Feliu Soler, A., Montesinos, F., Gutiérrez-Martínez, O., Scott, W., McCracken, L., & Luciano, J. (2018). Current status of acceptance and commitment therapy for chronic pain: A narrative review. *Journal of Pain Research, Volume 11*, 2145–2159. https://doi.org/10.2147/jpr.s144631

[58] Lai, L., Liu, Y., McCracken, L. M., Li, Y., & Ren, Z. (2023). The efficacy of acceptance and commitment therapy for chronic pain: A three-level meta-analysis and a trial sequential analysis of Randomized Controlled Trials. *Behaviour Research and Therapy, 165*, 104308. https://doi.org/10.1016/j.brat.2023.104308

[59] Pingo, J. C., Dixon, M. R., & Paliliunas, D. (2019). Intervention enhancing effects of acceptance and commitment training on performance feedback for direct support professional work performance, stress, and job satisfaction. *Behavior Analysis in Practice, 13*(1), 1–10. https://doi.org/10.1007/s40617-019-00333-w

[60] Littlehales, N. (2024, February 1). *ACT as a workplace intervention: A path to employee well-being and performance.* Contextual Consulting. https://contextualconsulting.co.uk/mental-health/act-as-a-workplace-intervention-a-path-to-employee-well-being-and-performance

[61] Fani Sobhani, F., Ghorban Shiroudi, S., & Khodabakhshi-Koolaee, A. (2021). Effect of two couple therapies, acceptance and commitment therapy and schema therapy, on forgiveness and fear of intimacy in conflicting couples. *Practice in Clinical Psychology, 9*(4), 271–282. https://doi.org/10.32598/jpcp.9.4.746.3

[62] Peterson, B. D., Eifert, G. H., Feingold, T., & Davidson, S. (2009). Using acceptance and commitment therapy to treat distressed couples: A case study with two couples. *Cognitive and Behavioral Practice, 16*(4), 430–442. https://doi.org/10.1016/j.cbpra.2008.12.009

[63] Speedlin, S., Milligan, K., Haberstroh, S., & Duffey, T. (2016, September). Using acceptance and commitment therapy to negotiate losses and Life Transitions | Request PDF. https://www.researchgate.net/publication/327382040_Using_Acceptan

ce_and_Commitment_Therapy_to_Negotiate_Losses_and_Life_Transitions

[64] Hayes, S. C., Pistorello, J., & Levin, M. E. (2012). Acceptance and commitment therapy as a unified model of behavior change. *The Counseling Psychologist, 40*(7), 976–1002. https://doi.org/10.1177/0011000012460836

[65] Zhang, C.-Q., Leeming, E., Smith, P., Chung, P.-K., Hagger, M. S., & Hayes, S. C. (2018). Acceptance and Commitment Therapy for Health Behavior Change: A contextually-driven approach. *Frontiers in Psychology, 8.* https://doi.org/10.3389\fpsyg.2017.02350

[66] Ray, J. (2024, March 22). *World Unhappier, more stressed out than ever.* Gallup.com. https://news.gallup.com/poll/394025/world-unhappier-stressed-ever.aspx

[67] Dochat, C., Wooldridge, J. S., Herbert, M. S., Lee, M. W., & Afari, N. (2021). Single-session acceptance and commitment therapy (ACT) interventions for patients with chronic health conditions: A systematic review and meta-analysis. *Journal of Contextual Behavioral Science, 20,* 52–69. https://doi.org/10.1016/j.jcbs.2021.03.003

[68] Ferreira, M. G., Mariano, L. I., Rezende, J. V., Caramelli, P., & Kishita, N. (2022). Effects of group acceptance and commitment therapy (ACT) on anxiety and depressive symptoms in adults: A meta-analysis. *Journal of Affective Disorders, 309,* 297–308. https://doi.org/10.1016/j.jad.2022.04.134

[69] Schreuder, E., van Erp, J., Toet, A., & Kallen, V. L. (2016). Emotional responses to multisensory environmental stimuli. *SAGE Open, 6*(1), 215824401663059. https://doi.org/10.1177/2158244016630591

[70] Dibdin, E. (2021, December 17). *How to connect with joy and happiness when you have depression.* Psych Central. https://psychcentral.com/depression/happy-when-depressed

[71] Willroth, E. C., Young, G., Tamir, M., & Mauss, I. B. (2023). Judging emotions as good or bad: Individual differences and associations with psy-

chological health. *Emotion, 23*(7), 1876–1890.
https://doi.org/10.1037/emo0001220

[72] Balban, M. Y., Neri, E., Kogon, M. M., Weed, L., Nouriani, B., Jo, B., Holl, G., Zeitzer, J. M., Spiegel, D., & Huberman, A. D. (2023). Brief structured respiration practices enhance mood and reduce physiological arousal. *Cell Reports Medicine, 4*(1), 100895.
https://doi.org/10.1016/j.xcrm.2022.100895

[73] Ewert, A., & Chang, Y. (2018). Levels of nature and stress response. *Behavioral Sciences, 8*(5), 49. https://doi.org/10.3390/bs8050049

[74] Torre, J. B., & Lieberman, M. D. (2018). Putting feelings into words: Affect labeling as implicit emotion regulation. *Emotion Review, 10*(2), 116–124. https://doi.org/10.1177/1754073917742706

[75] Wang, C., Schmid, C. H., Rones, R., Kalish, R., Yinh, J., Goldenberg, D. L., Lee, Y., & McAlindon, T. (2010). A randomized trial of Tai Chi for fibromyalgia. *New England Journal of Medicine, 363*(8), 743–754.
https://doi.org/10.1056/nejmoa0912611

[76] Tilbrook, H. E., Cox, H., Hewitt, C. E., Kang'ombe, A. R., Chuang, L.-H., Jayakody, S., Aplin, J. D., Semlyen, A., Trewhela, A., Watt, I., & Torgerson, D. J. (2011). Yoga for chronic low back pain. *Annals of Internal Medicine, 155*(9), 569. https://doi.org/10.7326/0003-4819-155-9-201111010-00003

[77] Kan, L., Zhang, J., Yang, Y., & Wang, P. (2016). The effects of yoga on pain, mobility, and quality of life in patients with knee osteoarthritis: A systematic review. *Evidence-Based Complementary and Alternative Medicine, 2016*, 1–10. https://doi.org/10.1155/2016/6016532

[78] Wu, Q., Liu, P., Liao, C., & Tan, L. (2022). Effectiveness of yoga therapy for Migraine: A meta-analysis of randomized controlled studies. *Journal of Clinical Neuroscience, 99*, 147–151.
https://doi.org/10.1016/j.jocn.2022.01.018

[79] Lee, A. (2020, April 7). *Why change is hard ... and good*. Columbia Business School. https://business.columbia.edu/cgi-leadership/ideas-work/why-change-hard-and-good

[80] Call, M. (2024, April 15). *Why is behavior change so hard?*. Why is Behavior Change So Hard? https://accelerate.uofuhealth.utah.edu/resilience/why-is-behavior-change-so-hard

[81] Harris, R. (2008). *The Happiness Trap*. Robinson.

[82] Cascio, C. N., O'Donnell, M. B., Tinney, F. J., Lieberman, M. D., Taylor, S. E., Strecher, V. J., & Falk, E. B. (2015). Self-affirmation activates brain systems associated with self-related processing and reward and is reinforced by future orientation. *Social Cognitive and Affective Neuroscience, 11*(4), 621–629. https://doi.org/10.1093/scan/nsv136

<u>BOOK 3 REFERENCES</u>

[83] Linehan, M. M. (University of W., USA). (2014). *DBT (R) skills training manual, Second Edition*. Guilford Publications.

[84] Walters, A. (2024). *The Radical Acceptance Workbook* (Ser. Acceptance Therapy). LifeZen Publications.

[85] Mah, L., Szabuniewicz, C., & Fiocco, A. J. (2016). Can anxiety damage the brain? *Current Opinion in Psychiatry, 29*(1), 56–63. https://doi.org/10.1097/yco.0000000000000223

[86] Staner, L. (2003). Sleep and anxiety disorders. *Dialogues in Clinical Neuroscience, 5*(3), 249–258. https://doi.org/10.31887/dcns.2003.5.3/lstaner

[87] *Obesity and anxiety disorder: Which one comes first?*. Obesity Medicine Association. (n.d.). https://obesitymedicine.org/blog/obesity-and-anxiety-disorder-which-one-comes-first/

[88] Abraham, M. (2020, October 10). *Can anxiety cause weight gain?*. Calm Clinic - Information about Anxiety, Stress and Panic. https://www.calmclinic.com/anxiety/symptoms/weight-gain

[89] Cherney, K. (2023, November 13). *Effects of anxiety on the body*. Healthline. https://www.healthline.com/health/anxiety/effects-on-body

[90] Ross, R. A., Foster, S. L., & Ionescu, D. F. (2017). The role of chronic stress in anxious depression. *Chronic Stress, 1*, 2470547016689472. https://doi.org/10.1177/2470547016689472

[91] Kalin, N. H. (2020). The critical relationship between anxiety and depression. *American Journal of Psychiatry, 177*(5), 365–367. https://doi.org/10.1176/appi.ajp.2020.20030305

[92] *Anxiety and heart disease*. Johns Hopkins Medicine. (2023, October 30). https://www.hopkinsmedicine.org/health/conditions-and-diseases/anxiety-and-heart-disease

[93] Ferguson, S. (2024, July 23). *Anxiety treatment: Self-help, therapy, medication*. Healthline. https://www.healthline.com/health/anxiety-treatment
Medically reviewed by Joslyn Jelinek, LCSW, ACSW, RDDP.

[94] American Psychiatric Association. (2022). *Anxiety disorders*. Diagnostic and statistical manual of mental disorders (5th ed., text rev., pp. 215-231). American Psychiatric Association.

[95] Booth, J. (2023, October 23). *Anxiety statistics and facts*. Forbes. https://www.forbes.com/health/mind/anxiety-statistics/
Expert Reviewed by Sabrina Romanoff, Psy.D. Psychology.

[96] U.S. Department of Health and Human Services. (n.d.). *Social anxiety disorder*. National Institute of Mental Health. https://www.nimh.nih.gov/health/statistics/social-anxiety-disorder

[97] Thompson, B. (2024, April 22). *Exploring the recent rise of Social Anxiety Disorder - Seattle psychiatrist*. Seattle Anxiety Specialists - Psychiatry, Psychology, and Psychotherapy.

https://seattleanxiety.com/psychiatrist/2023/2/24/exploring-the-recent-rise-of-social-anxiety-disorder

[98] Mayo Foundation for Medical Education and Research. (2018, May 4). *Anxiety disorders.* Mayo Clinic. https://www.mayoclinic.org/diseases-conditions/anxiety/symptoms-causes/syc-20350961

[99] Spitzer, R. L., Kroenke, K., Williams, J. B., & Löwe, B. (2006). A brief measure for assessing generalized anxiety disorder. *Archives of Internal Medicine, 166*(10), 1092. https://doi.org/10.1001/archinte.166.10.1092

[100] Cohen, S., Kamarck, T., & Mermelstein, R. (1983). Perceived stress scale. *PsycTESTS Dataset.* https://doi.org/10.1037/t02889-000

[101] *Women are more than twice as likely to develop anxiety disorders.* University of Utah Health | University of Utah Health. (2023, August 15). https://healthcare.utah.edu/the-scope/health-library/all/2016/12/women-are-more-twice-likely-develop-anxiety-disorders

[102] Remes, O., Brayne, C., van der Linde, R., & Lafortune, L. (2016). A systematic review of reviews on the prevalence of anxiety disorders in adult populations. *Brain and Behavior, 6*(7). https://doi.org/10.1002/brb3.497

[103] McLean, C. P., Asnaani, A., Litz, B. T., & Hofmann, S. G. (2011). Gender differences in anxiety disorders: Prevalence, course of illness, comorbidity and burden of illness. *Journal of Psychiatric Research, 45*(8), 1027–1035. https://doi.org/10.1016/j.jpsychires.2011.03.006

[104] Wieczorek, K., Targonskaya, A., & Maslowski, K. (2023). Reproductive hormones and female mental wellbeing. *Women, 3*(3), 432–444. https://doi.org/10.3390/women3030033

[105] *Menopause and your mental wellbeing.* NHS inform. (2022, November 29). https://www.nhsinform.scot/healthy-living/womens-health/later-years-around-50-years-and-over/menopause-and-post-menopause-health/menopause-and-your-mental-wellbeing/

[106] *Men's Mental Health*. Men's Mental Health | Anxiety and Depression Association of America, ADAA. (n.d.). https://adaa.org/find-help/by-demographics/mens-mental-health

[107] Thomas, D. (2024, May 3). *Why are men less likely to get mental health help?*. The Walker Center. https://www.thewalkercenter.org/blog-posts/why-are-men-less-likely-to-get-mental-health-help

[108] Keyes, K. M., McLaughlin, K. A., Vo, T., Galbraith, T., & Heimberg, R. G. (2015). Anxious and aggressive: The co-occurrence of IED with anxiety disorders. *Depression and Anxiety*, *33*(2), 101–111. https://doi.org/10.1002/da.22428

[109] Hawkins, K. A., & Cougle, J. R. (2010). Anger problems across the anxiety disorders: Findings from a population-based study. *Depression and Anxiety*, *28*(2), 145–152. https://doi.org/10.1002/da.20764

[110] *About*. Steven C. Hayes, PhD. (2024, June 10). https://stevenchayes.com/about/

[111] Khoury, B., Lecomte, T., Fortin, G., Masse, M., Therien, P., Bouchard, V., Chapleau, M.-A., Paquin, K., & Hofmann, S. G. (2013). Mindfulness-based therapy: A comprehensive meta-analysis. *Clinical Psychology Review*, *33*(6), 763–771. https://doi.org/10.1016/j.cpr.2013.05.005

[112] Mindful Staff. (2022, August 31). *The science of mindfulness*. Mindful. https://www.mindful.org/the-science-of-mindfulness/

[113] Isbel, B., Weber, J., Lagopoulos, J., Stefanidis, K., Anderson, H., & Summers, M. J. (2020). Neural changes in early visual processing after 6 months of mindfulness training in older adults. *Scientific Reports*, *10*(1). https://doi.org/10.1038/s41598-020-78343-w

[114] Jha, A. P., Krompinger, J., & Baime, M. J. (2007). Mindfulness training modifies subsystems of attention. *Cognitive, affective & behavioral neuroscience*, *7*(2), 109–119. https://doi.org/10.3758/cabn.7.2.109

[115] Roemer, L., Williston, S. K., & Rollins, L. G. (2015). Mindfulness and emotion regulation. *Current Opinion in Psychology, 3*, 52–57. https://doi.org/10.1016/j.copsyc.2015.02.006

[116] Heppner, W. L., Spears, C. A., Vidrine, J. I., & Wetter, D. W. (2015). Mindfulness and emotion regulation. *Handbook of Mindfulness and Self-Regulation*, 107–120. https://doi.org/10.1007/978-1-4939-2263-5_9

[117] Liu, T. (2018). The scientific hypothesis of an "energy system" in the human body. *Journal of Traditional Chinese Medical Sciences, 5*(1), 29–34. https://doi.org/10.1016/j.jtcms.2018.02.003

[118] Collins, N. (2018, June 11). *How the human mind shapes reality.* Stanford Report. https://news.stanford.edu/stories/2018/06/four-ways-human-mind-shapes-reality

[119] Vilhauer, J. (2020, September 27). *How your thinking creates your reality.* Psychology Today. https://www.psychologytoday.com/intl/blog/living-forward/202009/how-your-thinking-creates-your-reality Reviewed by Lybi Ma

[120] Hampton, D. (2022, October 24). *Science proves your thoughts influence your reality and shape your brain for better or worse. you choose.* The Best Brain Possible. https://thebestbrainpossible.com/thoughts-brain-neuroplasticity-reality/

[121] Kosslyn, S. M., & Thompson, W. L. (2003). When is early visual cortex activated during visual mental imagery? *Psychological Bulletin, 129*(5), 723–746. https://doi.org/10.1037/0033-2909.129.5.723

[122] Morewedge, C. K., Huh, Y. E., & Vosgerau, J. (2010). Thought for food: Imagined consumption reduces actual consumption. *Science, 330*(6010), 1530–1533. https://doi.org/10.1126/science.1195701

[123] Blanco, A.-L. (2020, April 2). *Our brain doesn't tell the difference between simulation and Reality.* SkillGym.

https://www.skillgym.com/2019/05/our-brain-doesnt-tell-the-difference-between-simulation-and-reality/

[124] Dijkstra, N., & Fleming, S. M. (2023). Subjective signal strength distinguishes reality from imagination. *Nature Communications, 14*(1). https://doi.org/10.1038/s41467-023-37322-1

[125] Wikimedia Foundation. (2024, June 8). *Gabriele Oettingen*. Wikipedia. https://en.wikipedia.org/wiki/Gabriele_Oettingen